CREATIVE HOMEOWNER PRESS®

Adding Value To Your Home

Projects That Make Your House & Yard Worth More

CREATIVE HOMEOWNER PRESS®, Upper Saddle River, New Jersey

Editorial Director: Timothy O. Bakke
Art Director: W. David Houser
Production Manager: Ann Bernstein

Editor: Joseph L. Fucci, A.I.A.
Copy Editor: Bruce Wetterau

Graphic Designers: Heidi Garner, Susan Hallinan
Illustrators: Vincent Alessi, Chuck Chezosky,
　　　　　Jonathan Clark, Wayne Clark,
　　　　　Mario Ferro, SFI, Cindie Wooley,
　　　　　Ian Worpole

Cover Design: Annie Jeon
Cover Photo: Four Star Color;
　　　　　Inset House Photo: Kim, Jin Hong
　　　　　Photo Studio
Photo Researcher: Craig Clark

Manufactured in the United States of America

Current Printing (last digit)
10 9 8 7 6 5 4 3 2 1

Adding Value To Your Home
Library of Congress Catalog Card Number: 97-07264
ISBN: 1-8011-011-8

CREATIVE HOMEOWNER PRESS®
A Division of Federal Marketing Corp.
24 Park Way, Upper Saddle River, NJ 07458
Web site: **www.creativehomeowner.com**

Photo Credits

Page 7: Left: APA-The Engineered Wood Association
Right: Freeze Frame Studios, CHP
Page 8: Sid Davis, CHP
Page 10: Both: Sid Davis, CHP
Page 11: Right & Bottom: Catriona Tudor Erler (Vienna, VA)
Left Top: Sid Davis, CHP
Page 12: Sid Davis, CHP
Page 14: Sid Davis, CHP
Page 16: Sid Davis, CHP
Page 17: Left: Elizabeth Whiting & Associates (London, England)
Right: Freeze Frame Studios, CHP
Page 18: Sid Davis, CHP
Page 20: Portland Cement Association
Page 24: Sid Davis, CHP
Page 33: Left: Anderson Windows, Inc.
Right: Freeze Frame Studios, CHP
Page 34: Therma-Tru
Page 36: Pease Industries Incorporated
Page 39: Pella Corporation
Page 41: Marvin Windows & Doors
Page 43: Andersen Corp.
Page 46: Top: Andersen Corp.
Bottom: Pella Corp.
Page 49: Left: APA-The Engineered Wood Association
Right: Freeze Frame Studios, CHP
Page 50: CertainTeed Corp.
Page 55: Left: CertainTeed Corp.
Right: Sid Davis, CHP
Page 61: Left: CertainTeed Corp.
Right: Freeze Frame Studios, CHP
Page 62: CertainTeed Corp.
Page 66: CertainTeed Corp.
Page 77: Left: CHP
Right: Freeze Frame Studios, CHP
Page 80: National Paint & Coatings Association
Page 87: Clarke Barre, CHP
Page 88: All: National Paint & Coatings Association
Page 91: Left: Dacor
Right: Freeze Frame Studios, CHP
Page 92: Wilsonart International, Inc.
Page 93: Picture This Home!
Page 99: Both: Formica Corp.
Page 100: Kohler Co.
Page 102: Kohler Co.
Page 104: Dacor
Page 106: Whirlpool Corporation
Page 107: In-Sink-Erator
Page 109: Left: John Schwartz (New York, NY)
Right: Freeze Frame Studios, CHP
Page 110: John Schwartz (New York, NY)
Page 112: Kohler Co.
Page 116: Robern, Inc.
Page 118: Kohler Co.
Page 122: American Standard, Inc.
Page 123: Left: Benjamin Moore & Co.
Right: Freeze Frame Studios, CHP
Page 124: Smith-Baer Studios, CHP
Page 128: National Paint & Coatings Association
Page 131: Thompson & Company
Page 139: Left: Bruce Hardwood Floors
Right: Freeze Frame Studios, CHP
Page 140: Bruce Hardwood Floors
Page 146: Armstrong World Industries, Inc.
Page 147: Formica Flooring
Page 148: Florida Tile Industries, Inc.
Page 155: Left: Georgia Pacific Corp.
Right: Freeze Frame Studios, CHP
Page 157: Jane Cornell Company
Page 158: Hurd Millwork Co., Inc
Page 160: Georgia Pacific Corp.
Page 164: Georgia Pacific Corp.
Page 165: Left: New England Stock Photo (Glastonbury, CT)
Right: Freeze Frame Studios, CHP
Page 168: Robert Perron (Branford, CT)
Page 169: Top: Paul Schumm, CHP
Bottom: National Paint & Coatings Association
Page 170: Top: CertainTeed Corp.
Page 172: Top: Crandall & Crandall (Dana Point, CA)
Bottom: Terry Wild Studio (Williamsport, PA)

Back Cover:
Right, Top: CertainTeed Corp.
Right, Center: Bruce Hardwood Floors
Right, Bottom: Dacor

S A F E T Y   F I R S T

Though all the designs and methods in this book have been reviewed for safety, it is not possible to overstate the importance of using the safest construction methods possible. What follows are reminders; some do's and don'ts of basic carpentry. They are not substitutes for your own common sense.

- *Always* use caution, care, and good judgment when following the procedures described in this book.

- *Always* be sure that the electrical setup is safe; be sure that no circuit is overloaded and that all power tools and electrical outlets are properly grounded. Do not use power tools in wet locations.

- *Always* read container labels on paints, solvents, and other products; provide ventilation, and observe all other warnings.

- *Always* read the manufacturer's instructions for using a tool, especially the warnings.

- *Always* use hold-downs and push sticks whenever possible when working on a table saw. Avoid working short pieces if you can.

- *Always* remove the key from any drill chuck (portable or press) before starting the drill.

- *Always* pay deliberate attention to how a tool works so that you can avoid being injured.

- *Always* know the limitations of your tools. Do not try to force them to do what they were not designed to do.

- *Always* make sure that any adjustment is locked before proceeding. For example, always check the rip fence on a table saw or the bevel adjustment on a portable saw before starting to work.

- *Always* wear the appropriate rubber or work gloves when handling chemicals, moving or stacking lumber, or doing heavy construction.

- *Always* wear a disposable face mask when you create dust by sawing or sanding. Use a special filtering respirator when working with toxic substances and solvents.

- *Always* clamp small pieces firmly to a bench or other work surface when using a power tool on them.

- *Always* wear eye protection, especially when using power tools or striking metal on metal or concrete; a chip can fly off, for example, when chiseling concrete.

- *Always* be aware that there is seldom enough time for your body's reflexes to save you from injury from a power tool in a dangerous situation; everything happens too fast. Be *alert!*

- *Always* keep your hands away from the business ends of blades, cutters, and bits.

- *Always* hold a circular saw firmly, usually with both hands so that you know where they are.

- *Always* use a drill with an auxiliary handle to control the torque when large-size bits are used.

- *Always* check your local building codes when planning new construction. The codes are intended to protect public safety and should be observed to the letter.

- *Never* work with power tools when you are tired or under the influence of alcohol or drugs.

- *Never* cut tiny pieces of wood or pipe using a power saw. Cut small pieces off larger pieces.

- *Never* change a saw blade or a drill or router bit unless the power cord is unplugged. Do not depend on the switch being off; you might accidentally hit it.

- *Never* work while wearing loose clothing, hanging hair, open cuffs, or jewelry.

- *Never* work with dull tools. Have them sharpened, or learn how to sharpen them yourself.

- *Never* work in insufficient lighting.

- *Never* use a power tool on a workpiece—large or small—that is not firmly supported.

- *Never* saw a workpiece that spans a large distance between horses without close support on each side of the cut; the piece can bend, closing on and jamming the blade, causing saw kickback.

- *Never* support a workpiece from underneath with your leg or other part of your body when sawing.

- *Never* carry sharp or pointed tools, such as utility knives, awls, or chisels, in your pocket. If you want to carry such tools, use a special-purpose tool belt with leather pockets and holders.

HOW TO USE THIS BOOK

Each step-by-step project in the book begins with a suggested list of the tools and materials necessary to complete the work. Each task also begins by rating the level of difficulty of the work to be done on each project. The level of difficulty is indicated by one, two, or three hammers:

   T   Easy, even for beginners.

  T T   Moderately difficult. Can be done by beginners who have the patience and willingness to learn.

T T T   Difficult. Can be done by the do-it-yourselfer but requires a serious investment of time and patience, as well as money for specialty tools. Consider consulting a specialist.

These difficulty ratings should help you decide whether or not you wish to tackle a particular project. In this way, you won't be too far into a project before discovering that you're in over your head.

Contents

Introduction 5

Chapter 1   Landscaping 7
Landscaping ✦ Lawns ✦ Trees and Shrubs

Chapter 2   Driveways and Walkways 17
Driveways ✦ Concrete Steps ✦ Concrete Walkways ✦ Dry-Laid Walkways

Chapter 3   Doors and Windows 33
The Front Doorway ✦ Replacement Windows ✦ Specialty Windows

Chapter 4   Exterior Repairs 49
Wood Siding ✦ Fiber-Reinforced Cement Shingles ✦ Vinyl Siding ✦
Aluminum Siding ✦ Stucco

Chapter 5   Roofing Repair and Replacement 61
Roofing Inspection ✦ Roofing Repair ✦ Roofing Preparation ✦
Underlayment and Flashing ✦ Shingle Replacement ✦ Gutters and Leaders

Chapter 6   Exterior Painting 77
Paints and Stains ✦ Painting Tools ✦ Ladders and Scaffolding ✦
Preparation ✦ Paint Colors ✦ Painting

Chapter 7   Kitchens 91
Kitchen Cabinet Improvements ✦ Kitchen Cabinet Replacements ✦
Kitchen Countertops ✦ Fixtures and Appliances

Chapter 8   Bathrooms 109
Lavatories ✦ Bathrooms Accessories ✦
Toilets ✦ Shower Enclosures

Chapter 9   Walls and Ceilings 123
Repairing Walls ✦ Repairing Ceilings ✦ Painting Walls and Ceilings ✦
Wallcovering ✦ Wall Tiling

Chapter 10   Floors 139
Repairing Floors ✦ Replacing Flooring ✦ Ceramic Tile Flooring

Chapter 11   Architectural Woodwork 155
Architectural Woodwork ✦ Door and Window Casings ✦
Floor and Ceiling Trim ✦ Wainscoting

Chapter 12   Investment Benefits 165
Your Home as an Investment ✦ Renting or Selling ✦
Selling Your Home ✦ Renting Your Home

Glossary 173

Index 174

Introduction

Your Home as an Investment

The intention of this book is to help homeowners get the most from their greatest investment in life—their home. This particular investment is measured not only by the magnitude of its initial cost but also by years of mortgage payments, taxes, operating costs, and the costs of ongoing maintenance. Unfortunately, many homeowners are more concerned with their investments in the stock market or their retirement fund than they are with the hundreds of thousands of dollars they are likely to spend on their homes over the course of a lifetime.

In view of the magnitude and importance of this investment, it would make good sense for every homeowner to pay serious attention to the potential benefits, as well as the pitfalls, of home ownership and to plan accordingly. This book reveals how to do this by focusing on those areas of home improvement and scheduled maintenance that will not only safeguard your investment but also enhance its value.

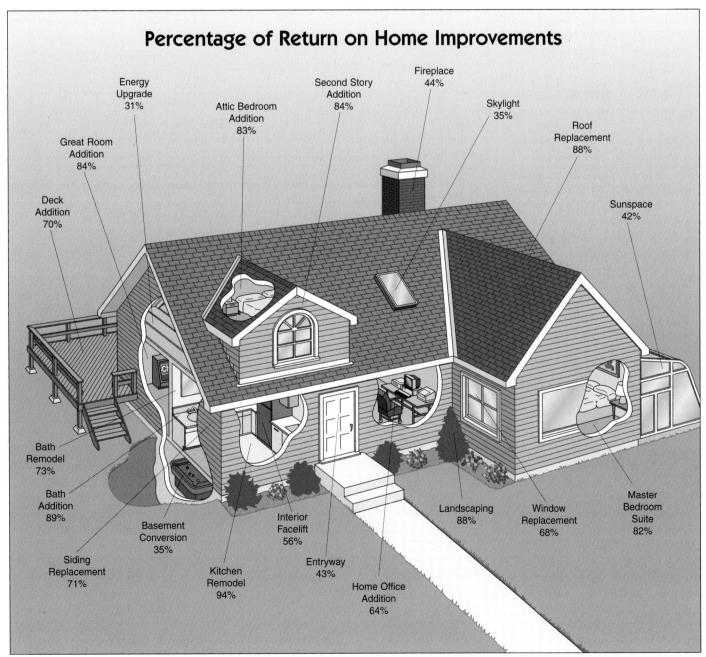

Percentage of Return on Home Improvements

- Energy Upgrade 31%
- Attic Bedroom Addition 83%
- Second Story Addition 84%
- Fireplace 44%
- Skylight 35%
- Roof Replacement 88%
- Great Room Addition 84%
- Sunspace 42%
- Deck Addition 70%
- Bath Remodel 73%
- Bath Addition 89%
- Basement Conversion 35%
- Interior Facelift 56%
- Landscaping 88%
- Window Replacement 68%
- Master Bedroom Suite 82%
- Siding Replacement 71%
- Kitchen Remodel 94%
- Entryway 43%
- Home Office Addition 64%

Source: National Association of Real Estate Appraisers.

Why Homeowners Lose on Their Home Investment

Nothing affects the value of a home more negatively than the home-owner's belief that he or she will live in the same home "forever." In today's mobile society, forever only averages about six years. This attitude causes delays in dealing with serious maintenance problems and the deferment of home-improvement projects. Worse, it may result in improvement projects that are stylistically appropriate for neither the home nor the neighborhood.

How to Get the Most Out of Your Home Investment

To maintain a home as a good investment, the homeowner must stay on top of both home maintenance needs and home improvement opportunities. For most, maintenance only occurs in response to an immediate emergency—a leaking roof, an overflowing toilet, exterior paint failure, rotting wood, crumbling plaster, or any of a hundred other crises to which homeowners are subjected. Many of these problems that go too long before being attended to become major expenses that easily could have been avoided.

This book shows you how to stay on top of critical maintenance projects in a way that will not only save on costs but actually add value to a home. It also delves into the importance of remodeling as a means of adding value to a home. The benefits of keeping pace with advances in technology and changes in stylistic preferences should be self-evident, especially as they affect the quality of your life. This is true whether you are updating a kitchen or bath, replacing obsolete fixtures, refinishing walls, installing maintenance-free siding, adding new energy-efficient windows and doors, adding or improving driveways and walkways, or upgrading a landscaping plan.

How *Not* to Lose Money on Maintenance and Remodeling

When planning maintenance or remodeling projects, it is of critical importance to view the big picture. This means considering the impact that a project may have on the remainder of the home. Will one area be modernized, while another area remains antiquated? Will new windows be out of character with the style of the home? What effect might the neighborhood have on design decisions? If all the neighboring homes have slate roofs, will a metal roof be appropriate on your home?

Consistency—of style, color, texture, and materials—or the lack of it can have a significant effect upon home values and must be an important consideration in any home improvement plan. And this consistency extends from the interior of a home to the outside, and even to the natural surroundings. All the elements of home and garden design must work and flow together in order to give the appearance of being part of a coherent whole. Failure to achieve this kind of consistency will almost certainly reduce the overall value of any home.

Which Home Improvements Yield the Greatest Returns?

This book highlights many of the most common maintenance and home improvement projects that a homeowner will either encounter or consider. But how do you know which projects are likely to yield the greatest return on your investment? You don't really know, since every case is different, but we can certainly make a reasonable assessment based on the experience of homeowners who have already completed such projects. Home improvement surveys, for example, are a good source of such information and provide a spotlight on current trends. Recent national surveys show that, on aver-

age, kitchen remodeling projects yield the greatest return, with bathroom improvements coming in a close second. To find information about the value of projects in your region, check with your local library, real estate broker, or home remodeling contractor. The information on the previous page is a compilation of such information gathered from recent surveys.

Selling or Renting a Home for Profit

The final chapter of this book explains why, after all, you might want to increase the value of your home. For one, most people are extremely mobile and really don't stay in the same home forever. Americans change jobs and move, retire and move, trade up to a better home and move, seek a different lifestyle and move, or move simply because they feel like it. Ultimately, moving means having to sell; selling means having something worth selling; and having something worth selling means adding as much attraction and value to a home as you reasonably can.

But what if you really don't want to sell? What if you move to another home but decide to keep the first as an ongoing source of income—as a rental property? You would still want to improve your home to make it more appealing to a potential tenant; to maximize rent returns; and to sell off eventually. The last chapter of the book also discusses this possibility. It makes clear how to convert a home into a profitable rental; how to modify a home to be damage-resistant, minimizing the need and expense of maintenance; how to advertise and find responsible tenants; and how to make an equitable rental agreement as a responsible landlord. A really ambitious home-owner might even continue this process, eventually owning several rental properties and having a steady source of income; an income that can continue even after retirement. What could be more valuable than that?

Chapter 1
Landscaping

The measure of a home's value, as well as its beauty, is seldom enhanced more than by well-planned and maintained landscaping. Trees and shrubs can provide privacy, cooling shade, a shield against wind and snow, a screen to block unwanted views, or a frame to bring a desirable vista into focus. Additionally, a well-balanced, carefully designed landscape will often create a pleasing composition of its own and further serve to create outdoor "rooms" that extend the living space of a home.

Make your property more attractive and valuable by designing a landscape appropriate to your region and to the size and style of your home. And if you prefer a natural look, select indigenous trees, shrubs, and grasses. Most importantly, develop a maintenance plan that will keep your landscape vibrant and healthy.

IN THIS CHAPTER

Landscaping

Planning a Landscape 8

Working with the Plan 10

Lawns

Adding or
Replacing a Lawn 12

Grass Seed 12

Seeding a Lawn 13

Sodding a Lawn 14

Trees and Shrubs

Pruning 15

Planting Trees and Shrubs 16

TODAY'S TRENDS

**Low-Maintenance
Landscapes**

Indigenous Plants

Low-Voltage Lighting

**In-Ground
Sprinkler Systems**

Landscaping

Nothing detracts from a beautiful home more than an unkempt yard or poorly planned landscape. But if you can't afford to hire a landscape architect to plan a beautifully organized yardscape, what can you do? The key to success is to develop a plan and stick to it. Start with a simple plan that is adaptable, and gradually add to it over time. The task need not be either complicated or overwhelming. Look around at other homes to get ideas, and do not be reluctant to ask for advice from professionals at your local garden center or garden club.

Planning a Landscape

Drawing a detailed site plan of a yard is the best way to start the design process. The act of drawing will itself engender ideas, and establish their feasibility. Having a plan will also save effort and money when the time comes to integrate future projects into the overall scheme or simply to estimate the quantity and cost of materials needed. And if you do hire a landscape architect, the site plan will serve as a point of departure for communicating your ideas and expectations.

Begin by drawing a base plan of the property. The plan should include property lines (*metes and bounds*) and the location and outline of the house, all other existing structures, driveways, walks, and important permanent features of the existing landscape (trees, rock outcroppings, etc.). Once this is done, simply sketch ideas on tracing-paper overlays. Develop a varied plan by providing space for lawns, planting beds, decks, patios, play areas, and storage areas. Take the best ideas, and then draw a final site plan.

1 Draw a base plan. If there is an existing deed map or site plan of your property, trace it exactly onto a large sheet of graph paper. For a large landscaping design, draw the entire property, showing the overall dimensions; the property orientation relative to north; the location of the house; easements; and setback distances from property lines, buildings, and the street.

2 Locate additional features. On the base plan, show the location of outbuildings and permanent features on the property, such as existing walks, walls, fences, garages, storage sheds, decks, patios, ponds, pools, etc. Also indicate the location of underground utility lines, pipes, and cables, if these are known. Be

Low-maintenance lawns, weed-free driveways and walkways, and well-kept flower beds all work together to create an attractive landscaping design.

sure to draw in the size and location of existing plantings, such as trees, hedges, and shrubs, as well as lawn areas, planting beds, and borders. Indicate which trees and shrubs are to be retained and which will need to be removed or relocated.

3 Show other relevant factors. On the base plan, indicate the direction of prevailing winds, existing sun/shade patterns in the yard (direction of morning and afternoon sun), existing drainage patterns, and any other factors that may affect the yard, such as noise or privacy problems or particular views that you wish either to preserve or to

block. If the base plan becomes too cluttered, show these features on a separate overlay clipped to the base plan.

4 Locate new features. Attach an overlay of tracing paper to the base plan, and then draw in the exact locations of proposed fences, flower beds, trees, shrubs, and other landscaping features. Note dimensions and construction materials on the overlay. (If the property requires extensive regrading, the building inspector may want to see spot elevations or contour lines on the final site plan. These must be provided by a licensed surveyor or landscape architect.) Use as many

overlay sheets as required to devise a suitable plan, taking this opportunity to experiment with different ideas. When the final plan is developed, place the overlay sheet(s) under the base plan, and then neatly trace in the new features. This final drawing must be submitted to the local building department to obtain a permit, if one is required.

Note: As an alternative to hand drawing a site plan, there are a variety of computer programs on the market that can simplify the process. Some landscaping programs enable the viewer to see a plan from different angles, while others include useful plant listings.

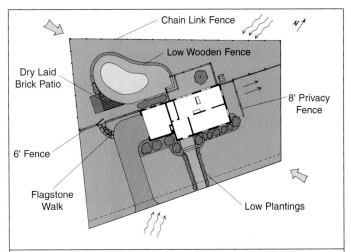

1. Trace the original site plan onto graph paper, showing boundaries, the house location and plan, and other major features, such as drives and walks, pools, direction north, etc.

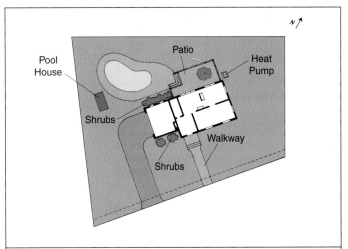

2. Add to the base plan other significant features, such as major trees, shrubs, rock outcroppings, patios, and outbuildings. Indicate those features that are to be removed or relocated.

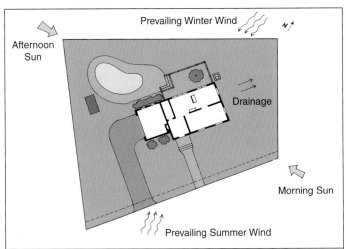

3. Complete the base plan by indicating the direction of morning and afternoon sun, prevailing summer and winter winds, and views you wish to preserve or eliminate.

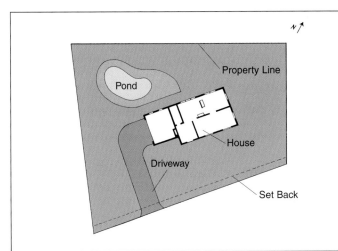

4. Overlay separate sheets of tracing paper on the completed base plan, showing the proposed landscape, including the locations of fences, gates, trellises, and other structures.

Working With the Plan

There are seven design elements that comprise a good landscape plan. Each of these elements must be carefully considered in the creation of a yardscape that is not only beautiful but also easily maintained. A well-designed landscape should also look natural, not surreal or out of character with its extended surroundings.

Composition. The first element of a good landscape design is composition. Trees and shrubs should be selected as though they were pieces in a puzzle; each piece must be fitted properly to complete the scene being constructed. Group landscape features into related components, and unite them into an overall scheme. The best way to ensure this is by working from a thoughtfully prepared plot plan.

Balance. The second element of landscape design is that of balance. Even though it may be difficult to define balance, it's easy to recognize the lack of it. An unbalanced landscape seems either to be missing something or to contain something that is out of place. Appropriate balance can only be achieved through the arrangement of trees, shrubs, and other plantings, from canopy to ground cover, in their proper relationships to each other. Man-made garden features and structures must also be included in this balance.

One way to create balance is to begin by dividing the base plan into roughly equal quadrants. Ideally, the quadrants should be somewhat symmetrical from side to side. For example, a large beech tree on the left side of the front yard might be balanced by a similar-sized maple tree on the right side, or a flower bed on one side of the backyard might be balanced by additional trees or shrubs on the other side. If symmetry is not appealing, try natural clustering.

Two oversized evergreen trees obscure this small home and cause the landscaping to appear both unbalanced and out of proportion.

Colorful hanging plants and properly sized shrubbery provide balance and add to the ordered appearance of this small home.

$ Value Tip

Eye Appeal

Not everything in a landscaping plan needs to be in the ground. You might want to consider hanging flowering plants on a front porch or placing hardy potted plants on outdoor steps and decks or strategically along a paved walkway. Even a window box, viewed from outside, becomes a part of the landscaping.

Scale. Scale is the third element of landscaping. Every feature in a landscape plan must be in the proper scale in relation to every other feature, especially those in close proximity. A small house in a small yard, for example, would appear dwarfed beside large trees. In this case, it would be preferable for the trees to be dwarfed and for other yard elements and outbuildings to be scaled down. Anticipate the mature height of trees and shrubs, and avoid planting them too close to the house. Overgrown plantings are not only distracting but also difficult to prune or have removed later.

Proportion. In nature, there is something called the "Golden Mean." Simply stated, it is the ratio of proportion that occurs most regularly in the natural world and that seems to be most pleasing to the eye. It is a ratio of three to five. Approximate this ratio when arranging trees, shrubs, and flower beds or when building fences, pools, and other structures, to achieve natural symmetry, the fourth element of design.

Color. This aspect of landscaping, the fifth, should not be overlooked. Even if it is low-maintenance, an all green yard might be boring to look at, as well as to be in. An easy way to bring color to a landscape is by adding foundation and border plantings, grape arbors, seasonal flower gardens, flowering ground ivy, and even simple window boxes.

Texture. Create a nicely textured landscape by organizing plants in groups with similar or related textures. To achieve this sixth element of landscaping design, avoid incompatible juxtapositions, like

delicately textured shrubbery next to sharp-needled scrub pines.

Harmony. Harmony, the seventh and final design element, is the synthesis of all the others. The design principles outlined here, if followed, will result in a yard that will be both beautiful to see and a joy to be in. The harmony and order inherent in the landscape will be self-evident.

CREATIVE LANDSCAPING

Pro Tip

There is probably no such thing as the perfect yard. Distracting views, utility boxes, nearby buildings, and a variety of other problems can pose a real landscaping challenge. With a little creativity, however, even big problems can be minimized. Include these problem areas on your base site plan, along with notes on how they affect the current landscape. Working out a problem on paper is often simpler than trying to visualize it in your head, and it's much easier than changing the landscaping!

EXAMPLES:

Problem: a transformer located in the front yard (above, right).

Solution: plant hedges or shrubbery to thoroughly block the view of the transformer. To keep the yard balanced, a second planting can be created at the opposite corner.

Problem: unsightly trash containers (below, right).

Solution: incorporate a bump-out into the fencing, to effectively hide the trash containers. The organized, tidy appearance of this solution works to improve the appearance of the home.

Color, proportion, and texture harmonize in this elaborate formal garden to form a welcoming retreat.

Lawns

The value of most homes will be enhanced tremendously by a landscape carpeted in lush, green grass. Although a comprehensive landscaping plan will include planting flowers, ground covers, shrubs, and trees—thick, green, healthy grasses still form the basis for even the most modest of landscaping designs. A lawn choked with weeds, covered with brown, burned-out grasses, or spotted with patches of bare dirt is not only unappealing but will detract from both the value and enjoyment of owning a home. Any decision to improve the condition of one's property must either begin with planting a new lawn or replacing an unhealthy one. For either of these attempts to be successful, you must satisfy three prerequisites: rich soil, good drainage, and a high-quality blend of grass seed.

Adding or Replacing a Lawn

Soil. To grow a healthy lawn, you must first have a good, rich soil. Soil not only provides the water and nutrients required for grass to grow, it also serves to anchor the roots of the grass. Nutrient-deficient or poorly managed soils will inevitably result in low-quality grass.

Soil Testing. Whether starting a new lawn or reviving an existing one, test the soil's acidity or alkalinity (pH level). Testing kits are available at home and garden centers. To collect soil samples, cut the soil to a depth of 6 inches, using a spade to expose the different layers of soil. Cut a ½-inch-thick slice from the edge of the cut. Take samples from different locations, mix them together, and then use a portion of this mixture for the soil test.

A neutral pH reading is 7. Any value below 7 indicates acid soil, and any value higher than 7 indicates alkaline soil. Turf grass usually does best in soil with a pH of 6.0

A healthy, green, low-maintenance lawn is perhaps the most important component of a well-designed landscaping plan.

to 6.5. Acid soil may be sweetened with ground limestone or oyster shell lime, while dolomitic limestone also adds magnesium. The addition of sulfur will make soil more acidic.

Seeding vs. Sodding. Once the soil is prepared to support a healthy lawn, the next task is to decide whether to plant grass seed or to lay down sod.

Grass Seed

Most growers of quality grass seed offer custom blends that suit a variety of climates and conditions. One blend of bluegrass, for example, may provide deep color, high density, and thick texture, while another blend may be designed for shady areas, heavy foot traffic, and quick covering of bare spots.

Ingredients. Beware of cheap grass seed. Avoid seed that includes weeds and inert materials that may be difficult to remove from your lawn. Carefully read the label on a bag of grass seed before purchasing it. By law, seed growers and packagers must print an analysis of the contents of each bag of seed, which rates the seed by the following six criteria:

Purity. Purity denotes the percentage by weight of the types of grass seed included in a particular blend. A purity of 35 percent or more of the primary grass type (e.g., Kentucky bluegrass) is best.

The seed analysis may include two subcategories: *Fine-Textured Grasses* and *Coarse-Textured Grasses.* Fine-textured grasses include bluegrass, bentgrass, fine fescue, and such strains as Windsor, Merion, and Victa. Common coarse-textured grasses include perennial ryegrass, red-top, timothy, tall fescue, and Kentucky 31. The seed mix should include at least 40 percent ryegrass seed or other strain of coarse-textured grass seed.

Germination. Germination is an indication of the percentage of seed in a mix expected to grow under ideal conditions. Germination should be in the 85 percent range. Keep in mind that this percentage is determined through laboratory testing, and that not all seeds will germinate at the same time.

Crop. *Crop seeds* are also listed as a percentage of total weight. These are what the name implies: seeds for crops, such as oats, wheat, and rye.

If crop seeds account for more than 5 percent by weight, then "Crop Seed" must appear somewhere on the package label.

Weeds. All seed mixes contain some weed seeds. Look for a low percentage of weed. Even 0.1 percent chickweed in a pound of seed can result in 560,000 chickweed plants in a 10,000-square-foot lawn. Aside from the added cost of weeding and weed killers, these inhibitors can slow the germination of your primary seed mix.

Noxious Weeds. These seed types must be listed by name and count on the label. Noxious weeds are mostly of concern in farm and grazing fields, but to be safe, look for mixes without noxious weeds.

Inert Matter. Inert matter can consist of sand, ground-up corn cobs, empty seed hulls, and anything else that might add extra weight to a seed package. Read the package labels carefully, and purchase the seed mixture that contains the least amount of inert matter that you can select.

Seeding a Lawn

Difficulty Level: 🔨

Required Tools:

❑ **Basic tools:** garden hoe, hose, spade, steel or wooden leveling rake, string and stakes, wheelbarrow

❑ **Special tools:** hay rake, rototiller, seed spreader, sprinkler

1 Prepare the seed bed. If the bed to be seeded is very uneven, hire a professional with a tiller or backhoe to level the area. If you wish, do it yourself with a spade, a hoe, and a wheelbarrow. Or use a small rototiller, if you have one.

After leveling the earth, remove loose debris, such as rocks and sticks. Next, loosen the soil by tilling it to a depth of 3 to 4 inches.

Allow about a week for the soil to settle. Sprinkle the ground with water to hasten the settling process. Once the soil is properly prepared, seeding is a relatively simple task. Carpet the entire area with a *new grass* fertilizer, a mixture with a high phosphorus content, to help establish a strong root system.

2 Sow the seed. For consistent seed distribution use a spreader instead of sowing the seed by hand. This will ensure even coverage and

minimal waste. Approximately 3 to 6 pounds of seed are needed to cover 1,000 square feet of lawn. Exact coverage will depend on the seed quality, grade characteristics, and spread recommendations found on the seed package.

3 Rake and water the seed. After the seed is applied, rake it gently into the soil, covering as much seed as possible. This will transport the seed below the surface, where it can germinate. It will also safeguard the

1. Remove loose debris from the area to be seeded. Till the soil to a depth of 3 to 4 in., and then rake it lightly. Next, water the soil, and apply grass fertilizer.

Drop Spreader

2. Distribute seed using a spreader for even coverage, with the spreader at the setting that is recommended on the label of the grass seed bag.

Hay

3. Rake seed lightly into the soil, covering the seed as much as possible. Cover the seed bed with burlap or hay, and then water it lightly. Keep the area damp with daily waterings for the first few weeks, to hasten growth.

SEED VS. SOD

	Advantages	Disadvantages
Seed	◆ Relatively inexpensive per square foot. ◆ Variety of specific seed types: for shade, heavy foot traffic, low maintenance, etc.	◆ Long waiting period to establish a lawn. ◆ Washes away on steep slopes or uneven ground before it can germinate. ◆ Can be planted only in fall or spring.
Sod	◆ Instant landscaping. ◆ Can be applied at almost any time of year. ◆ Erosion resistance; stability on slopes.	◆ Relatively expensive per square foot. ◆ Specialty grasses for shaded and heavy traffic areas are difficult to obtain.

seed against hungry birds and the wind. After raking, cover the seed bed with burlap or hay. Then lightly water it. Dampen but do not muddy the ground. Moisture is essential for germination, so water the seed bed every day, at first, to hasten growth.

Refertilize 30 days after the initial seeding, and then fertilize the lawn regularly, once in the spring and once in the fall. Use a *starter* fertilizer until the lawn is established. For the first year, cut new grass to a height of about 3 inches, to help to crowd out weeds.

Sodding a Lawn

Difficulty Level: 🔨

Required Tools:

❑ <u>Basic tools:</u> **garden hoe, hose, knife, spade, steel rake**

❑ <u>Special tools:</u> **rototiller, tamper, wheelbarrow**

Applying freshly cut sod on cultivated ground is a fast and easy way to establish a lawn. It is also the most expensive way. If sod is too expensive, a compromise is to use it only to fill bare spots or to prevent soil erosion on newly graded slopes.

1 Prepare the soil. Cultivate the soil just as for seeding. Level it, and then mix in a growth-boosting fertilizer. (See sidebar on fertilizer.)

2 Lay down the sod. Begin applying sod along a straight edge, such as a walk or a driveway, butting the ends tightly together and staggering them as you go. On slopes, peg sod in place with wood stakes to prevent it from slipping.

3 Tamp down and water the sod. After the sod is in place, tamp, water, and fertilize it. Water encourages roots to bond with the soil.

F.Y.I. HYDRO-SEEDING

An alternative to traditional seeding is hydro-seeding. In this process, a slurry of grass seed, wood fibers, and fertilizer is spray-applied in one step. Hydro-seeding is relatively inexpensive. Compared with seeding by hand, hydro-seeding is also very fast.

1. Use a rototiller to thoroughly cultivate the soil. Then use a steel rake to remove large rocks and other debris.

2. Lay sod along a straight edge, such as a walk or string line. Cut excess sod and piece it into odd-shaped lawn areas.

3. Tamping the sod helps embed roots into the soil. After 2 weeks, you should not be able to lift individual pieces.

Keep the sod damp but not soaked for several weeks. If any sod appears dead or dying after this time, remove and replace it with a new section of sod. After this initial growth period, mow the lawn to a height of about 2½ inches, and then spread another application of a growth-boosting fertilizer.

Trees and Shrubs

As trees and shrubs grow, so does their value. Mature trees provide shade, privacy, and a sense of permanence. However, homes with overgrown trees and bushes can be unappealing. For security reasons, too, it is not a good idea to have windows and doors obscured by bushes and trees. Break-ins often occur at entry points where thieves can work undetected. If you desire greenery at these locations, plant prickly bushes and trees that will act as a natural deterrent.

Pruning

To protect your landscaping investment, regular maintenance is essential. Healthy trees and shrubs must

---

FERTILIZER

F.Y.I.

Fertilizers contain nutrients balanced for different kinds of growth. The ratio of nutrients is indicated on the package by three numbers (for example, 10-10-10). The first specifies nitrogen content; the second, phosphorus; and the third, potash.

Nitrogen. Nitrogen helps grass blades to grow and improves the quality and thickness of the turf. *Quick Green* fertilizers contain up to 30 percent nitrogen.

Phosphorus. Phosphorus helps grass to develop a healthy root system. It also speeds up the maturation process of the plant.

Potash. Potash helps grass stay healthy by providing amino acids and proteins to the plants.

---

be pruned, dead wood removed, and hanging branches cut back from a house to let in more sunlight and air. Dark, dreary yards and heavily shadowed homes will appear quite uninviting, even forbidding.

Pruning will also benefit the health of most trees and shrubs. Older, densely overgrown plants may be reinvigorated if they are thinned to admit more light and air.

Knowing some basic plant physiology helps with understanding the effects of pruning. Plants produce growth hormones, called auxins, in the tips of their shoots. Auxins stimulate tip growth and suppress side growth. Removing the growing tip and its supply of auxins releases some of the buds along the shoot, called lateral buds, from dormancy, creating side shoots. Although auxin strength varies among plants, pruning a growing tip generally induces growth on the remaining shoot, stem, or branch. Seek advice from experienced gardeners or your local nursery for information about specific plants.

Pruning trees is no different from pruning shrubs, except for their size. Removing a 6-inch diameter branch growing 30 feet above the ground, however, can be challenging and dangerous. It is best to hire a professional to handle such difficult pruning jobs.

Thinning Shrubs. Branches may be cut back to encourage growth in a

---

particular area. Find a bud facing in the direction you want a branch to grow, and then cut just above it. Pinch or cut off growing tips in the spring to make shrubs bushier and more compact. Some shrubs can be pruned every year to produce new growth the following season. Heavy pruning may also rejuvenate old shrubs. To reduce the risk of losing a shrub, cut it back in stages, one-third every year for three years.

Pruning Trees. Columnar trees often have a dominant, or leader, trunk. If a tree has two leaders when it is young, one can be trimmed back so that the tree will grow in the desired shape. Never "top" the central

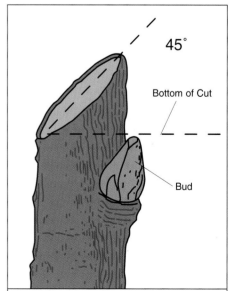

Cut a stem above the bud at 45°. Keep the bottom of the cut level with the top of the bud on the opposite side of the stem.

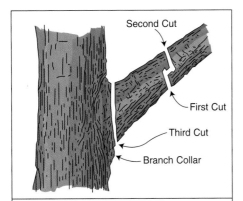

To prevent tearing, cut large branches in three stages. The final cut lets the tree close the wound efficiently.

Attractive, well-maintained shrubs and planting beds enhance this modest home.

leader of a tree, however. If a tree is too tall, remove it, and then replace it with a tree that won't grow as tall. To remove large branches, make a series of cuts to prevent tearing. Do not cut flush at the trunk, but cut along the branch collar, instead.

Planting Trees and Shrubs

Difficulty Level: 𝐓

Required Tools:

❑ <u>Basic tools:</u> **garden hose, pitchfork, shovel**

❑ <u>Special tools:</u> **clamshell digger**

1 Dig the hole. Make a hole large enough for the root ball but no deeper than its current growth, or the trunk will be too deeply placed. Place the dug-up soil on a tarp, and then remove any rocks and debris. Using a rake or pitchfork, loosen the soil on the sides of the hole to encourage root penetration.

2 Plant the tree. To remove the tree from its container, soak the container first. Then, without disturbing the root ball, slide or cut off the container, and gently untangle the roots. Once the roots are bared, the tree or shrub must be planted as soon as possible. If the roots appear dry, soak them for a day in a weak solution of liquid fertilizer.

With the tree in place, fill the hole halfway, working the soil in with your hands. Brace the tree upright, fill the hole with water, and then let it drain. When the water has drained, add the remaining soil, mounding some around the base to absorb water. Cover the ground with mulch to retard evaporation.

1. Dig a hole large enough for the root ball. Place the soil on a tarp. Using a pitchfork, loosen soil remaining in the hole, and screen out rocks and debris.

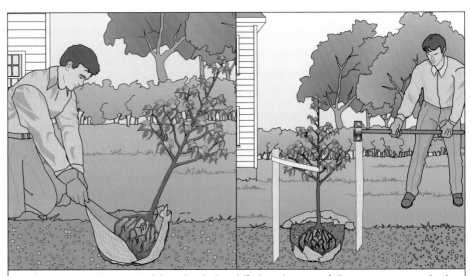

2. After placing the root ball into the hole, shift the plant carefully to remove *synthetic* wrapping or to fold back *burlap*. Fill half of the hole with soil, and soak it thoroughly. After the water has drained, shovel in the remaining soil. Stake the tree, add a mulch of chipped bark or compost at the base, and then water the tree once again.

Chapter 2
Driveways and Walkways

If green lawns and luxuriant shrubs are the primary elements of an appealing landscape, then the next in line must be attractive driveways and walkways. Their high visibility commands visual attention, offering casual passersby a first impression of your home. If you already have a beautifully paved driveway and nicely laid out walkways, you will certainly want to make sure that they are kept in good repair. If not, adding a brick walk or an extra carport may be a good idea. Look around your neighborhood. If large lawns and gardens are favored, then a major paving project could end up actually reducing the value of your home. But if spacious driveways and decorative walkways are popular in your area, an addition or improvement of this kind might well be worth the investment.

In This Chapter

Driveways

Asphalt Paving 18

Repairing Asphalt Paving 18

Concrete 19

Cleaning Concrete 19

Repairing Concrete 20

Laying Out a New
Concrete Driveway 21

Ordering Concrete 22

Concrete Steps

Repairing Step Edges 24

Repairing Step Corners 25

Concrete Walkways

Laying Out a New Walkway 26

Building Formwork 27

Pouring and
Finishing Concrete 29

Resurfacing Concrete 30

Dry-Laid Walkways

Paving Units 30

Edging Systems 30

Installing a Brick Walkway 31

Today's Trends

Paving Bricks

Garden Walks

Textured and Colored
Concrete

Cobblestones

Driveways

Driveway deterioration is a universal problem, and sooner or later every homeowner must either repair or replace a driveway. Simple repair work will seldom involve a change of material, but if a driveway is going to be replaced, you may want to know which material is best, asphalt or concrete? The answer may be as simple as looking at your neighbor's driveway. Certainly, if everyone else has concrete, you may reduce the value of your home by selecting asphalt. Ultimately, the choice depends almost entirely upon whether or not you wish to do the work yourself.

Asphalt Paving

Asphaltic concrete is widely used as a driveway material because it is more flexible than regular concrete and therefore more durable in extreme temperatures. In winter, its dark color absorbs heat faster than concrete, enabling it to shed ice and snow quickly. Asphalt does not require formwork or long curing times. If it is damaged, asphalt paving is easy to repair. The disad-

vantage of asphalt is that it must be spread by a paving contractor. The contractor must excavate 6 to 9 inches of grade and lay down 4 to 6 inches of compacted gravel for a solid road base. Some homeowners believe omitting the base can cut costs, but without a good base, drainage problems and sinkholes will almost certainly develop.

After laying down a base, the contractor must install a 2- to 3- inch deep bed of compacted asphalt. The driveway must have at least a 1-percent slope or crown so that water will drain off the surface. In cold climates, steeper grades prevent water penetration, freezing, and pothole formation.

Repairing Asphalt Paving

Difficulty Level: ⏐

Required Tools:

❑ **Basic tools:** scrub brush and cleaner, sealing brush, tamper

❑ **Special materials:** asphalt filler and sealer, cold-mix asphalt

Asphaltic concrete is a mixture of asphalt and graded aggregate. Because asphaltic concrete is more flexible and easier to repair than regular concrete, it is an ideal paving material for roads and driveways.

Because of their flexibility, asphalt driveways can be easily damaged by cars, bicycle kickstands, and seasonal freeze–thaw cycles. Water percolating beneath the asphalt or through surface cracks can undermine the gravel base, creating sinkholes. Cracks should be sealed as soon as they appear, before water penetration and freezing can create problems.

A driveway that is not too badly deteriorated can usually be patched or resealed in about one weekend. For the best results, however, maintenance and repairs should be done in warm weather, when asphalt materials are malleable and will form a better bond.

1 **Clean the surface.** For patching compounds and sealers to bond properly, the asphalt must be clean. Broom-sweep the driveway, and then use a wire brush to remove loose debris from cracks. Use a trisodium phosphate (TSP) solution or a commercial asphalt cleaner to remove surface oil and dirt. Rinse the pavement using a hose or power washer.

2 **Caulk the cracks.** Narrow cracks, less than ³⁄₈ inch, can be filled with latex-based crack filler. Apply the filler with a caulking gun.

3 **Fill the potholes.** Fill larger holes and cracks with cold-mix asphalt, commonly sold in 60-pound bags. The material should be loose in the bag. If it is stiff, leave it in the sun for a few hours. As with small cracks, clean out loose debris. Shovel in the asphalt, filling the hole in 1-inch layers. Firmly tamp each layer to remove air bubbles. Overfill the hole about ½ inch to allow for settling. Allow the patch to set for at least 36 hours before applying a sealer coat.

4 **Seal the driveway.** Sealing the driveway will protect it from water damage and give it a uniform appearance. A 5-gallon pail of sealer will typically cover about 400 square feet. Before sealing the driveway, clear away dirt and debris. Pour an 8-inch wide ribbon of sealer across the width of the driveway, starting

1. Sweep the driveway thoroughly with a broom, and then remove debris in the cracks using a wire brush.

2. Using a caulking gun, apply a latex-based asphalt crack filler to fill and seal any narrow cracks in the pavement.

3. In 1-in. layers, fill the larger holes with cold blacktop mix. Tamp each layer firmly into the hole to remove air bubbles.

4. Clean away dirt and debris, and then seal the driveway to protect it from water damage and give it a uniform appearance.

at the high end. Using a broom or squeegee, spread the sealer until it is even. Avoid splashing sealer on walls or sidewalks by using a cheap 4-inch brush to cut in edges. Allow the surface to cure for 24 hours before walking or driving on it.

Concrete

Concrete is an excellent material for driveways because of its plasticity, durability, and strength. Although the neutral color of natural concrete

blends easily with most architectural and landscaping styles, concrete can also be tinted, embedded with decorative stone finishes, textured in a variety of patterns, or even formed to resemble brick, tile, slate, or stone.

Cleaning Concrete

Although concrete can last for decades, it does require periodic cleaning and maintenance. There are several ways to remove stains from concrete. First, try a household detergent with a fiber scrub brush. Avoid steel wool or steel-bristle brushes because the metal fiber particles they leave behind may rust and discolor the concrete. For really stubborn stains, mix ½ cup of trisodium phosphate (TSP) and ½ cup of household detergent to 1 gallon of warm water. Be sure to wear protective gloves and glasses when applying this solution.

Stain-specific cleaning agents are available and can be purchased at many home-improvement centers. Read labels carefully to determine what the correct use is for a particular stain remover. Avoid acids or acidic solutions that may etch the surface of the concrete. If the cleaning agent contains a weak acid, soak the area first to minimize potential etching. Be aware that removing a stain can leave a bright spot that is more noticeable than the original stain. To prevent future stains and moisture-related damage, apply a sealer to the concrete. Thoroughly wash the concrete surface with a TSP solution before applying the sealer. The sealer may be applied with a paint roller, squeegee, or garden sprayer.

Repairing Concrete

Difficulty Level:

Required Tools:

- ❑ **Basic tools:** bucket, cold chisel, putty knife, whisk broom
- ❑ **Special tools:** masonry trowels, sledgehammer

STAIN REMOVAL
Pro Tip

Stubborn oil or grease can be removed with a solution of baking soda and water. Make a paste, apply it to the stain, and then cover it with plastic to keep it moist. The paste should absorb the stain in about 24 hrs.

Concrete is made from portland cement, sand, stone aggregates, and water. It is a durable material, and it is extremely strong in compression. The plastic properties of concrete make it especially suitable for a variety of design purposes, including driveways.

Concrete exposed to repeated cycles of freezing and thawing can crack or *spall* (flake). Uneven settling of the soil can also cause concrete to crack. To repair minor cracking, you must remove the damage and patch the area with a cement-based patching compound.

1 Remove the damaged concrete. Using a cold chisel, remove the cracked or crumbling concrete. Wear work gloves and safety goggles to protect yourself from serious injury.

2 Undercut the edge of the patch. Form a *keyway* between the patch and the existing concrete by holding the chisel at an angle and undercutting the edge of the patch area.

3 Remove the debris. Sweep out debris with a whisk broom, and then hose down the area to be repaired. Sponge out any standing water, but keep the area relatively moist for at least several hours before proceeding further.

1. Using a cold chisel, remove any cracked or crumbling concrete. Wear gloves and safety goggles for protection against flying concrete chips.

Angled Undercut, or Keyway

2. Form a keyway between the patch and the existing concrete. Do this by undercutting the edges of the area to be patched using a cold chisel.

3. Sweep out debris with a whisk broom, and then hose down the patch area. Sponge out any standing water, but keep the area relatively moist.

4. Coat the edges of the patch area with a cement slurry. Then pack cement paste firmly into the patch using a putty knife or trowel.

5. Level the mixture using a straight-edged concrete-finishing trowel. Allow the patch to set for at least 1 hr., and then float the finish.

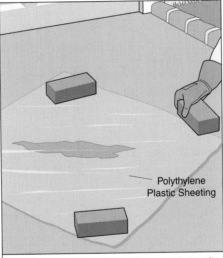

Polythylene
Plastic Sheeting

6. After troweling, allow the patch to sit for a few hours, and then cover it with a plastic tarp. Use heavy objects to hold down the corners.

4 Mix the patching cement. In a large bucket, mix one part portland cement and three parts sand with enough water to make a stiff *paste*. In a separate container, mix a small amount of portland cement with water adequate to make a cement *slurry*. Using this slurry, thoroughly coat the area to be patched. This coating will serve as a primer. Next, pack the cement paste firmly into the patch using a putty knife or trowel. Agitate the cement thoroughly with the putty knife to remove trapped pockets of air.

5 Fill and smooth the patch. Level the mixture using a straight-edged concrete-finishing trowel. Allow the patch to set for at least 1 hour, and then float or trowel the finish to match the surrounding surface.

6 Cure the patch. After troweling, allow the patch to set for a couple of hours, and then cover it with a sheet of plastic to let it cure. Secure the plastic with bricks or rocks. For the next week, lift the plastic cover daily and sprinkle water on the patch.

Laying Out a New Concrete Driveway

Difficulty Level: ⚒

Required Tools:

❑ **Basic tools:** line level, mason's string, measuring tape, sledgehammer, stakes

If you wish to replace an entire driveway that has cracked or collapsed because of frost heave, or if you simply wish to construct a new driveway where previously there was none, then either asphalt or concrete may be selected. As stated earlier, applying asphalt requires specialized machinery and professional skills. Although it may be difficult, homeowners can conceivably do their own concrete work. Doing this can save 50 percent or more of what it would cost to have a concrete driveway installed professionally. Furthermore, a properly constructed concrete driveway will provide long-lasting service.

Whether it will be constructed from asphaltic concrete or from regular concrete, you must plan your new driveway using the same layout method.

Before doing anything, however, make sure you have a building permit, if one is required. Also ask your local utility company to mark the location of any underground utilities in the path of the proposed excavation. When all of this has been completed, take the following steps to lay out the proposed driveway.

1 Erect batter boards. Using a measuring tape, locate and mark the perimeter dimensions of the proposed concrete slab using temporary stakes. Erect batter boards at right angles to each other, about 2 feet outside each corner of the planned driveway. Batter boards provide support for string guidelines to mark exact corner locations. They can be made from scrap lumber, about 2 feet long, supported by wooden stakes. Use a line level to set the horizontal boards at the same height.

2 Set string guidelines. Set up string guidelines to mark the perimeter of the proposed concrete driveway slab. Be sure the lines are level and secured to the batter boards. Use mason's twine for the guidelines, as it is specifically designed to resist sagging.

To set precise right angles at each corner, use a 3-4-5 method of triangulation. Beginning at a point A, measure 3 feet along one line and mark a point B. Again from point A, run a second line perpendicular to the first, and measure 4 feet along this line to mark a point C. Adjust string line AC so that the distance BC becomes exactly 5 feet in length. Angle BAC will be a 90-degree angle.

After all the string guidelines are in place, double-check them for accuracy by measuring the diagonal distance between opposite corners. The distances should be equal. If they are not, readjust the layout.

3 Reposition the corner stakes. To reposition the temporary stakes in their precise corner locations, use a plumb bob to transfer the string-guideline intersection points down to the ground.

Excavation. Concrete slabs must be supported on soil that is compact, uniformly graded, and well-drained. Check the local building code for the required load-bearing capacity of soil in your area. Inadequate subgrading may cause uneven settling and cracking in the concrete.

Excavation work is labor intensive and strenuous. For a large-scale driveway excavation, it may be best to hire a contractor who has heavy-duty excavation equipment. If the project is not too large, you may choose to do the excavation yourself. Remember to have your utility company mark any utility lines that you need to avoid. When you excavate, start 8 to 10 inches outside the string guideline to allow room for the formwork. Remove grass, roots, large rocks, and other debris from the excavation area. Dig out soft or spongy areas, and fill them in with compacted soil, gravel, crushed stone, or sand. Excavate enough soil to accommodate the thickness of the slab plus base materials. Leave virgin grade undisturbed where possible. Natural soil will be more compacted than fill material. Level the surface soil using a rake, and then fill the voids left by debris removal with sand or gravel. Next, compact the soil using either a hand-operated tamper, a mechanical roller, or a vibrating compactor.

Drainage. In regions with poor drainage, excavate deeply enough to lay 4 inches of gravel beneath the concrete. Plan to finish the slab 2 to 3 inches above the adjacent grade. Local building codes will specify the depth of gravel base typical for your region. Pour, level, and tamp the gravel in several layers. Use compactible gravel to form a firm, well-drained base. Crushed limestone, ¾ inch or less, is an ideal material. If needed, slope the adjacent grade away from the driveway to ensure good drainage and reduce the likelihood of frost heave or washout.

Ordering Concrete

Concrete mixes can be purchased by the bag, but for large jobs it is more practical, as well as economical, to have the concrete delivered to your home by a mixing truck. Concrete mixes may vary, depending upon their use, weather conditions, drying time, and the properties of admixtures. Local concrete suppliers will be able to advise you about these mixture variations.

To estimate the amount of concrete required, first determine the rough dimensions of the proposed driveway. The precise layout for the formwork is not critical at this stage. Allow for waste and irregular concrete thickness by rounding up to the next whole or half cubic yard of measure. Add a 5 to 10 percent margin of error to your concrete order.

1. Drive temporary stakes at the corners of the proposed slab. Set up level batter boards 2 ft. outside each corner.

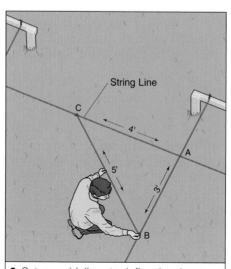

2. Set up guidelines to define the shape of the project. Test whether it is square by using the 3-4-5 method of triangulation.

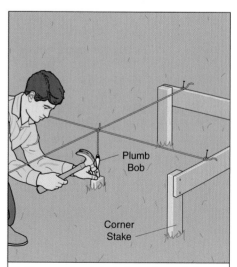

3. Drop a plumb bob from the point where the strings intersect. Stake this location to mark the exact corner.

TABLE OF USEFUL FORMULAS

Volume of a Square or Rectangle (cu. yd.)

$$V = \frac{(w \times l \times d)}{12 \text{ in.}} \div 27$$

To calculate the volume of a square or rectangular area, multiply the width (w) in feet by the length (l) in feet, and then multiply the product by the depth (d) of the proposed concrete slab in inches. Divide the result by 12 inches, to calculate the number of cubic feet of concrete required. Round this up to the nearest whole number, and then divide by 27 to determine how many cubic yards of concrete to order, adding 10 percent as a margin of error.

Volume of a Triangle (cu. yd.)

$$V = \frac{(^1/_2)(w \times l \times d)}{12 \text{ in.}} \div 27$$

To calculate the volume of a triangular area, multiply the width (w) in feet by the length (l) in feet, multiply by $^1/_2$, and then multiply this product by the depth (d) of the proposed concrete slab in inches. Divide the final number by 12 inches to calculate the number of cubic feet of concrete required. Round up, divide by 27, and add 10 percent as a margin of error, to calculate the total cubic yards of concrete needed.

Volume of a Cylinder (cu. yd.)

$$V = \frac{(3.14 \times r^2 \times d)}{12 \text{ in.}} \div 27$$

Circular driveways are actually cylindrical due to the slab depth. To find the volume, multiply *pi* (3.14) by the square of the radius in feet. Multiply the result by the slab depth (d) in inches; then divide by 12 inches to obtain cubic feet. Round up to the next whole number, divide by 27, and add 10 percent as a margin of error to determine how many cubic yards of concrete to order.

Volume of Irregular Shapes.

To find the volume of an irregular shape, break it down into squares, rectangles, triangles, and circles. Use the formulas above to determine the volume of each component in cubic yards, and then add them together.

CALCULATING CUBIC YARDS OF CONCRETE

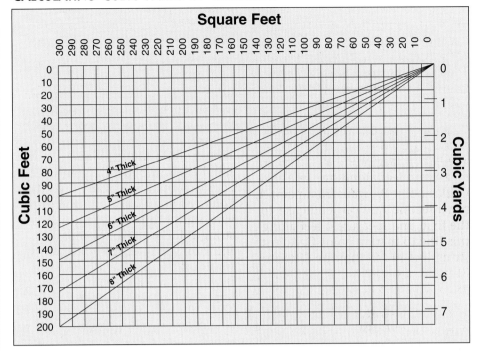

Sample problem: As an example, consider the driveway illustrated at right. The concrete slab will be 5 inches thick, except for the apron, which will be 7 inches thick. Begin by calculating the volume of the main driveway (A), which is a rectangle. The formula for A yields:

$20 \times 55 \times 5$ inches = 5,500

$5,500 \div 12 = 458$ cubic feet

$458 \div 27 = 16.98$ cubic yards

The main driveway will, therefore, require 17 cubic yards of concrete.

The turnaround can be treated as a rectangle (B) plus two triangles (C_1 and C_2). The formula for B yields:

$12 \times 18 \times 5$ inches = 1,080

$1,080 \div 12 = 90$ cubic feet

$90 \div 27 = 2.25$ cubic yards

The volume of triangles C_1 and C_2 is equal to one square having the same width and length as the triangles:

$10 \times 10 \times 5$ inches = 500

$500 \div 12 = 41.66$ cubic feet

$42 \div 27 = 1.55$ cubic yards

$2.25 + 1.55 = 3.8$ cubic yards

The turnaround will require 4 cubic yards of concrete.

The apron volume may also be calculated as the total of a rectangle (D) and two triangles (E_1 and E_2), combined into one square having the same width and length as the triangles.

Apron rectangle:

$20 \times 5 \times 7$ inches = 700

$700 \div 12 = 58.3$ cubic feet

$59 \div 27 = 2.2$ cubic yards

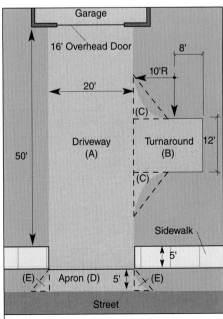

Sample Problem. This sample driveway is reduced to simple shapes to calculate the cubic volume of concrete needed.

Two triangles (One square):

5 × 5 × 7 inches= 175

175 ÷ 12 = 14.6 cubic feet

15 ÷ 27 = 0.6 cubic yard

Total apron:

2.2 + 0.6 = 2.8

The total apron will require 3 cubic yards of concrete.

Lastly, add these quantities to get the total amount of concrete needed:

17 + 4 + 3 = 24 cubic yards

Adding 10 percent as a margin of error, the total order is then rounded to 26.5 cubic yards of concrete.

Although these formulas are easy to apply, the chart "Calculating Cubic Yards of Concrete," on page 23, can be used to estimate the volume of concrete needed. First, calculate the area of the project in square feet by employing the formulas for rectangles and cylinders. It is not necessary to multiply the area by the slab depth or divide by 12 inches. Next, locate the square-foot quantity on the chart, and follow this line down to where it intersects the line representing the slab depth. Follow the intersecting horizontal line across to the left column of the chart, which will indicate the number of cubic feet of concrete required for the project. Follow the horizontal intersection across to the right side of the chart to get the amount of concrete required. If it exceeds the limits of the chart, the total may be extrapolated.

Concrete Steps

Concrete steps receive a great deal of wear and tear during normal use. For example, heavily loaded dollies and handtrucks can do significant damage to the edges of steps, making minor repairs necessary.

Repairing Step Edges

Difficulty Level: 🔨

Required Tools:

❏ **Basic tools:** bucket, cold chisel, 4-lb. sledgehammer, garden hose, gloves, goggles, paintbrush, whisk broom

❏ **Special tools and materials:** masonry trowel, edging trowel, finishing trowel, plywood formwork, portland cement, sand

1 Chip away the damaged concrete. Using a small sledgehammer and cold chisel, remove loose or damaged concrete at the edge of the step. Hold the chisel horizontally

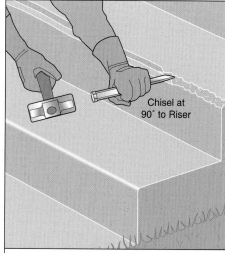

1. Use a small sledgehammer and a cold chisel to remove loose or damaged concrete at the edge of the step.

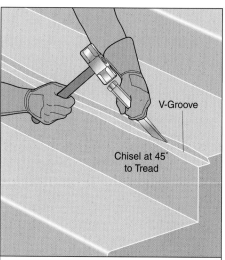

2. Using a cold chisel, undercut the damaged area, forming a V-groove to interlock with the new concrete.

and parallel to the stair tread, to better control chipping. Be sure to wear heavy gloves and safety goggles to protect your hands and eyes.

2 Undercut the edge. Hold the chisel at a sharp angle to the step, and undercut the area to be repaired, forming a V-groove, or keyway, to interlock with the new concrete. Use a whisk broom and water spray from a hose to remove loosened debris from the edge of the damaged step.

3 Set the form board in place. Cut the plywood formwork to the height of the riser on the dam-

An integrated driveway and walkway adds textural and dimensional appeal to this suburban house, bringing unity and harmony to the overall home and landscape design.

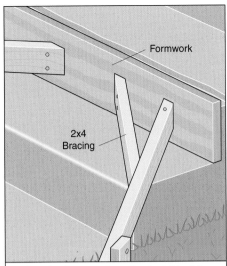

3. Cut the formwork to the height of the stair riser, and then brace it firmly against the riser with 2x4 stud reinforcing.

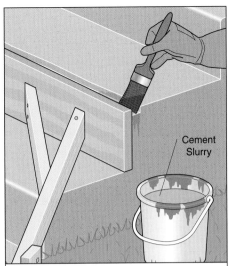

4. Make a stiff cement repair mix. In a separate bucket, make a watery cement slurry to moisten the edge being repaired.

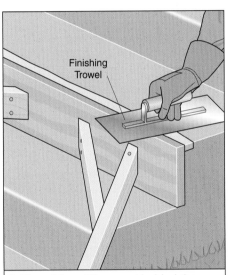

5. Trowel the stiff cement behind the formwork, and level it. Allow the surface to set, and then give it a float finish.

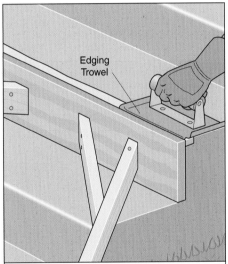

6. Round repaired edges using an edging tool. Remove the formwork, and then smooth out the finish using a trowel.

Repairing Step Corners

Difficulty Level: 🔨

Required Tools:

❑ **Basic tools:** bucket, cold chisel, 4-lb. sledgehammer, garden hose, gloves, goggles, paintbrush, whisk broom

❑ **Special tools and materials:** edging trowel, plywood formwork, pointing trowel, portland cement, sand

Prepare damaged step corners for patching in the same way as for a damaged step edge. Remove loose concrete with a chisel, and clean away all debris. Then mix one part portland cement with three parts sand. Add enough water to create a stiff cement mix for the repair work. In a separate container, combine a small amount of portland cement with water to make a cement slurry to moisten the area before patching.

1 Build up the corner. Coat the damaged area with the cement slurry, and then trowel in a new corner with the stiff cement mix. Brace a piece of plywood formwork against the riser of the damaged step to shape the work on one side of the patch. Smooth out and level the cement with the rest of the step. Repeat the process for the adjacent side of the corner repair.

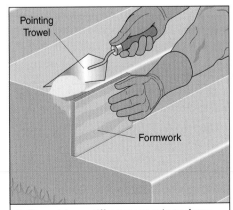

1. Trowel in a stiff cement mix to form the new corner. Secure the cement with plywood formwork braced tightly against the step riser.

aged step, and then brace it firmly against the riser with bricks, concrete blocks, or 2x4 stud bracing staked securely into the ground.

4 Mix the patching cement. In a bucket, mix one part portland cement and three parts sand with enough water to make a stiff cement mix for the repair. In a separate container, mix a small amount of portland cement with water to make a watery cement slurry, and use it to coat the cleanly chiseled step edge.

5 Fill and smooth the repair. Trowel the cement mix behind the formwork, agitating the mixture to break up air pockets. Form the concrete using a steel finishing trowel, making sure the repair is even with the rest of the step. Allow the concrete to set for about 1 hour, and then give it a float finish.

6 Edge the repair. Using an edging trowel, shape the edge of the concrete repair. Carefully remove the formwork after several hours, and smooth the finish if necessary. Keep the patch moist for at least one week, sprinkling it with water every day. Avoid heavy use for another week or more after this.

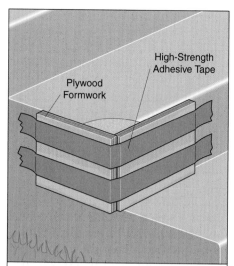

2. Use scrap plywood secured with duct tape to keep the cement work from slumping or collapsing while it sets.

2 **Brace the repair.** Brace the repair work with plywood formwork secured with adhesive duct tape. Remove the formwork after about 1 hour, and then smooth the surface, if necessary, with a float trowel. Allow the repair to cure for a week, sprinkling it with water daily. Avoid subjecting the step repair to heavy use for at least three weeks.

Concrete Walkways

Concrete walkways are durable and long lasting. If they are well constructed, they will require little maintenance. Concrete is also an extremely versatile material that can be broom finished, troweled, pressed or stamped, finished with exposed aggregates, or given a nonslip surface.

Laying Out a New Walkway

Difficulty Level: 🔧

Required Tools:

❏ **Basic tools:** line level, rake, shovel, sledgehammer, stakes

❏ **Special tools:** mason's string, tamper or compactor

Before constructing a walkway, check local ordinances with regard to work near street curbs. Also, contact your utility company, and have them mark the location of underground utilities before you do any excavation work.

To begin, draw a scaled plan of the proposed walkway. If there are no steps, plan the top of the slab to be 3 to 6 inches below the door sill to prevent water infiltration, and about 2 inches above the adjacent grade. Walkways are generally 3 to 4 feet wide, although a narrower width of 2 feet can be used for a garden path or service access. Primary entrance walks will look best between 4 and 6 feet in width, depending on the size, style, and design of your home.

Concrete slabs must be supported on bearing grade that is reasonably hard and stable, uniformly level, and well-drained. Check local building codes for the soil-bearing capacity required in your area. A poorly or improperly prepared subgrade will result in uneven settling and cracking. It is a good idea to support a walkway on a gravel base to improve drainage and reduce heaving. Ask the local building inspector or a land-

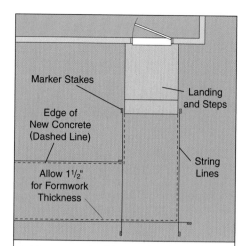

1. Use mason's string and stakes to lay out the perimeter of the walkway, allowing 1½ in. for the thickness of the formwork.

scape architect for the appropriate thickness to make your gravel base.

The concrete slab itself should be 4 to 6 inches thick, and reinforced with 6x6-inch–#10x10 gauge welded-wire mesh. Slope the slab ¼ inch in 12 inches toward drainage to carry off surface water.

1 **Lay out the sidewalk.** Lay out the perimeter of the walkway using stakes and mason's string. Set your stakes to mark the edge of the concrete, allowing 1½ inches for

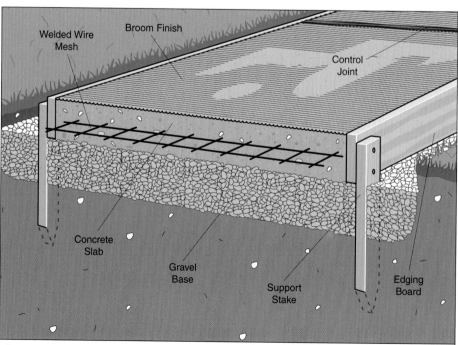

Concrete Sidewalk. A typical concrete sidewalk rests on a bed of gravel and is held in place by wooden or premolded composite formwork until the concrete is properly cured.

2. Temporarily remove the string guide, and then excavate enough soil to accommodate the slab and base material.

the thickness of the formwork. Set the outside corners a bit beyond the proposed edge so that they will not be in the way of excavation. Use the 3-4-5 method of triangulation for squaring the corners, as described in "Laying Out a New Concrete Driveway," on page 21. Outline curved walkways with old garden hoses or plastic sidewalk edging. Sprinkle sand around the perimeters. This will leave a line on the ground to guide your excavation work.

2 Excavate the soil. Temporarily remove the string guideline, and then excavate widely enough to allow room for the formwork. Dig out spongy areas, and fill them in with crushed stone or sand. Loosen and tamp hardpan to provide uniform support. Excavate enough soil to accommodate the thickness of the slab plus the base material. In areas with poor drainage, provide a 4- to 6-inch layer of gravel beneath the slab. In better-drained areas, a 2-inch-deep layer of sand might be sufficient.

3 Smooth and tamp surface. Leave virgin soil undisturbed where possible, because it is packed firmer than compacted fill. Level loose surface soil with a rake, and fill voids left by removed stones and roots with sand or gravel. Compact the soil with a hand-operated tamper or vibration compactor.

3. Fill the voids and level the loose soil. Compact the subgrade with a hand tamper or vibration compactor.

Building Formwork

Difficulty Level: 🔨

Required Tools:

- ❏ **Basic tools:** line level, sledgehammer, stakes
- ❏ **Special tools:** formwork, mason's string

1 Set the elevation. After the subgrade is prepared, begin the formwork at the stakes nearest to the house. If these have been loosened or moved during excavation, reset them firmly into the ground. Use either a board with a mason's level or a string with a line level to set the elevation

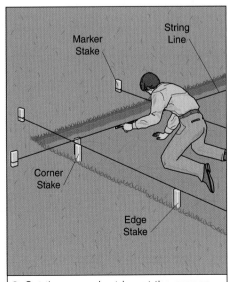

1. Mark the elevation of the slab on the layout stakes for the string guideline.

for the top of the new concrete walkway. This elevation should be set in relation to the height of the bottom step or, if there are no steps, at least 3 to 6 inches below the door sill. Mark the stakes, and then tie mason's string to them at the height marked.

2 Set the string lines. Using a line level, stretch a string guideline between the layout stakes to mark the perimeter of the proposed walkway. Be sure that the corners are square. If necessary, drive intermediate stakes at intervals of 10 to 15 feet along the perimeter to keep the string from sagging. (Stakes for the formwork will be placed 4 feet apart.) If the grade change is significant, adjust the string guide so that it follows the slope of the ground. To ensure proper drainage, slope or crown the walkway surface a minimum of ¼ inch for every 12 inches of run. For example, a walkway 3 feet wide sloped at ¼ inch per foot of run should be ¾ inch lower along one edge than along the other. To set the string guidelines at the correct slope, measure the required distance down on each stake along what will become the lower side of the walkway. Reset the string on that side at the lower height.

3 Stake the formwork. Drive additional stakes along the string guideline, spacing them at

2. Set the mason's string at the proper slab height between the layout stakes.

approximately 4 feet on center. Make sure the tops of these stakes are set somewhat below the string line so that they will not interfere with leveling and finishing the top of the concrete walkway slab, but also be sure to leave room to drive nails into the forms. At the corners, drive a stake parallel to each side. If necessary, use extra stakes to ensure that the formwork won't flex during the pour.

4 **Make curved formwork.** To make curved formwork, if needed, use ¼-inch plywood to form the short-radius curves. Align the grain of the plywood face vertically so that it will bend more easily. Space the support stakes no more than 1 to 2 feet apart. Use 1x4 or 1x6 lumber for longer-radius curves. Wet the wood first, to make it more flexible for bending. Curved formwork must be nailed to the support stakes from the inside for it to be held securely. Use common nails, rather than double-headed nails, so that the nailheads will not be stuck in the concrete when the stakes and forms are removed.

5 **Attach boards to the stakes.** After the stakes are in place, align the top of the formwork with the string. For straight forms, hold the boards tightly against the stakes and nail the stakes to the formwork from the outside. Use double-headed nails for ease of removal. Butt the formwork tightly together to prevent any wet concrete from leaking out. Where the ends of boards adjoin, be sure that each board is staked.

6 **Mark locations for control joints.** After the formwork is completed, mark the locations for the control joints. These will be tooled or saw-cut later. Mark the top of the formwork using a wax crayon or other marker that will still be easy to read when the forms are wet and splattered with concrete.

7 **Add the base material.** Add the sand or gravel base appropriate for local conditions. For a gravel base, add half of the base material

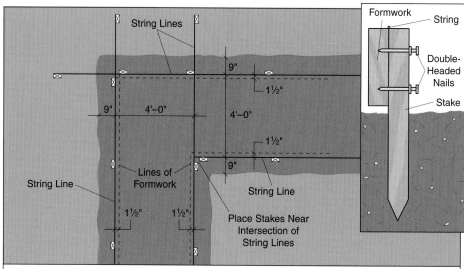

3. Just below the string line, drive wooden stakes at a maximum of 4 ft. on center to support the formwork.

4. Secure curved forms to the support stakes from inside with common nails.

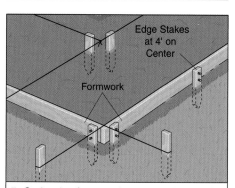

5. Stake the formwork at a maximum of 4 ft. on center to prevent flexing.

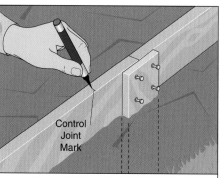

6. Indicate the location of the control joints using a wax crayon or marker.

7. Add a gravel base to ensure adequate drainage beneath the slab.

to the inside of the formwork, level it, and then tamp it firmly into place. Add the remaining gravel, and then tamp it once again. For a sand base, pour in all the material at once, and then tamp it thoroughly. Use a 2x4 to screed the sand or gravel, leveling it to a depth that will bring the concrete pour even with the top of the formwork.

8 **Lay the wire mesh.** Concrete is strong in compression, while steel is strong in tension. Due to its tensile strength, steel is typically used to reinforce concrete against cracking. Usually, walkways are reinforced with welded-wire mesh for the same reason. The mesh is placed in the middle of the concrete pour. Stones, bricks, or pieces of

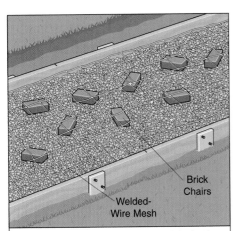

8. Install 6x6-in.–#10x10 ga. welded-wire mesh 2 in. below the top of the formwork. Where the reinforcing mesh must be spliced, lap one full row of squares, and then tie the overlap with wire.

concrete can be used as chairs to support it during the pour. If the mesh must be spliced, lap one full row of wire squares and tie the laps together with steel wire. If the concrete mix will be trucked in, order a mix that contains fiber reinforcement to provide the concrete with additional resistance to cracking.

Pouring and Finishing Concrete

Difficulty Level: 𝍏 𝍏

Required Tools:

❏ **Basic tools:** broom, shovel, wheelbarrow, work gloves

❏ **Special tools:** darby, edging trowel, finishing trowel, float trowel, jointing trowel, mason's hoe, screed (2x4)

Before mixing or pouring concrete, check the layout of the formwork for accuracy. Once it is in place, lightly wet down the formwork and the base material to keep them from drawing water from the concrete mix, which would weaken it.

Mix the concrete, or have it delivered as near to the work as possible. If necessary, use a wheelbarrow to move the concrete to the formwork. Be sure to fill the forms completely. Fill low areas using a shovel, and

agitate the concrete using a hoe to eliminate voids and fill corners. Gently tap the outside of the formwork with a mallet to settle the concrete along the perimeter of the walkway. After the concrete has all been placed, it will be ready for leveling and texturing.

1 Screed the concrete. As soon as a few feet of the formwork have been filled and agitated, begin striking off, or *screeding*, the concrete. Use a straight 2x4 screed slightly wider than the walkway, and pull it across the top of the formwork to level the surface of the concrete. Fill low areas using a shovel, and screed them once again, if necessary.

2 Level the concrete with a darby. Using a wooden darby, make wide sweeping arcs across the surface to initially level the concrete. Keep the darby edge slightly raised to avoid gouging the concrete. This *floating* process will be continued after the water has evaporated from the concrete surface. How long this takes varies with the weather and the type of cement used.

3 Edge the slab. Use an edging trowel to separate the concrete from the formwork and to produce a clean, finished edge.

Handling Concrete. Place the concrete into the formwork with a wheelbarrow and shovel, and then agitate it using a mason's hoe to eliminate air bubbles.

1. Screed the concrete by dragging a 2x4 across the top of the formwork.

2. Using a darby, make sweeping arcs across the surface of the concrete.

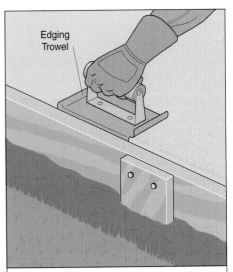

3. Separate the concrete from the formwork using an edging trowel.

4. Use a 2x4 as a guide for tooling control joints. Bridge the formwork with a 2x12 to create a kneeling surface.

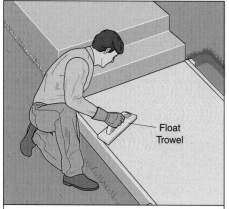

5. Use a wood float to smooth the concrete surface. If any water rises to the surface, let it evaporate before floating.

4 Form the control joints. Using a jointing trowel, make control joints at the points marked earlier on the formwork. Use a 2x4 as a straightedge to guide the cutting of the control joints. If necessary, bridge the formwork with a 2x12 supported on concrete blocks. This will create a surface to kneel on.

5 Float the finish surface. When the surface water has completely evaporated, move the float trowel in wide, nearly-flat sweeping motions across the concrete to finish the surface. Be sure to smooth away any gouges left by either the edging or jointing trowel. Go over the edges and the control joints with the edging and jointing trowels one more time, after the surface has been floated.

Pull a damp broom across the floated finish, perpendicular to the direction

of traffic to produce a nonskid surface. For a more finely textured surface use a soft-bristled brush. For a coarser texture use a broom with stiff bristles.

Curing concrete. After the concrete has cured for one day, carefully remove the formwork. Do not pry or hammer against the concrete itself. It will continue to cure gradually until it reaches its full strength after 28 days. It can, however, be walked on after the first day.

Resurfacing Concrete

Replacing damaged concrete should be done only as a last resort. If the concrete is generally sound, resurfacing it will be less expensive than replacing it altogether.

To add a new layer of concrete over an existing one, dig a shallow trench along the perimeter of the old concrete to accommodate new formwork. The formwork should project 2 inches above the existing surface to form a new concrete cap. Pour and finish the concrete in the same way as for a new walkway. Before pouring the cap, however, be sure the old concrete is free of major fracturing, frost heaving, or other structural problems. If such problems are not first corrected, then the new cap will crack or heave again in the same place.

Dry-Laid Walkways

To construct a dry-laid walkway, masonry units, or *pavers*, are laid down on a bed of compacted sand or gravel. No mortar is needed.

Paving Units

The paving units are typically brick or concrete and may be interlocking. They are laid tightly together, and then fine sand is swept between the joints creating a stable and durable walkway, even in climates subject to moderate frost heave. With dry-laid paving, it is easy to replace damaged pavers and reposition uneven sections of the walkway. The sand, however, must be periodically replenished because it gradually washes away.

The ideal base for pavers is a bed of sand *over* gravel. Only when soil is stable and well-drained should sand be placed directly on grade. The depth of a gravel base depends on the strength of the underlying soil. A 2-inch sand bed over 4 inches of gravel or crushed stone is typical.

Edging Systems

Dry-laid pavers require edging to prevent them from slipping apart.

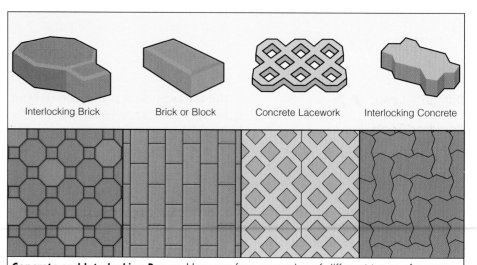

Interlocking Brick   Brick or Block   Concrete Lacework   Interlocking Concrete

Concrete and Interlocking Pavers. Here are four examples of different types of pavers. Below each type is the pattern that it produces.

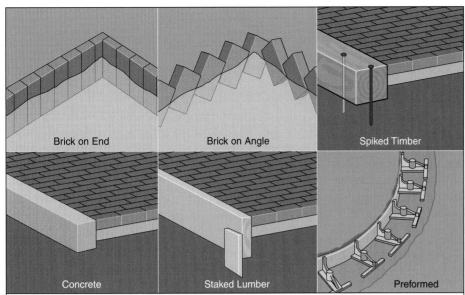

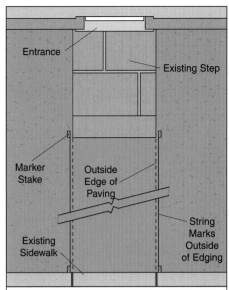

Edging Systems. Dry-laid paving units must be contained by an edging system, several of which are illustrated here, including brick, wood, concrete and preformed edging.

1. Mark out the boundaries of the walkway, and then set stakes at the corners. Use mason's string between the stakes.

Brick, treated wood, concrete, or pre-formed curbs can all provide stability, provided that they are properly installed. Metal or plastic edging systems are especially easy to install. This type of edging is usually conceal-able below grade, and it will not change the appearance of the paving pattern. For interlocking pavers, check the manufacturer's literature to see whether or not edging is required.

If an edging material will be used, it should be installed upon comple-tion of the excavation work. The gravel base should be applied next, followed by landscaping fabric, a sand bed, and lastly, the pavers.

Installing a Brick Walkway

Difficulty Level: 🔨🔨

Required Tools:

❑ **Basic tools:** 4-ft. level, garden hose, line level, mallet, mason's string, push broom, sledgehammer, screed, stakes, tamper

❑ **Basic materials:** brick pavers, gravel or crushed stone, landscaping fabric, mason's sand

1 **Lay out the walkway.** Using wooden stakes and mason's string, lay out the perimeter of the proposed walkway. Set the outside corner stakes a bit beyond the pro-posed paving edge to allow for the thickness of the edging material. Use the 3-4-5 method of triangula-tion described earlier to ensure that everything is square. (See page 22.)

2 **Excavate the soil.** Sprinkle some sand over the string guidelines to transfer the boundaries of the excavation to the ground, and then remove the strings. The depth of the excavation must accommodate the gravel base, the sand bed, and the paver thickness. Excavate along the marked boundaries of the walkway, removing grass, roots, rocks, and other debris as necessary.

To best weather the elements, build the walkway on a 2-inch bed of sand over a 4-inch gravel base. Check your local building codes to see if a gravel base is mandatory. In any case, the gravel should be compactable so that it will make a firm, well-drained base. Crushed limestone, ¾ inch in diameter or less, is ideal for this purpose. Avoid smooth riverbank or pea gravel. One cubic yard of gravel will cover approximately 80 square feet of walkway area. Lay down half of the gravel, tamp it with a hand

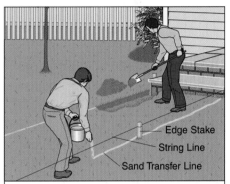

2. Sprinkle sand over the string to show the walkway boundaries. Remove the string, and excavate the bounded area.

3. Replace the string line to mark the edge, and then excavate the perimeter to accommodate the edging bricks.

tamper, add the rest of the gravel, and then tamp it down again.

3 **Install brick edging.** Replace the string line as a guide for the ele-vation and alignment of the edging.

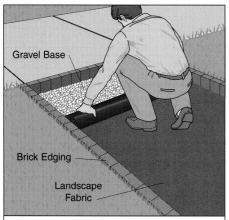

Gravel Base

Brick Edging

Landscape Fabric

4. Lay landscaping fabric or perforated polyethylene over the base material.

Sand Bed

Wood Screed

5. Shovel in the sand bed, and then screed it to the level of the paver depth.

6. Lay the pavers on the sand bed, and then gently tap them into position.

If the edging bricks will be set on end, dig a narrow trench around the perimeter of the excavation area deep enough to allow for the gravel, the sand, and the height of the edging bricks. Place the bricks on end against the string line, and then tap the pavers into place using a trowel handle. Fill around the edging with sand. Set the edging high enough to cover the depth of the sand bed and the thickness of the brick pavers. Be sure that the edging bricks are snugly butted together.

Before laying down the sand bed, do a dry run of the proposed brick pattern between the edging bricks to test how well the bricks will fit. After confirming that the layout will work, remove the test bricks.

4 **Install a weed barrier.** To keep weeds from growing between the dry-laid pavers, install a layer of landscaping fabric or perforated polyethylene sheeting between the gravel base and the sand bed. Roll out sections of fabric, lapping adjoining pieces by at least 6 inches. A weed barrier between the gravel base and the sand bed will also keep the sand from settling.

5 **Spread and screed the sand bed.** Install the sand bed. Use 1 cubic yard of sand for each 150 square feet of walkway. Tamp the sand to a level that will bring the surface of the pavers 2 inches above the adjoining finished grade. Cut a 1x4 to the width of the walkway,

7. Tamp the positioned pavers into the sand bed. Check and level the pavers.

and attach it to a 2x4 that is cut wider than the walkway to make a *screed*. Screed the sand only in one direction. Avoid walking on it.

6 **Install pavers.** Place the pavers on the compacted sand, butting them tightly together and tamping them into place with a rubber mallet or trowel handle. Use string lines to keep the brick coursing straight. If necessary, put down plywood on which you can kneel to avoid making depressions in the sand.

7 **Check for level and bed the pavers.** After installing several linear feet of pavers, lay a length of 1x6 on the walkway, and tap the wood down over the surface using a mallet to uniformly set the brick pavers into the sand bed. Tap individual units gently into place with the mallet. If any pavers sit too low,

8. Sweep mason's sand in between the paver joints using a stiff push broom.

then place more sand beneath them. Check the surface of the walkway periodically with a 4-foot level to ensure that the pavers are either level or uniformly sloped in the correct direction for proper drainage.

8 **Fill the joints with sand.** After all the pavers are in position, spread a layer of dry mason's sand evenly over a section of the walkway. Using a stiff broom, sweep the sand into the joints between the pavers, filling them completely. Scoop up any excess sand for reuse. Lightly wet down the walkway using a garden hose to compact the sand and to wash off the surface of the bricks. Do not use a heavy spray, or the sand from the brick joints will be dislodged. Allow the surface to dry, and then repeat the process until all of the brick joints are filled with sand.

Chapter 3
Doors and Windows

Little says "Welcome to my home" more effectively than an elegant entryway with a beautifully styled door. Stately, yet inviting, a well-crafted entrance that is adorned with sidelights lets in a bit of light while giving a hint of the light and warmth within. Likewise, windows not only hint at what is within but also reveal what is outside, whether beautiful scenery, a welcome guest, or children playing in the yard. Doors, windows, and skylights add security, beauty, and light to a home. Smooth-working, energy-efficient doors and windows also add value by reducing heating and cooling costs. Add to this the psychological benefits of light and air, which help to promote a sense of brightness and spaciousness, and this value becomes inestimable.

IN THIS CHAPTER

The Front Doorway

Refinishing the Door 34

Replacing the Door 35

Replacement Windows

Replacing
Sash and Jambs 38

Replacing the
Entire Window Unit 41

Installing a Jamb-
Supported Window 41

Installing a Flange-
Supported Window 42

Specialty Windows

Installing a Skylight 44

Installing a Bay Window 46

TODAY'S TRENDS

Custom Carved Doors

Stained Glass

Special Hardware

Curved Windows

Roof Windows

The Front Doorway

Refinishing the Door

It isn't always necessary to buy a new door to create a beautiful entrance. If the front door is in good condition, it may need only refinishing or perhaps the addition of a sidelight or two. Consider also replacing exterior light fixtures or adding a planter or two around the entranceway or on the porch steps.

Difficulty Level:

Required Tools:

❏ **Basic tools:** paintbrush, putty knife, sander, scraper

❏ **Special Materials:** mineral spirits, paint, wood filler

1 Remove the door. While it might seem easier or faster to paint a door in place, it is better to remove the door from the hinges and paint it on a horizontal surface. This also makes it easier to sand or scrape off dried paint that may have been causing the door to stick.

The Front Doorway. A front door is the gateway to a home. How it is designed will determine whether or not those who approach it will feel welcome.

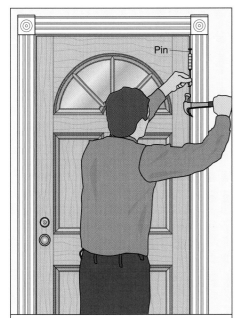

1. Using a hammer, tap the pins out, and then lift the door free of the hinges.

2. Use a power sander to remove old, thick, blistered, and flaking paint.

3. Paint the raised panels, brushing first across the grain and then with the grain.

To remove the door, insert a nail in the bottom of the hinge and tap the pin out with a hammer. Tap out all the pins, and then lift the door slightly to free it from the hinges. Lay the door on a workbench or between two sawhorses, and then remove and label all hardware to ease reassembly.

2 Scrape and sand the door. To prepare the door for refinishing, scrape away paint drips and thick paint. If the finish coat has failed, scrape off blistering or flaking paint. For speed, use an electric sander with 60-grit paper to feather away major chips. Finish sanding with 100-grit paper, and then clean the wood surface with mineral spirits or a liquid deglosser.

3 Paint the door. Panel doors are finely detailed, compared with flush doors, and therefore they are more difficult to paint. Beginning with a 2-inch brush, paint the center panels. For even coverage, first paint the wood across the grain, and then paint it with the grain. Work quickly to keep a smooth, ripple-free finish. Once the panels are done, finish painting the remainder of the door in a logical sequence. For example, paint the panels first, then the rails, and lastly the stiles.

Replacing the Door

Difficulty Level: 🔨🔨🔨

Required Tools:

❑ **Basic tools: caulking gun, circular saw, hammer, power drill, pry bar, reciprocating saw, spirit level**

❑ **Special materials: aluminum flashing, caulking, insulation, lumber, shim stock, nails, and screws**

Value Tip

Paint or Polyurethane Clear Finish?

It usually does not pay to strip the finish off a painted door in the hope of obtaining a wood-grained look. It is extremely difficult to remove all of the paint, and the effort spent stripping, sanding, staining, and sealing isn't worth the time and expense. It is best either to paint the door in a traditional color, such as white, to provide a fresh look, or to coat it with an opaque stain over the existing finish. Consider adding a brass kick plate or letter slot for an elegant touch.

Pro Tip

PAINTING DOORS

To protect the door finish while working, cover the sawhorses with towels or carpet scraps. Be sure to allow sufficient time for the door to dry before flipping it over.

To paint both sides of the door at one time, drive a pair of 16d nails into the top and bottom edges of the door, and then rest the door on the sawhorses, as shown below. After painting one side, simply flip the door over to paint the other side. (Note: This method may not work quite as well with very heavy wood or steel doors.)

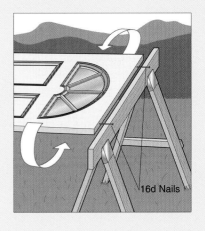

16d Nails

A Grand Entrance. An elegant door with sidelights says "Welcome" and at the same time provides light and security.

Prehung Doors. A door that comes prehung in a frame can be easier to install than a new door in an existing frame.

If your front entryway lacks liveliness and charm or seems hopelessly out-of-date, perhaps it's time for a complete replacement. Even if your entrance isn't in particularly bad shape, upgrading the door with a leaded-glass panel or sidelights can give a home an attractive and interesting facelift.

Although you can choose to simply replace the door itself, purchasing a complete prehung unit, including the frame, is probably a better value. Prehung doors are easy to install because the door is already hinged in its frame, which has an aluminum threshold and factory-applied weatherstripping attached.

All you need to do is remove the old door and door frame, exposing the end studs in the wall (the *rough opening*), and then nail the new door assembly into place. If you choose to install a larger door, of course, the doorway will need to be reframed and a longer header installed. Because this involves cutting into the side of your house and adding framing, this type of work should be reserved only for experienced do-it-yourselfers.

1 Remove the frame. Whether installing a replacement door of the same size or wider, start by removing the casings and frame. If the door is the same size, the existing rough opening, with minor modifications, will suffice. If the new door is wider, then frame the opening as needed.

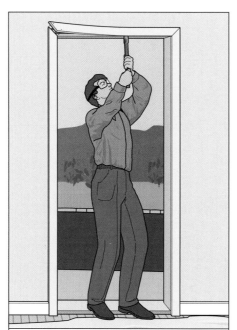

1. To establish the rough opening for the door, remove the existing casings, and then cut back the drywall as needed.

Begin reframing by marking out the rough opening on the inside wall. (The *rough opening* is equal to the width and height of the door unit plus ½ inch.) Next, cut back the drywall (or plaster) and the baseboards as needed. It is easier to remove the drywall all the way to the first stud on each side of the rough jamb opening. Cut back to at least 12 inches above the rough head opening to accommodate a new header.

2 Erect a temporary wall. If the ceiling joists run perpendicular to the door opening, erect a temporary stud wall to support the weight bearing on the wall being opened. If the ceiling joists run parallel to this wall, a temporary support wall may not be necessary. Check with the local building inspector or a licensed architect before removing or opening any bearing walls.

If a temporary wall is necessary, position it about 3 feet in from the door opening. This should allow sufficient room for working comfortably. Erect the wall directly beneath the joists.

3 Replace the header. Once the old door has been removed and

2. If the ceiling joists run perpendicular to the door opening, erect a temporary support wall to bear the ceiling load.

the ceiling braced, pry out the old header and any studs that interfere with the proposed new opening. Use a reciprocating saw to cut through nails holding studs to the sheathing.

Frame in the new trimmer studs, header, and support posts as necessary. Use a level to ensure that the new studs are plumb.

Note: The size of a header depends upon the width that it must span and the load that it must carry. Consult with a licensed architect or local building inspector to determine the correct size beam to use.

4 Rough-cut the opening. From inside, drill a hole through the wall in each corner of the proposed opening. From outside, draw a pencil line to connect the drill holes. Using a circular or reciprocating saw, cut through both the siding and the plywood sheathing.

5 Test-fit the door. With the rough opening cleared and the subsill exposed, test-fit the new door unit. If the old door frame was notched into the floor joists, use plywood to build the joist up to the level of the subfloor. If necessary, shim the subfloor with plywood strips to bring it level.

Next, tilt the door into the rough opening, checking to make sure that the base is level and that the sides are plumb. The installed door should swing clearly about ½ inch above the finish floor or carpeting. Lastly, outline the position of the exterior casing on the siding to determine how far back you'll need to trim it.

6 Trim back the siding. Set your saw-blade depth to cut through the siding, and then cut the siding back to the trimline, using a board to support the saw and guide a straight cut.

Next, flash the subfloor, and then tuck felt paper at least 2 inches behind the siding to prevent water penetration. Lastly, install a metal drip cap over the head casing.

3. After you've braced the ceiling, frame the doorway. Install a new header as needed to span the opening.

4. Drill pilot holes from the inside, and then use these holes as a guide to cut the opening from outside.

5. After you've cut the rough opening, test-fit the new door. It should swing about ½ in. above the finished floor.

6. Set the saw blade to cut through the siding, and then trim it back to accommodate the exterior casing.

$ Value Tip

Door Styles

Before replacing any doors in your home, decide upon an appropriate style. Will you be able to match the existing door style? If not, it may be necessary either to get a door custom-made or to replace all of the doors in your home. It is important to have a unified and consistent style throughout your home, in order to avoid the appearance of haphazard design.

7 Set the door. Before lifting the door unit into place, run a bead of exterior caulking on the sheathing around the perimeter of the opening. Tilt the frame into place, and then shim it to make sure that the sides are perfectly plumb. Next, tack the frame into place with three 16d galvanized finishing nails on each side. Install the door into the frame, and then open it to see whether it works properly. If necessary, shim the frame along the sides and top, and then drive the nails into the wall studs at 16 inches on center. Drive the nails through shims.

8 Insulate and caulk the opening. Use a bead of low-expansion foam or fiberglass insulation to fill the jamb shim space. Outside, use exterior caulk to seal between the siding and casing.

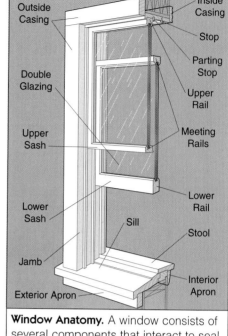

Window Anatomy. A window consists of several components that interact to seal out wind and rain, yet operate smoothly.

Replacement Windows

Replacing obsolete windows will not only beautify a home but will also result in savings on heating and cooling. In addition, airtight windows make a home more comfortable by eliminating unwanted drafts, and they can be purchased in a tilt-in version that is easy to clean.

If old window frames are in good condition, sash-and-jamb replacement windows are a sensible and economical choice. Simply remove the existing sash and stops, and then replace the interior window components. The existing frame, drywall, and trim remain intact.

If the jambs and sills have begun to rot, however, then a complete frame and window replacement may be required. Look for signs of rot and deterioration by poking the frame in several places with an awl. If the frame seems solid, you can probably salvage it and just replace the sash. But if any part of the frame seems spongy, offering little resistance to a sharp object, then replace the entire window, both sash and frame.

Replacing Sash and Jambs

Difficulty Level: 🔨

Required Tools:

❑ **Basic tools:** chisel, hacksaw, hammer, measuring tape, nail set, pry bar, screwdriver

❑ **Special materials:** 8d finishing nails, sash replacement kit, vermiculite or foam insulation

Shop around to determine the types of replacement sash available. Some require a precise fit into an existing frame, while others come with adjustable frames. Modern replacement sash ride in jamb liners, rather

7. Run caulking around the opening, and then set the new door frame into place. Be sure the sides are plumb.

8. To create an airtight seal, insert a bead of low-expansion foam or fiberglass insulation in the shim spaces at each jamb (left). Use a high-grade exterior caulk to seal the gap between the cut edges of the siding and the edge of the exterior casing (right).

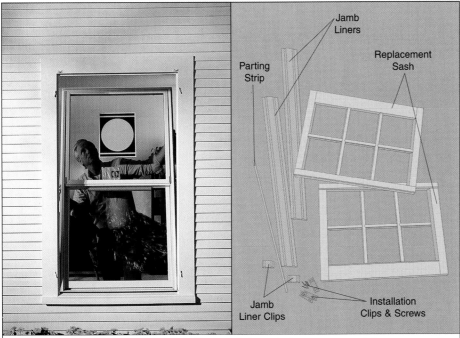

Replacement Windows. Simply pry off the existing window stops, and then remove the existing sash to install the components of a modern window replacement.

Parting Strip

Jamb Liners

Replacement Sash

Jamb Liner Clips

Installation Clips & Screws

than being suspended with concealed pulleys and weights. This type of window sash also may tilt inward on a pivot for easy cleaning.

1 Measure the sash opening width. Using a measuring tape, measure the sash opening dimensions, beginning with the actual width between the jambs (not the stops). Take one measurement across the top and another across the bottom. If the two dimensions are different by more than ⅛ inch, you will need the type of replacement sash that has an adjustable frame width.

2 Measure the sash opening height. To obtain the sash opening height, measure from the top frame to the topmost part of the sill. Measure the sash opening width

and height for all the windows to be replaced—even though they look the same size they probably vary, especially in older homes with site-built windows. Using the widths and heights obtained, order the replacement sash.

3 Remove the existing stops. If the existing stops are secured to the head and jambs with screws and not stuck in place by layers of paint, simply remove the screws. If the stops are painted in place and fastened with nails, first score the joint between the stop and the frame using a utility knife to loosen the paint. Then use a pry bar or chisel to pry the stops from the head and jambs of the window frame.

Measuring Tape

1. Carefully measure the distance between jambs at both the top and the bottom to get correct sash opening width.

Measuring Tape

Sill

2. To obtain the sash opening height, measure the distance between the top frame and the topmost point on the sill.

Stop

Pry Bar

3. To free the existing sash, remove the stops from each jamb and from the head of the window.

4 **Remove the existing sash.** First pry off the window stops at the head and side jambs of the existing window, and then remove the bottom sash from the frame. Disconnect the sash cords and sash weights from the bottom sash, if there are any, being careful to lower the weights before letting go of the sash cords. Finally, disconnect and remove the top sash.

5 **Insulate the frame.** Open the sash weight covers at the lower end of each jamb, and then remove and discard the ropes and weights. After replacing the cover, remove the pulleys, and fill in the voids with vermiculite or foam insulation. If necessary, enlarge the openings with a hole saw in a power drill or a key-hole saw. This step is important because it makes little or no sense to install an energy efficient window in an uninsulated window frame.

6 **Install the new jamb liners.** Measure the jamb liners, and then cut them to the proper length using a hacksaw. Place the jamb liners into position, and attach them to the existing frame. This is typically done with nails preset at the top and bottom of the jambs.

7 **Install the new top sash.** Holding the sash at an angle, insert the top sash into the jamb liners. Be certain that the clutch pivot (the projecting hardware at the side of the sash) is above the clutch and in the outside track on both sides.

Next, rotate the top sash into a horizontal position, and then tilt it up into a vertical position. Press the sash into the liners while pushing it to the outside track, one side at a time. Slide the sash down until the clutches are engaged, and then slide it back up again. Install the bottom sash by the same method but using the inside tracks of the jamb liners.

8 **Replace the stops.** Replace the original or install new window stops. In order to prevent sticking, use a $1/16$-inch spacer to set the stops.

4. Pry off the window stops on the head and jambs of the frame, and then re-move the bottom sash from the frame.

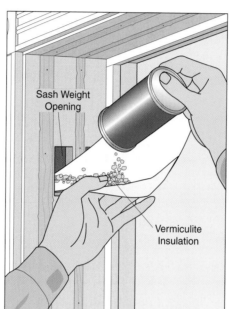

5. Remove and discard sash weights, ropes, and pulleys, and then insulate the frame using vermiculite or foam.

6. Measure and cut the new jamb liners, and then position and nail them to the window frame.

7. Insert the top sash into the jamb liners, lift it horizontally, and then tilt it verti-cally into position.

8. Lastly, install the new window stops in place of the original stops, and discard the old window components.

Window Replacement. Replacing an entire window unit requires considerably more effort than installing a simple sash-and-jamb replacement kit.

Installing a Jamb-Supported Window

Difficulty Level: 𝕋 𝕋 𝕋

Required Tools:

❑ <u>Basic tools:</u> caulking gun, circular or reciprocating saw, hammer, nail set, spirit level

❑ <u>Special materials:</u> aluminum flashing, caulking, foam insulation, 10d casing nails

1 Place and level the window.
Unpack the window, and check it for damage or missing parts. Next, measure the window diagonally. The diagonal measurements must match for the window to be square. Leave bracing, if there is any, on the window until it has been secured in place. Some manufacturers recommend that the sash be removed before installation, to prevent glass breakage, while others recommend leaving it in place to stiffen the jambs. Following the manufacturer's recommendations, lift the window into position. While an assistant braces it, check the sill for level, and then shim it as needed. For windows wider than 36 inches, also shim midway under the sill. Check the sill frequently during installation to be sure it stays in position.

Replacing the Entire Window Unit

Replacing an entire window unit is more complicated than installing a simple sash-and-jamb replacement kit. All of the existing window components must first be removed, including the sash, trim, and frame. It may then be necessary to alter the rough opening to accommodate the size or shape of the new unit. The steps taken to install a new window in a wood-frame wall also apply to brick veneer walls, but to avoid having to alter the brick, you may opt for a replacement window that fits the same rough opening.

Complete window units may be installed in several different ways.

Some are installed by driving nails through the jambs into the stud framing. This type of window has a narrow casing, called a "brick molding," on the outside face.

Metal, vinyl, aluminum-clad wood, vinyl-clad wood, and some all-wood windows are secured by nailing through a perforated perimeter flange into the exterior sheathing and stud framing. This system requires that the siding, but not the sheathing, be cut back to accommodate the nailing flange. A window casing may also be needed.

Other window units come with a heavier outside casing that is nailed directly to the stud framing. To install these, the sheathing must be cut back, as well as the siding.

1. Lift the window into the rough opening, level it, and then shim it as needed.

2 Set the window. Tip the window slightly away from the opening while an assistant runs a bead of exterior-grade caulking behind the brick molding. Next, insert aluminum flashing over the head casing, and slip it under the siding. Then press the window firmly into place. Using 10d galvanized casing nails, attach the casing, temporarily securing the lower end of the brick molding to the wall.

3 Shim and nail the jambs. Check the window once again to be sure it is both plumb and square. If necessary, readjust the shims, and then tack the window into place. Then, if the sash was removed, put it back into the frame. Open and close the sash a few times to be sure it doesn't bind. If it does, you may need to reposition the frame. Once the window works properly, secure the frame by nailing through the

jamb and shims into the wall studs.

4 Insulate and caulk. Using a high-quality exterior-grade caulking, fill the gap beneath the sill and between the window casings and the siding. From the inside, use fiberglass batting or an expandable foam sealant to seal the shim space between the window frame and the stud wall. If foam is used, inject it incrementally to prevent it from expanding too much and pushing the jambs out of position. After insulating, install the interior casing.

Note: For 6-inch stud walls, extension jambs will be required to bring the jambs flush with the interior wall edge. Usually, extension jambs can be ordered with the window unit. If they are not supplied, you can make them on-site.

Installing a Flange-Supported Window

Difficulty Level: ⚒⚒

Required Tools:

❏ **Basic tools: caulking gun, hammer, spirit level**

❏ **Special materials: aluminum flashing, caulking, 15 lb. felt paper, foam insulation, 1¾-in. roofing nails**

Windows with perimeter nailing flanges are easier to install than jamb-supported windows. For one thing, shimming is less critical because, once secured, the flange supports the window. With less shimming, the rough openings for flanged windows are also typically smaller than they would be for standard windows of the same size.

1 Set and nail the window. Attach 15-pound felt paper to the exposed sheathing around the rough opening, wrapping it around and over the top, bottom, and sides of the framing, as well. Apply a bead of caulking to the exterior

2. Install flashing around the window frame. Then, using 10d casing nails, temporarily secure the lower end of the brick molding to the wall.

3. Check the window to be sure it is both plumb and square, and then shim it as needed. Next, nail the jambs into the stud framing.

4. Using a high-quality exterior-grade caulking, seal the exterior of the window unit between the siding and the sill, head, and jambs. On the interior side, either stuff fiberglass batt or inject foam insulation into the shim spaces between the window frame and the stud wall.

1. Apply caulk, and then position the window. Nail one flange, plumb and square the unit, and then nail the opposite flange.

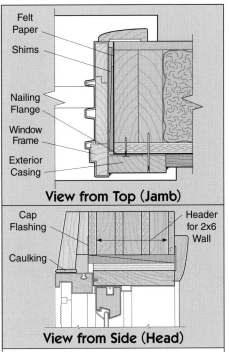

Felt Paper
Shims
Nailing Flange
Window Frame
Exterior Casing

View from Top (Jamb)

Cap Flashing
Caulking
Header for 2x6 Wall

View from Side (Head)

2. Flash around the window, and then install exterior casings or extend the siding to the window frame. Finish by caulking around the entire window.

around the perimeter of the window, and between the casing and the ends of the siding.

Note: To install a window in a wall where there is no existing window, consult the manufacturer's literature to determine the rough opening dimensions before cutting the wall.

Specialty Windows

A skylight or roof window is an excellent way to bring light and air into a space. Skylights typically allow 30 percent more light into a room than vertical windows of the same size. For this reason, they are especially beneficial in spaces like renovated attics that don't have side walls. They are also good for focusing light in a particular area, such as a niche. They are frequently installed in kitchens and bathrooms, as well, where wall space may be limited.

Adding a bay window to your home can also be beneficial. A bay window not only adds light to a room but can also add needed floor space.

wall, around the perimeter of the opening, and then place the window unit into position. Next, check to see that the window unit is plumb and square. If necessary, insert shims from the interior side. Fasten the window into place, on one side only, using 1¾-inch roofing nails through the slots in the window flange. Double check to see that the window is plumb and square. If necessary, shim the sill to hold the window unit in the proper position, and then nail the opposite flange into the sheathing and stud frame. After driving several nails through the flange, check the operation of the sash. Insert the top flange nails at the lowest end of the nailing slots, and hammer them in, but not tightly, in case the header should sag. This reduces the likelihood that pressure will transfer to the window frame and cause the sash to bind or the glass to crack.

2 **Trim the window.** Be sure to flash the top of the window, and then install a drip cap and exterior casings or extend the siding to the edge of the window

frame, whichever is necessary to match the rest of the house. If you apply casings, they should fit snugly between the ends of the siding and the edge of the window frame. Finish the installation by caulking

Speciality Windows. A skylight or roof window is an excellent way to bring light and air into a space that has no side walls, such as a renovated attic.

Installing a Skylight

Difficulty Level: 𝐓 𝐓 𝐓

Required Tools:

❏ **Basic tools:** adjustable bevel gauge, circular saw with carbide-tipped blade, drywall knife, drywall saw, hammer, measuring tape, plumb bob, power drill with screwdriver attachment, safety goggles, spirit level, utility knife

❏ **Special materials:** aluminum step flashing, drywall, fiberglass batt insulation, framing ties, joint compound, roofing compound, 6-mil polyethylene vapor barrier, 12d and 16d common nails

To achieve the optimal balance between room size and quantity of light penetration, the square foot area of the skylight should be at least 10 percent of the total square footage of the room. Nevertheless, check your state and local building codes before determining what size unit to purchase. Many building codes have natural light and ventilation requirements that are tied directly to floor area. Once the correct daylight area is calculated, this requirement may be satisfied by installing one large skylight or by clustering two or more smaller skylights to create an interesting design element or light focus.

Installing a skylight or roof window (an operable skylight) can be either very difficult or fairly easy, depending upon the location proposed for the unit. Working inside a cramped attic space, crawling around on a steep roof, or building a complicated angular light shaft does not appeal to everyone. If this does not appeal to you, then perhaps you should consider hiring a professional contractor to complete this project. If you choose to do it yourself, however, be certain to read and follow the manufacturer's instructions very carefully, and be aware that many steps are not likely to be included in the instruction booklet.

1. Using a drywall saw, cut a test hole in the ceiling at the center of the area where you want the proposed skylight or roof window to go.

2. Inspect the framing around the test hole, and then mark the position of the full opening. Position the opening to minimize joist cutting.

3. Brace the ceiling, if you're cutting joists, and then cut along the marked outline. Remove the ceiling material, and then cut through the ceiling joists.

4. Double the uncut joists at each side of the full opening, taking care to keep the rough opening dimensions required for the shaft.

1 Make a test hole. Using a drywall saw or saber saw, cut a test hole in the ceiling, about 2 feet square, near the center of the proposed skylight shaft.

2 Locate and mark the opening. Inspect the ceiling and roof framing around the test hole to determine the optimal opening location. Position and mark the opening so that the need for cutting existing framing will be minimized.

3 Cut the opening. Cutting along the guideline with a drywall saw, remove the ceiling material. Install temporary bracing before cutting through the ceiling joists, and then cut through the ceiling framing for the skylight opening.

4 Frame the ceiling opening. Double up the last uncut joist on each side of the full ceiling opening. Install double headers across the opening, perpendicular to the ends of the cut joists. Be sure to use lumber of the same depth as the existing ceiling framing. Next, nail trimmer joists to frame the exact opening for the skylight shaft. Using 12d common nails, nail through metal framing ties to connect joists more securely than with simple toenailing. (Use 4-inch ties for 2x4s, 6-inch ties for 2x6s, etc.)

5 **Locate and mark out the roof opening.** Hang a plumb bob from the bottom edge of the roof rafters down to each corner of the ceiling opening. Transfer the corner locations vertically to the rafters, and then project these points perpendicular to the rafters and up to the underside of the roof. This will locate the rough opening to be cut through the roof. Drive a pilot nail up through the roof at each corner of the opening to be cut. The corners should fall on the inside of the skylight curb framing.

6 **Cut the roof opening.** Most prefabricated skylights and roof windows come pre-mounted on their own curb assembly. Take the assembly up to the roof. Using the pilot nails as a guide, outline the curb opening on the roof. Next, cut away the asphalt shingles with a utility knife, baring the roof sheathing below. Using a circular saw, cut through the sheathing. If you are cutting through wood shingles, place a board beneath the saw. This will allow the saw to glide forward without bumping the bottom of the shingles.

CAUTION: Wear protective goggles when using a circular saw to cut through roofing.

7 **Frame the roof opening.** Double the rafters at the sides of the roof opening. At the ends of the cut rafters, install double headers across the opening at each end.

8 **Install the skylight curb.** Follow the manufacturer's instructions for installing the skylight. Secure it in only one place until the entire skylight unit is properly positioned. If it is not aligned correctly, it will

5. Using a plumb bob, transfer the corners of the ceiling opening up to the roof rafters, and then project them to the roof.

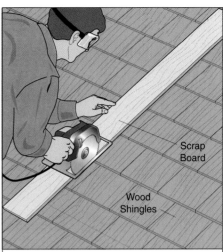

6. With the pilot nails as your guide, outline the window curb on the roof, and then cut the roof opening for the skylight.

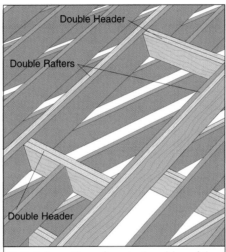

7. Reinforce the rafters to the sides of the skylight opening, and add double headers across the head and sill.

8. Align the window unit, and then install it in accordance with the manufacturer's recommendations.

be very noticeable when the interior side is finished.

9 **Flash the curb and repair the roofing.** Install aluminum step flashing as recommended by the window manufacturer, carefully interweaving the flashing and the replacement shingles as you move along. Be sure to apply roofing compound under both the flashing and the shingles as you proceed. Lastly, caulk around the perimeter of the window unit.

10 **Frame the shaft.** Frame the sides of the shaft with 2x4s. Using an adjustable bevel gauge, carefully mark and cut the framing, and then insulate the side walls

9. Install step flashing, interwoven with the shingle replacements, applying roofing compound beneath each.

with fiberglass batts. Staple a 6-mil polyethylene vapor barrier on the interior sides.

11 **Finish the interior.** Finish the light shaft with drywall. Hide the joint between the skylight and the walls with wood molding.

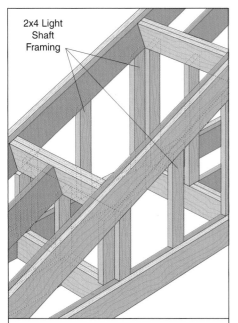

2x4 Light
Shaft
Framing

10. Use a bevel gauge to mark the framing cuts, and then cut the framing for the skylight shaft. Be sure to insulate the side walls.

11. Finish the interior of the skylight shaft with drywall. Cover the joint between the skylight and the drywall with wood molding.

Installing a Bay Window

Difficulty Level: 𝕋 𝕋 𝕋

Required Tools:

❏ <u>Basic tools:</u> adjustable bevel gauge, circular saw with carbide-tipped blade, drywall knife, hammer, keyhole saw, measuring tape, plumb bob, power drill with screwdriver attachment, safety goggles, spirit level, utility knife

❏ <u>Special materials:</u> aluminum step flashing, drywall, fiberglass batt insulation, framing ties, joint compound, roofing compound, roofing felt, 6-mil polyethylene vapor barrier, ³⁄₈ x 5-in. lag screws, 12d and 16d common nails

Before deciding to install a bay window, overlay a sketch of it on an enlarged photo of your home to get some idea of what the window might look like on your house. The sketch may also help to resolve particular questions, such as what type of roofline to make or whether to include decorative brackets under the window or carry the bay down to a foundation wall.

Once these issues have been settled, the framing will be fairly straight-forward. If you are making a new opening or enlarging an existing one, you will need to do some additional framing. Check the manufacturer's literature to establish the rough-opening dimensions and the suggested methods of construction.

1 **Install the window.** Installing a bay window is definitely not a job for one person. As a general rule, lifting a bay window requires at least one person for every two linear feet of window length. This is necessary so that the unit doesn't twist or warp during installation. Lifting the window into position must be accomplished in two steps. The bottom of the window unit must first be rested on the sill of

Bay Windows. A bay window projects from an exterior stud wall and has three sides, typically angled out from the wall at 30, 45, or 60 degrees.

Bow Windows. A bow window also projects out from an exterior stud wall but has only one curved side with a large radius, rather than three angled sides.

the wall opening, and then it must be tilted up and into the opening. Once the window is positioned, brace it with T-braces, or rest it on sawhorses.

2 **Shim the window.** Working from inside, temporarily secure the upper edge of the window sill, or seat, with either double-headed nails or 3-inch trim screws. Shim between the window seat and the

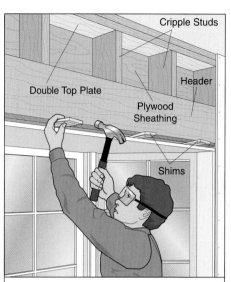

2. Shim the sill, jambs, and head of the bay window unit to get it properly positioned. If the unit is wide, use slate shims under the sill.

3. Be especially certain to insulate the window seat to prevent cold-air infiltration. Use an insulating panel or fiberglass batts.

1. Lifting and installing a bay window requires several people. It is a good idea to have at least one person for every 2 linear ft. of window length. First, lift the unit and rest the inner edge on the sill of the wall opening, and then carefully lift it all the way up into its final position, supporting the outer edge on sawhorses. Secure the unit in place.

rough sill, adjusting the bay window unit until it is level and plumb. Be careful, while doing this, not to bow the window frame. If the window unit is 8 feet wide, or wider, it should be shimmed with either slate or hardwood shims. Softwood shims are likely to compress under the weight of the bay window.

Plumb the jambs by holding a level against the edge of each jamb, while helpers on the outside adjust the window until it is properly positioned. Nail through the jambs and the shims and into the stud framing at approximately 12 inches on cen-

ter vertically. Secure the window head last, shimming and then nailing the head frame into the header at approximately 8 inches on center.

3 Insulate around the window.
If the bay window is not properly insulated, it will allow cold air to infiltrate through the base, the ceiling, and the wall behind the bay roof. To prevent this, install an insulating panel or fiberglass batt insulation beneath the base before closing it. After framing out the bay roof, be sure to use fiberglass batt insulation here also, especially up against the back wall of the "attic" space.

Value Tip

Mix and Match

Windows, both fixed and operable, are made in various styles and shapes. While mixing styles should be carefully avoided, a variety of interesting window sizes and shapes may nevertheless be combined to achieve symmetry, harmony, and rhythm on the exterior of a home.

4 Install support brackets. If the bay window does not come with a cable support system, then install structural support brackets beneath the base of the unit to carry its weight. Each bracket should be attached to the stud framing with at least two ⅜x5-inch lag screws. Attach the brackets to the base with 2½-inch wood screws.

5 Install support strapping. Provide metal strapping at 16 inches on center to secure the window to the stud framing along the top plate of the unit. Fasten the straps to the house with ⅜x5-inch lag screws. Make certain that these screws are secured into a stud or joist. Next, fasten each strap to the top of the window unit with another lag screw. Generally, these straps are attached approximately 10 inches above the window head. Make certain that the location of the strapping will not interfere with the position of any of the rafters.

6 Frame the roof. A bay window can usually be purchased with a prefabricated roof kit. However, custom-framing the roof will not only save on costs but permit the layout of framing to match the pitch and style of existing roof(s).

To frame the roof, first cut a template from ¾-inch plywood, profiling how the rafters will join with the wall of the house. This template will serve as a guide, allowing you to determine the proper angle and length of the rafters.

Align the template with the top corners of the window unit, and secure it in place. Use a measuring tape and bevel gauge to double-check the final measurements and angles. Next, construct a flat 2x4 (or 2x6) ledger profile flush with the top edge of the template, nailing the framework in place with 16d nails. (As an alternative, measure and cut the rafters on the ground, if this is more convenient.)

After all the cuts have been made, either assemble the frame in place, or preassemble the rafters on the ground, and then lift the completed assembly into position, and secure it to the wall of the house.

7 Finish the roof and siding. As mentioned earlier, the enclosed space above the ceiling of the bay window should now be insulated. When this is done, apply ¾-inch exterior-grade plywood sheathing over the roof rafters. Next, cut and install the fascia, drip edge, and any other trim pieces around the roof perimeter. Finally, staple down 15-pound roofing felt, and then shingle the roof. Where the roof slopes join the house wall, slide aluminum or copper step flashing under the siding. Along the top edge of the center roof section, install a continuous strip of aluminum flashing. Lastly, repair the exterior siding and trim around the new bay window to match the rest of the house, and refinish the interior drywall surfaces.

4. Install structural support brackets beneath the base of the bay window. Use ⅜x5-in. lag screws to secure the brackets to the wall.

5. Use metal strapping to secure the top of the window unit to the stud-bearing wall. Fasten the straps with ⅜x5-in. lag screws.

6. Make a template of the desired roof profile, and then use this as a guide to determine the angle and length of the rafter framing.

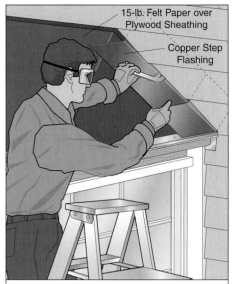

7. After insulating and sheathing the roof, apply roofing felt. Next, install aluminum or copper step flashing, and then shingle the roof.

Chapter 4
Exterior Repairs

Appearances certainly *do* matter when it comes to a house. Because the exterior view of a home is the first thing we see, it will invariably influence our impression of the entire home, as well as our impression of its value. As an investment, then, it makes good sense for homeowners to keep the exterior of their residences looking as beautiful as possible.

Keeping the exterior of a house looking its best usually requires little more than doing normal maintenance and making minor repairs. Usually, this means cleaning, painting, gluing, or patching. But, occasionally, the condition of siding may be so deteriorated that it merits being completely replaced. If this is the case, it is important to select a siding in the style and material that are appropriate for both your home and your neighborhood.

IN THIS CHAPTER

Wood Siding

Replacing Clapboard 50

Repairing Wood Shingles 51

Replacing Hardboard
or Plywood Panels 53

Patching Wood with Epoxy 53

Fiber-Reinforced
Cement Shingles

Repairing Fiber-Reinforced
Cement Shingles 54

Vinyl Siding

Repairing Vinyl Siding 55

Installing Vinyl
Soffits and Fascia 57

Aluminum Siding

Repairing Aluminum Siding 58

Replacing Aluminum Siding . . .58

Stucco

Repairing Stucco 59

TODAY'S TRENDS

Premium-Grade Vinyl
Siding

Textured-Vinyl Siding

Naturally Rot-Resistant
Woods

Aluminum Soffits

Wood Siding

Clapboard is a traditional form of wood siding, noted for its ability to withstand weathering, its classic look, and its paintability. Nevertheless, clapboard siding has the disadvantage of needing periodic maintenance in order to keep its good appearance and durability intact. Clapboard siding is subject to splitting, cracking, and rotting. Replacing siding that has been damaged is imperative for the homeowner who is serious about maintaining the beauty of a home.

Replacing Clapboard

Difficulty Level: 🔨 🔨

Required Tools:

❏ **Basic tools: backsaw, hammer, keyhole saw, measuring tape, pry bar, utility knife**

1 Avoid chipping the paint. If the siding is painted, score along the bottom edge of the damaged board and wherever it meets a trim board to avoid chipping paint off the adjoining undamaged boards.

2 Loosen the clapboard. Insert a pry bar under the board that is just above the damaged clapboard, and then pry out the board about ¼ inch to loosen the nailing.

Clapboard is a form of horizontally-lapped wood siding that has a classical appeal, weathers well, and is paintable.

3 Remove the nails. Tap the siding back toward the wall by hammering on the end of a pry bar to avoid marring the clapboard. This will cause the nailhead to protrude. Then cushion the hammer claw using a wooden shim, and pry out the nails. Loosen the bottom of the damaged board the same way.

4 Mark a cut line. If an entire board is not damaged, then cut out only the damaged section. Cut vertically over wall studs to provide a nailing surface for the replacement

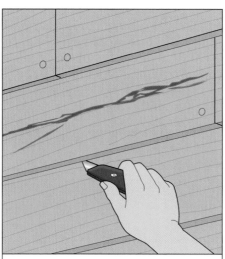

1. Use a utility knife to score between siding boards. This reduces or eliminates paint chipping on the adjoining boards.

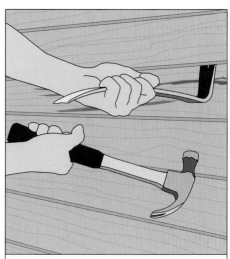

2. Tap the end of a pry bar under the clapboard above the damaged board. Pry up the board and nails about ¼ in.

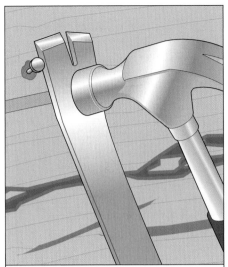

3. Tap the siding back into place using a hammer against the flat end of a pry bar.

Replacement Board

4. Using the new board as a template, trace the vertical cut lines over wall studs.

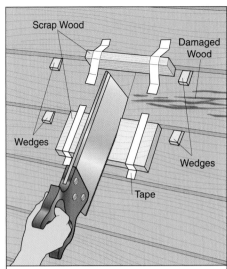

Scrap Wood

Damaged Wood

Wedges

Wedges

Tape

5. Use scrap wood to protect adjacent siding when cutting damaged boards.

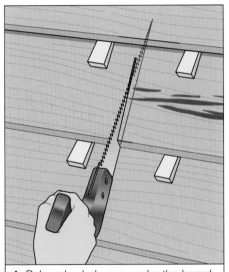

6. Poke a keyhole saw under the board above the damage, and finish the cut.

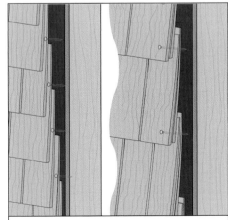

7. Set the exposure; then align and tap in the primed replacement board.

board. Remove nails from the area to be cut, and then measure between the two closest studs bracketing the damaged board, center to center. Cut a replacement board to size, and use it as a template to score an outline over the damaged area.

Pro Tip

AVOID SPLIT WOOD

To avoid splitting wood siding when nailing it, either drill pilot holes in the boards or blunt the nails by hitting the tip of them with a hammer.

5 **Cut the siding.** Using a backsaw, neatly cut the damaged board along the guidelines made previously. If necessary, use wooden wedges to separate the damaged board from the adjoining boards.

6 **Complete the cut.** Poke a keyhole saw under the siding, just above the damaged board, and then complete the cut. Once the damaged board has been loosened, remove any remaining nails.

7 **Replace the damaged board.** Prime both sides of the replacement board before nailing it in place. Slide the top edge of the replacement board snugly under

the next board above. Be sure that the end joints do not leave gaps more than ¼ inch wide. Seal these with paintable caulking after securing the replacement board with hot-dipped galvanized 8d box nails. Nail through only one layer of siding, about an inch above the bottom edge.

Repairing Wood Shingles

Difficulty Level: 🔨🔨

Required Tools:

❑ **Basic tools: chisel, hammer, handsaw, pry bar, utility knife**

❑ **Special tools: block plane, mini-hacksaw**

Nailing Wood Shingles. Single-course nailing is concealed, while double-course nailing remains exposed.

Cedar shingles are another traditional wood siding that weathers well and has an attractive appearance. They are relatively simple to repair or replace. New shingles can be easily feathered into the existing siding. Because shingles can be installed only one at a time, shingling is a labor-intensive job. Nevertheless, if you own a home with wood shingles, it makes sense to preserve the original siding, rather than replace it with aluminum or vinyl.

Wood shingles may be installed in either single or double courses. Single-course shingles are fastened with concealed 5d or 6d box nails through one course at 2 inches above the *beltline* of the previous course. For double-course shingles, the nails penetrate through four shingles. The nailheads remain exposed.

1 Remove the damage. Wood shingles may be damaged by impact, moisture, prolonged exposure to sunlight, or natural aging. The difficult part of replacing damaged shingles is removing the nails without damaging other shingles. Using a wood chisel or pry bar, split out the damaged pieces, and then carefully cut the nails that held them in place.

2 Remove the nails. After removing the damaged shingles, a space will be created under the good shingle above. If the shingles are double-coursed, place a wood block against the good shingle and gently tap it down. This will allow you to get a hammer claw or pry bar under the nailhead without damaging the good shingle. Removing the dam-

aged shingle will detach the undercourse. If it is not damaged, reuse it. An alternative that must be used for single-coursed shingles is to remove the nails by cutting them with a mini-hacksaw slipped beneath the good shingle.

3 Cut a replacement. Using a handsaw or a utility knife, cut a replacement shingle about ⅛ inch narrower than the space to be filled. If necessary, smooth the edge with a block plane or sandpaper.

4 Nail the replacement. If you're replacing a double-coursed shingle, first reinstall the undercourse saved earlier. Nail the new shingle with 5d or 6d galvanized box nails. Reattach the shingle above. The old nailholes may be reused, but

1. Use a 1- to 2-in. chisel to split out damaged shingles. Remove them, and then pull out any exposed nails.

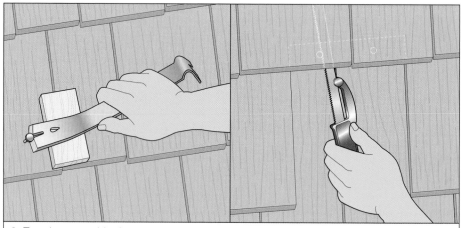

2. Tap down on shingles to expose nailheads on double-coursed shingles. Remove the nails using a pry bar on a wood block to protect the adjacent shingle. For single-coursed shingles, slide a mini-hacksaw under the shingle to cut the concealed nails.

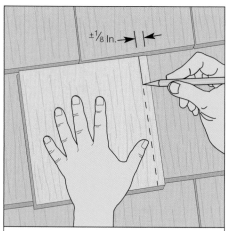

3. Hold the replacement shingle against the wall, and then mark it to fit the empty space, minus approximately ⅛ in.

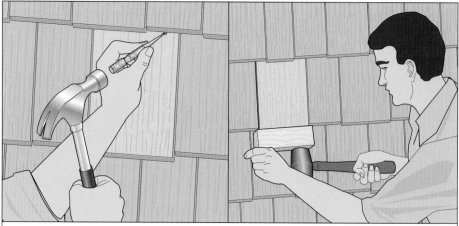

4. To conceal the nailheads on single-coursed shingles, toenail 5d or 6d galvanized nails at the course line (left), and then use a scrap piece of wood and a hammer to gently tap the shingle upward, setting the nailheads under the course above (right).

1. Using a cat's paw, remove nails along the top edge, and then use a crowbar to pry off the panel and remaining nails.

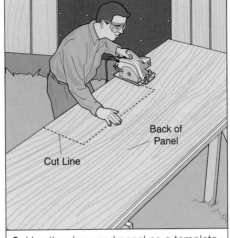

Cut Line

Back of Panel

2. Use the damaged panel as a template to mark the cutouts on the new panel. Cut it from the back using a circular saw.

3. Use 8d galvanized nails to install the new panel. Caulk the seams, and then finish the panel to match the rest.

only if the new nails are slightly larger in diameter than the originals

Single coursing requires that nails be concealed. Use 5d or 6d galvanized box nails, 2 inches above the top of the previous course. Hold the shingle about ¼ inch below its course line while nailing. Using a block and hammer, tap upward to force nailheads under the course above.

Replacing Hardboard or Plywood Panels

Difficulty Level: 🔨🔨

Required Tools:

❑ **Basic tools:** cat's paw or pry bar, caulking gun and caulk, crowbar, hammer

❑ **Special tools:** circular saw, saber saw

Minor damage to hardboard or plywood siding can easily be patched with epoxy compound. This will not work, however, if more extensive damage has been caused by faulty gutters, open seams around doors and windows, or mud, rain, and snow splashed up from the ground. Wood panels may also become damaged if they are left unpainted and exposed to moisture.

For major damage or any damage involving veneer delamination, it is

best to remove and replace the entire panel. Be sure to match the existing panel thickness when purchasing a replacement.

Prime new panels before installing them, and then paint or stain them to protect them from the weather.

1 **Remove the damaged panel.** Using a utility knife, score any caulked areas along the upper and lower panel edges. Remove battens, if there are any, and then use a cat's paw to remove all but two nails. These nails will hold the panel in place until it can be removed. If you use a crowbar to lift the edges, do not use a good panel as a fulcrum. As one person braces the panel, another should loosen it and then take it down.

2 **Cut a replacement.** If you remove a whole panel, no cutting will be necessary. If the panel was cut to width or to fit around a wall opening, use it as a template to mark the cut on the new panel. When cutting, support the panels on 2x4s laid across two sawhorses.

3 **Nail the replacement.** Inspect the building paper for damage, and patch it as required. Then, using 6d casing or siding nails, install the replacement panels. Be certain to caulk the seams along all of the panel edges and between the panels and the trim boards. As soon as possible, apply the finish coating to the siding panels.

Patching Wood with Epoxy

Difficulty Level: 🔨

Required Tools:

❑ **Basic tools:** putty knife, hammer, rasp, sandpaper and sanding block, wood chisel

❑ **Special materials:** plastic sheeting, epoxy

Not every damaged board needs to be replaced. Damage, such as minor rotting or staining around a rusty nail, can be patched with an epoxy-based patching compound.

1 **Remove the damage.** Using a chisel, remove loose or rotten wood from damaged boards. Dig

1. Chisel out the damaged board just enough to reach sound wood, and then clean the area thoroughly using a wire brush.

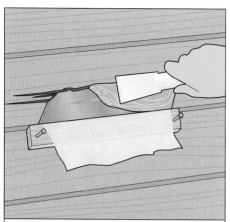

2. Mix the compound, and press it firmly in place. Scrap wood covered with plastic wrap will help maintain a clean bottom edge.

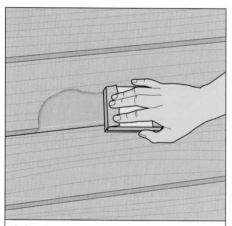

3. Let the epoxy dry for at least 24 hrs., and then file, sand, and prime the repair before applying a finish coat of paint.

just deep enough to reach sound wood. Clean the area thoroughly using a wire brush.

2 Combine the epoxy. Mix the epoxy patching compound as directed by the manufacturer. Two applications may be necessary if the cavity is deep. If the damage is located along the edge of the siding, then cover a piece of scrap wood with thin plastic (so the epoxy won't stick to it later), and use it as a mold by tacking it to the siding. Make sure the final layer is as smooth and even as possible to save yourself filing and sanding time later on.

3 Smooth the patch. Allow the epoxy at least 24 hours to dry. When it is completely dry, smooth the area using a wood file or rasp. Sand and prime the repair, and then give it a coat of finish paint.

Fiber-Reinforced Cement Shingles

Many homes built in the middle of the twentieth century were sided with fiber-reinforced cement shingles, or mineral siding. It was manufactured as a low-cost, maintenance-free, fireproof alternative to wood shakes and shingles.

Cement shingles have several advantages. They are not subject to rotting; they are fireproof; and they are able to stand up well to the effects of weathering. However, cement shingles are decidedly brittle and can therefore be easily cracked or shattered by impact. As a consequence, individual shingles may need to be replaced periodically.

Another potentially serious drawback to cement shingles is that they were originally manufactured with asbestos fibers. (Now they are made of fiberglass.) Because these particles can be released when cutting or removing shingles, proper safety equipment is mandatory. Large jobs should be handled by a professional who is licensed to remove and dispose of hazardous materials. For minor shingle repairs, just replace old shingles with new ones, and avoid cutting to prevent asbestos dust.

Repairing Fiber-Reinforced Cement Shingles

Difficulty Level: ⫟

Tools & Materials:

❑ **Basic tools: hammer, mini-hacksaw, pry bar, utility knife**

❑ **Special tools: drill with masonry bit, shingle breaker**

1 Remove the damaged shingles. Because fiber-reinforced shingles are brittle and inflexible, nails cannot easily be removed from them without damaging the shingles. It may be necessary to break a damaged

shingle in order to remove it. A mini-hacksaw blade may then be used to cut away the nailheads if they cannot be removed with a prybar.

2 Replace the shingles. To cut replacement shingles, either use a *shingle breaker* or score the shingles by pulling a utility knife repeatedly against a straightedge abutting the cut line. To prevent hazardous dust, do not use a saw on asbestos shingles. Predrill nailholes with a 1/8-inch masonry bit because fiber-reinforced cement shingles cannot be directly nailed without breakage. Nail the replacement shingles in place with 3d galvanized box nails.

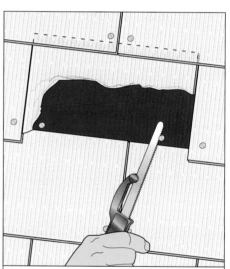

1. Break damaged shingles with a hammer, and then pull out the nails or cut away the nailheads using a mini-hacksaw.

Top of Shingle

2. Bore nailing holes in the new shingle, using a 1/8-in. masonry bit, and then face-nail it with 3d galvanized box nails.

Vinyl siding is a popular choice among homeowners, primarily because it is economical and relatively maintenance-free.

A look of distinction may be created by combining vinyl siding with brick masonry. Each is a low-maintenance material.

Vinyl Siding

More than one-third of all new homes are now sided with vinyl. Vinyl siding is relatively maintenance-free. Unlike wood, it does not need periodic repainting. It is also more economical than either wood or aluminum siding.

Vinyl does have its disadvantages, however. Low-quality vinyl may crack under impact, especially in low temperatures. Small cracks can be repaired by removing the damaged piece and gluing on a vinyl patch from behind. For larger areas of damage, though, an entire section may need replacement. Vinyl also fades, so a patch or replacement may not match perfectly. Vinyl can be painted, however, if it is first cleaned and primed. You should use a good-quality acrylic paint to paint over vinyl siding.

Repairing Vinyl Siding

Difficulty Level: 🔨

Required Tools:

❏ **Basic tools:** cat's paw, hammer, utility knife, roofing nails, tin snips

❏ **Special tools:** PVC primer and cement, power saw, vinyl siding tools (see pg. 56)

1 **Detach the damaged siding.** Each course of vinyl siding locks into the course below it or adjacent to it. The siding is nailed through a flange molded into the top of each piece. A special tool, called a *zip tool*, can be used to unlock the courses. You insert the zip tool beneath the lower edge of the siding, and then pull it horizontally to unzip the locked piece. For vertical siding, you pull the zip tool downward instead of across. Use the zip tool to disengage the damaged course from the course below or adjacent to it. Next, expose the nailing flange by disengaging the course above from the

damaged course. Pull out the nails, and then remove the damaged section of siding.

2 **Patch the siding.** Cut a vinyl patch large enough to cover the damaged area of the removed siding. Thoroughly clean the siding, and then coat both the patch and the siding with clear PVC primer. Lastly, glue the patch to the back of the siding with PVC cement. As an alternative, purchase a length of replacement siding. Using the damaged piece as a guide, cut it to the proper size with a utility knife.

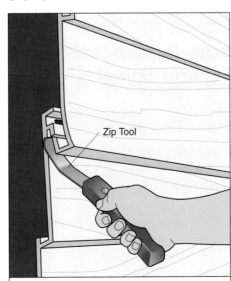

1. Pry up on the siding with a zip tool. Drag the tool sideways to unlock the bad piece, and then remove the nails.

2. Coat both the patch and the damaged piece of siding with PVC primer and then glue the patch in place with PVC cement.

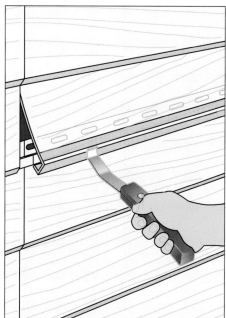

CUTTING VINYL

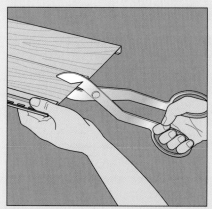

Utility Knife. Score vinyl face up, using a utility knife. Bend it to crack it apart.

3. Lock the bottom edge of the siding, and then nail the top flange into place. Do not hammer the nails in completely, to allow for expansion and contraction.

4. Using the zip tool, pull the overlapping siding course down and out at the bottom, and then lock it into the upper edge of the replacement section of vinyl siding.

Tin Snips. For a clean edge, don't close the snips completely at the end of a cut.

3 Replace the siding. Lock the lower edge of the patched siding back in place. Lift up the overlapping course of siding, and then nail the patched piece through the center of each flange slot. Use corrosion-resistant nails that will penetrate at least ¾ inch into the sheathing. Nailheads must be a minimum of ⁵⁄₁₆ inch in diameter. Do not hammer the nails in completely. Instead, leave them slightly raised so that the siding can slide easily due to expansion and contraction caused by atmospheric changes.

4 Relock the overlapping course. Using the zip tool, lock the overlapping course of siding back into place. Pull the siding downward, and then release it when it is engaged by the channel of the replacement piece.

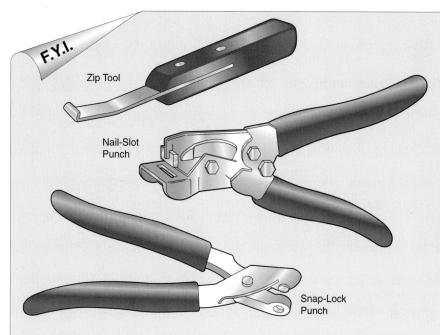

F.Y.I.

Zip Tool

Nail-Slot Punch

Snap-Lock Punch

VINYL SIDING TOOLS

Zip Tool. A zip tool hooks underneath the lip of a section of siding. It is then pulled down and out along the seam to lock or unlock the siding course.

Nail-Slot Punch. If slots are needed where there are none in cut sections of vinyl siding, then the nail-slot punch can be used to make them.

Snap-Lock Punch. This handy tool can make small lugs along the top edge of a cut section of vinyl siding so that the cut edge can engage the edging trim beneath windowsills and eaves.

1. Snap a level chalkline, and then nail the F-channel to the wall along the line.

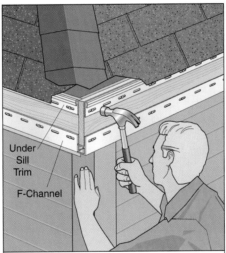

2. Slip the soffit panels into the F-channels, beginning at one of the corners.

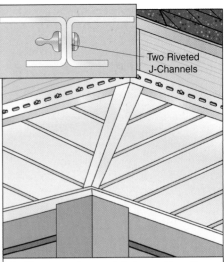

3. Rivet two pieces of J-channel together to create a mitered corner joint.

Installing Vinyl Soffits and Fascia

Difficulty Level: ⸯⸯ

Required Tools:

❑ **Basic tools:** hammer, pencil, spirit level, utility knife

❑ **Special tools:** chalk line, pop riveter, snap-lock punch

Vinyl soffits and fascia are typically used to finish vinyl siding applications, but they can also be used on homes with other types of siding to reduce the need for maintenance. Unlike wood, vinyl will not rot, peel, or split from weathering.

1 Attach the F-channels. Attach the F-channels to the fascia, nailing through the flange slots at 6 to 12 inches on center. Using a pencil,

Value Tip

Cleaning Vinyl

You should wash vinyl siding periodically to keep it looking its best. Products are made specifically for cleaning vinyl, but a mild household detergent and water will do just as well. To remove mildew mix 1 part bleach and 3 parts water to the detergent. If it is a commercial detergent, be sure to read the instructions carefully.

4. Attach an undersill J-channel along the top edge of the fascia.

mark a level line on the wall to align the bottom inside edge of the F-channel, and then nail it in place.

2 Cut and install the panels. Cut the panel sections to the required width, minus ¼ inch. Slip each panel into the F-channels from one end of the soffit, and then slide them into their final position.

3 Miter the corners. Where they meet at corners, cut the panels to make a mitered joint. Support the joint with two pieces of J-channel riveted together with a pop riveter. At gable ends, continue the soffit to the gable fascia, and use a double J-channel for the transition joint.

4 Cover the fascia. Attach undersill J-channels along the top edge of

5. Use a snap-lock punch to add friction lugs to the fascia at 6 to 12 in. on center.

the old fascia. Like the F-channels along the bottom edge, these should be nailed at 6 to 12 inches on center. Allow for temperature expansion and contraction by cutting the trim ¼ inch less than the length of the fascia.

5 Install the fascia panel. Cut a length of fascia panel to the correct width. Use a snap-lock punch to add lugs along the top edge at 6 to 12 inches on center. Lock the fascia panel tightly into place by inserting its upper edge into the finishing trim of the J channel. At the same time, carefully hook the bottom of the fascia panel over the F-channel. Push upward until the cover flange and lugs are locked into place.

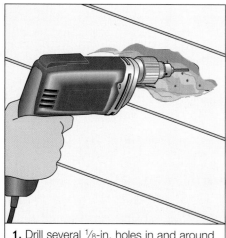

1. Drill several ⅛-in. holes in and around the dented area of the siding.

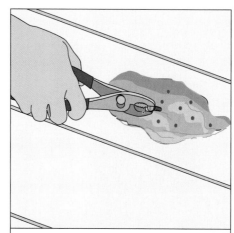

2. Insert one or two #8 sheet-metal screws; then use them to grab and pull out the dent.

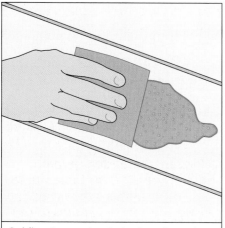

3. Mix a two-part auto-body putty and apply it to the dent, feathering the edges.

4. After the patch has hardened, sand, prime, and then spray paint it.

Aluminum Siding

Aluminum is also a low-maintenance siding material, somewhat more durable than vinyl, although it can be dented by impact. Minor damage to aluminum can be easily repaired. The technique is similar to repairing a car dent. Seriously damaged siding, however, must be replaced.

Repairing Aluminum Siding

Difficulty Level: 🔩

Required Tools:

❑ **Basic tools:** pliers, drill with ⅛-in. bit, emery cloth

❑ **Special tools:** auto-body putty and filler, #8 sheet-metal screws, primer and paint

1 Drill pulling holes. Using a ⅛-inch drill bit, drill several small holes in and around the perimeter of the area of the damaged aluminum siding.

2 Pull the dent. Insert a #8 sheet-metal screw partway into one or more of the drilled holes near the deepest part of the dent. Grab the head of the sheet-metal screw with a pair of pliers, and pull out the dent.

3 Patch the dent. After you have pulled out the dent, remove the screws, and sand the damaged area with an emery cloth. If any dents are ⅛ inch deep or more, apply a two-part auto-body putty. Use auto-body filler for small imperfections.

4 Sand and paint. Once the filler has hardened, sand, prime, and then paint the surface with a matching color spray paint.

Replacing Aluminum Siding

Difficulty Level: 🔩🔩

Required Tools:

❑ **Basic tools:** caulking gun, hammer, sheet-metal snips, utility knife

❑ **Special materials:** aluminum siding, butyl caulking

Replacement sections of aluminum siding are not as easily installed as vinyl because aluminum does not have the same flexibility as vinyl. If the damaged area is significant, it is best to cut out and replace the entire damaged section. If you don't happen to have any extra pieces of siding stored away, look for a siding distributor who can match the style and color you need and is willing to sell you only the number of sections needed. An alternative would be to repaint the siding. Several paint manufacturers have exterior paints formulated to recoat aluminum siding.

1 Cut away the damage. Use either sheet-metal snips or a utility knife to cut away the damaged siding. Leave at least a 1-inch lip along the upper edge to be used as a gluing surface for the replacement siding. The new section must extend at least 3 inches beyond each side of the damage.

1. Use sheet-metal snips or a utility knife to cut away damaged aluminum siding.

2 Cut the replacement siding.

Cut a section of replacement siding to the length required. Using sheet-metal snips or a utility knife, trim off the nailing strip from the piece. The patch should be just deep enough to fit snugly up against the overlapping course of siding.

3 Secure the replacement siding.

Run a heavy bead of butyl caulking just beneath the bottom edge of the overlapping siding and where the vertical edges of the patch course overlap the adjoining siding. Lock the bottom edge of the replacement siding into the top of the siding course below it, and then tape it firmly into place until it is dried.

Stucco can be applied in a wide variety of surface textures. It is an attractive, durable siding material, which if properly maintained, will protect a home for many years.

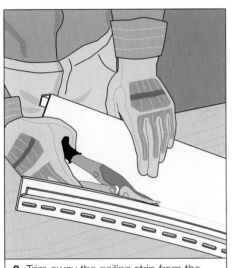

2. Trim away the nailing strip from the section of replacement siding.

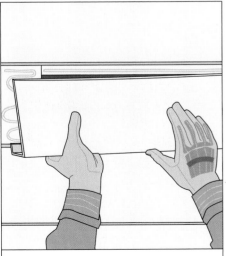

3. Apply butyl caulking to adhere the new siding, and then press it into position.

Stucco

Doing stucco repair is not that difficult, and it will save you the expense of having to hire a professional contractor. The hardest part is preparation. Minor surface damage often indicates a more serious underlying problem, such as rotten sheathing. Try to identify the cause of any problems. Remove rotted underlayment to provide a solid base for the stucco. It is almost impossible to match the color and texture of the old stucco—so the less patching you have to do, the better.

Generally, if cracks are not causing harm, leave them alone. As for painting stucco, it is not advisable. Think twice before doing so. Once the paint peels, it will become very difficult to scrape the surface adequately enough to prepare it for repainting. If you do paint, however, use porous paint such as latex or acrylics.

Repairing Stucco

Difficulty Level: 🌴🌴

Required Tools:

❑ **Basic tools: gardening claw, hammer, heavy-duty stapler, rubber gloves, safety goggles, steel cement trowel, stiff-bristled brush, straightedge**

❑ **Special tools and materials: 15-lb. felt paper, galvanized-wire lath, masking tape, metal-cutting shears, mist sprayer, 1¼-in. roofing nails, sponge trowel**

1 Prepare the underlayment.

Chop out all of the loose stucco. When stable material is reached, undercut the remaining stucco. This will provide a good bonding surface, and a key to improve the adhesion of the patch. Snip away any rusted or damaged lath, and then replace or repair any damaged underlayment. Staple two thicknesses of asphalt-impregnated felt over the exposed sheathing. Lap the new felt

1. Repair the sheathing, cover it with felt paper, and then nail new lath into place.

2. Apply the scratch coat with a trowel. Groove the stucco after it stiffens.

3. Level the stucco with a straightedge, and then smooth it with a sponge trowel.

4. Stir a soupy mix for the finish coat. Using a large brush, apply it like paint.

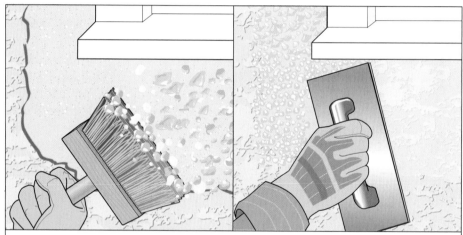

5. Texture the new stucco by flicking mix from a stiff-bristled brush. Lightly trowel over the new surface to reduce the peaks and simulate the texture of the original stucco.

paper over the existing felt paper by at least 6 inches each way, to cover the sheathing. Cut new galvanized-wire lath, and lap it over the edges of the existing lath by at least 2 inches. Nail the new lath into place with 1¼-inch roofing nails at 6 inches on center.

2 Apply the scratch coat. The first coat of stucco is called the *scratch* coat. It is used to fill a patch almost to the level of the adjoining stucco. After you've mixed the stucco for the scratch coat, apply it to the moistened edges of the old stucco, pushing it into the wire lath with the steel trowel. Continue doing this until the scratch coat is about ⅜ inch deep. After the surface stiffens, score it with horizontal grooves ⅛ inch deep to provide better adhesion for the next coat. Allow the scratch coat to dry overnight. Avoid working in hot, dry conditions that are likely to cause the stucco to dry too quickly. In hot weather, moisten the stucco periodically with a fine-mist sprayer, or cover it with a plastic sheet to slow down the drying time.

3 Apply the brown coat. Spread a second layer, or *brown* coat, of stucco over the first using a steel trowel. Apply the brown coat flush with the surrounding stucco. Use a 2x4 board in an upward and back and forth motion to slough off the excess material. Use a sponge trowel to smooth ridges, fill holes, blend

edges, and roughen up the surface for the finish, or *dash*, coat. Allow the stucco to harden overnight.

4 Apply the dash coat. Mix the final coat of stucco to the consistency of a very dense soup, and then apply it to a depth of about ⅛ inch with a large brush, as if it were thick paint. Be especially careful to stir the mixture frequently so that the sand will be prevented from settling to the bottom.

5 Texture the patch. Match the texture of old stucco as closely as possible. Texture the new finish by flicking stucco mix onto the wall with a stiff-bristled brush. Flatten the peaks by drawing a steel trowel lightly across the surface. To ensure the effect that you want, practice first on a piece of scrap wood.

Chapter 5
Roofing Repair and Replacement

Your number-one home-maintenance priority should be your roof. The roof and its components, along with siding, constitute the first line of defense in protecting the value of a home. Roofing problems often evoke images of water dripping into buckets on a rainy day—not to mention water-damaged ceilings and walls or rotting fascia boards, sheathing, and soffit panels. And these images are likely to be framed by visions of winged dollar signs fluttering rapidly out of your savings account.

As a major visible element on a home, the roof should be kept in top condition. Corroded flashing, curled or missing shingles, and clogged gutters are simple and inexpensive problems to fix. Left unrepaired, the roof's protective value can be quickly and adversely affected.

IN THIS CHAPTER

Roofing Inspection

Inspecting a
Roof for Damage 62

Roofing Repair

Fixing Built-Up Roofing 63

Replacing Composite Shingles . .64

Repairing Rake and Eaves
Fascia and Soffits 65

Roofing Preparation

Inspecting a Shingle Roof 66

Preparing a Roof
for Reshingling 67

Removing Shingle Roofing 67

Underlayment and Flashing

Applying Underlayment 68

Installing Metal Flashing 69

Shingle Replacement

Installing Composite Shingles . . .70

Roofing an Open Valley 72

Roofing a Ridge 73

Sealing and Trimming 74

Gutters and Leaders

Repairing Gutters 74

Replacing Gutters 75

Maintaining Gutters 76

TODAY'S TRENDS

Metal Roofing

Simulated Slate

Patterned and
Dimensional Shingles

Ceramic or Clay
Roofing Tiles

Roofing Inspection

Never delay repairing or replacing damaged roofing. Water can be one of the most destructive forces in nature. A leaky roof can wreak havoc in your home, costing more than would timely repair and maintenance. To avoid problems, inspect your roof at least twice a year.

Caution: Before beginning, read "Ladders and Scaffolding," page 82.

Inspecting a Roof for Damage

Difficulty Level: 🔨

Required Tools:

❑ <u>Basic tools:</u> **awl or ice pick, extension ladder, flashlight**

Knowing what to look for is the only prerequisite for inspecting a roof. With checklist in hand, examine your roof, and weigh each of these questions:

1. Can you see the underlayment or plywood sheathing through worn shingles? If so, then the shingles must be replaced as soon as possible.

2. Are any shingles cracked or curled up at the edges? If the shingles have reached this stage of wear, patches of asphalt will most likely be visible. If the surface granules have worn off this much, then it is time to seriously consider replacing the shingles.

3. Do the shingles easily crumble or break apart in your hands? Dried-out shingles easily split and leak. They should be replaced fairly soon.

4. Is the caulking or roofing compound around skylights, vents, pipes, or valleys, cracked or missing? Remove and replace cracked or crumbling caulk, and then fill the cracks with roofing cement.

5. Is the metal flashing around chimney walls, valleys, and dormers worn or cracked? Replace it. Remove loose nails, fill the holes with roof cement, and then set new nails off to the side of the old nailholes.

6. Do you have mildew or green mold on shaded areas of your roof? Remove it by spraying the area with detergent and pressurized water. Be careful not to damage the shingles.

Algae damaged roofing contrasts starkly with the new shingling on this roof.

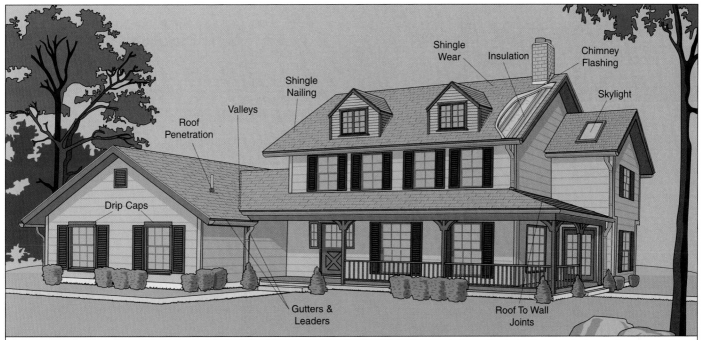

Shingle Wear

Insulation

Chimney Flashing

Shingle Nailing

Skylight

Valleys

Roof Penetration

Drip Caps

Gutters & Leaders

Roof To Wall Joints

Roof inspection requires knowing what to look for. Prepare a handy checklist of areas to investigate before venturing onto your roof.

Roofing Repair

Many homes were once constructed with flat built-up roofs (BURs). This type of roofing is relatively inexpensive but difficult to maintain. Worn roofing, separated seams, and popped nails are common problems on BURs. Standing water can readily cause leaks. The only advantage to having a leak on a flat roof is that it may be easy to work on, compared with a leak on a pitched roof.

F.Y.I.

Repairing a Ridge Shingle

If a ridge (or hip) shingle is cracked or otherwise damaged, repair it with a shingle tab. Bend the tab gently to match the curvature of the ridge, and slip one end under the ridge shingle above the damaged one. Cement the tab in place.

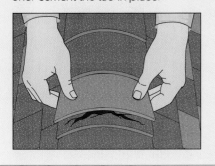

Fixing Built-Up Roofing

Difficulty Level: 🔨

Required Tools:

- ❏ **Basic tools:** gloves, hammer, putty knife, utility knife

- ❏ **Special materials:** asphalt roofing compound, asphalt shingle or piece of roll roofing repair patch, roofing nails

1 **Cut away damaged roofing.** A tear or crack in built-up roofing can be repaired with a rectangular patch. Cut a piece of composite shingle or roll roofing for the repair patch. The repair patch must be cut larger than the damaged area. Use the patch piece as a template for cutting away the existing roofing material. Cut and remove the damaged roofing.

2 **Cement the patch.** Using a putty knife, spread some roofing compound onto the roof area that has been cut out. Be sure to work the roofing compound thoroughly beneath the cut edges of the roofing material. If there is more than one layer of roofing, add layers of roofing compound and repair material until the surface of the patch is even with the overall roof surface.

1. Cut a patch of repair material larger than the damaged area, and use it as a template to cut away the damaged roofing.

2. Use a putty knife to spread roofing compound. Fill the cutout completely, working the compound under the edges of the cut.

3. Nail the repair patch in place with roofing nails, and apply another layer of roofing compound. Lap the edge joint at least 2 in.

4. Add another, larger repair patch over the first, lapping it by at least 2 in. Do not nail it down. Apply roofing compound.

3 **Nail the patch, and apply roofing compound.** Nail down the edges of the roof patch, and then lap another layer of asphalt roofing compound over the repair joint by at least 2 inches.

4 **Add a cover layer.** Add a final layer of roof patching material overlapping the initial patch by at least 2 inches. Apply asphalt roofing compound again, as in Step 3. Press the patch firmly into place, but do not nail it down. Where any roof nails have popped out, nail them back in and fully cover the nailheads with roofing compound. Sprinkle shingle granules over all your repairs.

Replacing Composite Shingles

Difficulty Level: 🔨
Required Tools:

❑ **Basic tools:** gloves, hammer, pry bar, putty knife

❑ **Special materials:** asphalt roofing compound

The most widely used roofing today is composite shingling. Composite shingles are available in a variety of weights and colors. Most are warrantied for 15 to 20 years or more. If your roofing is nearing the end of its life expectancy, consider

replacing it. If the roofing is basically sound but has isolated damage, then it might be more economical to replace just the damaged shingles. It is important to match the original style and color, which is why it is always a good idea to keep extra shingles stored away.

1 **Remove nails.** Shingles are typically fastened with eight nails; four directly through the shingle, and four through both it and the next overlapping shingle. To loosen damaged shingles, you must remove the nails from the overlapping shingle, and then pull the nails from the damaged shingle. To access the nails, pull back on the shingle tabs.

2 **Replace the shingle.** Slip a new shingle in place, aligning it carefully at each end. In warm weather, bend the overlapping shingle tabs up; then nail the new shingle with galvanized roofing nails. If the weather is cool, slip the flat end of a pry bar on top of the nailhead under the overlapping shingle. Hammer the pry bar as near as possible to the nailhead without hitting the shingle.

3 **Seal the shingle.** Apply some asphalt roofing compound under the shingle tabs, and press them down firmly. This will hold the shingle in position until it softens and settles in warm weather.

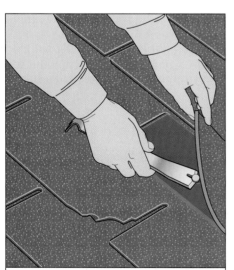

1. Use a pry bar to remove the nails in the shingle overlapping the damaged one, and then remove the nails holding down the damaged shingle.

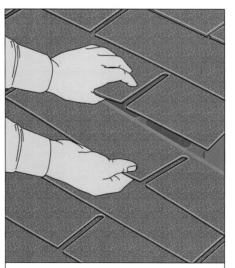

2. Slip a replacement shingle into position, aligning it carefully at both ends. Nail the new shingle in place with galvanized roofing nails.

3. Apply asphalt roofing compound underneath the replacement shingle, and then press the shingle down firmly into the compound.

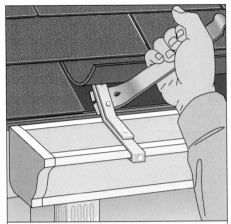

1. To repair fascia, first remove the gutter. Support both ends until it is lowered.

2. Remove damaged fascia. Cut the damaged boards at the rafter-end centerlines.

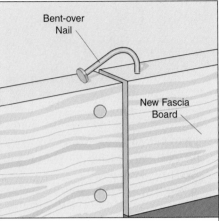

3. A bent nail will hold one end of the new fascia board while you nail the other end.

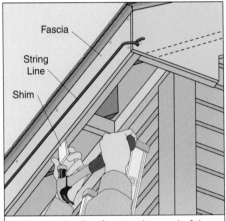

4. Run a string line from end to end of the fascia. Align the new fascia with the line.

5. Remove and replace damaged soffits, again cutting between rafter centerlines.

6. Tack a new soffit in place; then carefully align it with the fascia before final nailing.

Repairing Rake and Eaves Fascia and Soffits

Difficulty Level: 𝄞𝄞

Required Tools:

❏ **Basic tools:** hammer, handsaw, pry bar or cat's paw

❏ **Special materials:** 8d galvanized nails, wood for soffit

If rake and eaves fascia or soffits are compromised, the entire roof may become vulnerable to weather, nesting animals, and insects. Fascia and soffits should be repaired before you install any new roofing.

1 Remove the gutter. To repair the fascia, you must remove the gutters. First remove the mounting screws; then detach the gutter from the leader. Support both ends of the gutter until it's lowered to the ground.

2 Remove damaged wood. Pry off damaged fascia boards. If a whole board isn't damaged, mark a cut line at the center of a rafter end. Pull nails out with a *cat's paw*; then make the cut with a handsaw. If the rafter is too damaged to provide nailing, double the rafter end or add a nailing block to one side of it.

3 Replace the fascia. Cut new fascia boards, and prime them on both sides and edges. With the help of a co-worker, nail the boards in place. If you are working alone, a bent-over nail in the top of a new fascia board will hold it in place while you nail the other end.

4 Align the fascia. The new fascia should be nailed to every rafter with two 8d galvanized nails, one above the other, where the fascia touches the rafter end. Because rafter ends are seldom exactly even,

run a string line from end to end of the fascia. Where the board cups inward, tap it out and insert a shim between the rafter and the fascia.

5 Replace damaged soffits. Remove damaged soffits in the same way as damaged fascia. Be sure to cut away damaged areas at the rafter centerlines so that there will be a surface for nailing. Use the damaged piece as a template for cutting a replacement. Mark the rafter locations on the new soffit, and hammer starter nails in place before lifting up the soffit. If you're alone, tack a nail in the wall to support one end of the soffit while you slide it into place from the opposite end.

6 Make a tight fit. Tack the soffit in place temporarily. With a pry bar, pull the soffit outward until it is tight against the fascia. Do the final nailing, and then replace the trim.

Roofing Preparation

Reshingling simply means applying new material over existing roofing. This is much less costly, as well as easier, than stripping off and then replacing the old roofing. However, if the existing roofing material is tile or slate, it cannot be covered over. These materials must be removed. Even asphalt or fiberglass shingles must be removed if a roof has already been reshingled twice, because of the weight of the combined layers. If your roof can accommodate another layer of lightweight shingles, be sure it is structurally sound before applying them.

Composite shingle roofing can typically be reshingled twice before a complete *tear-off* is needed, depending on the weight of the shingles and local code requirements.

Inspecting a Shingle Roof

Difficulty Level: 🪜

Required Tools:

❑ <u>Basic tools:</u> awl, ice pick, or screwdriver, extension ladder, flashlight, work gloves

1 Count the shingle layers. To determine whether or not a roof can be reshingled, look along the gable rake, and count the number of existing shingle layers. Be sure the drip edge is not hiding any layers.

Check local building codes and the manufacturer's literature for the maximum number of layers permitted. This may vary according to the shingle material and the roof pitch. Typically, wood shingles can only be shingled over once. Asphalt shingles can usually be shingled over twice before they must be replaced.

2 Check the sheathing. Rotten sheathing boards beneath old roofing must be replaced. If the attic is unfinished, examine the underside of the roof from inside. Check for voids and delaminated plywood. Using an awl, ice pick, or screwdriver, poke into the rafters

and sheathing to check for rotten wood. If rot is limited, remove the old roofing and replace just the rotten boards. If necessary, build up roofing over replacement sheathing with layers of shingles to make the roof surface even.

3 Check the surface conditions. New roofing will not level dips, bumps, or curling shingles on an existing roof. If the surface of the roofing is not uniformly flat, then the existing roofing must be completely removed. For this reason, wood shakes, curled composite shingles, and old-style interlocking shingles should not be roofed over.

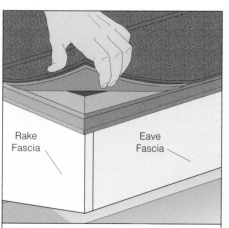

1. Check along the gable rake, at the edge of the roofing, to determine the number of existing shingle layers on the roof.

Rake Fascia

Eave Fascia

2. With an awl, ice pick, or screwdriver, poke into rafters and sheathing to check for soft, rotten wood in need of replacement.

3. Check the roof surface for badly curled shingles and uneven spots. If the roofing is not uniformly flat, it must be removed.

1. Remove the ridge shingles using a pry bar or flat shovel, and then remove the loose nails and debris from the work area.

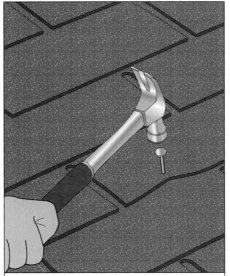

2. Nail down curled shingles, and fill in voids where shingles have broken off. Nail down or remove any protruding nails.

3. Remove damaged flashing around roof vents and other exposed areas. If valley flashing is in good shape, leave it in place.

Preparing a Roof for Reshingling

Difficulty Level: 🔨

Required Tools:

❑ **Basic tools: extension ladder, hammer, pry bar**

1 Start at the ridge. If existing shingles do not need to be entirely removed, you must still do preparation work before reshingling. Begin by removing the ridge shingles using a pry bar or flat shovel, and then remove the loose nails and debris from the work area.

2 Repair the surface. To ensure a smooth, even roof, nail down curled shingles and fill in voids where shingles have broken off. Protruding nails should either be hammered in again or removed. Carefully remove loose nails and debris, which if wedged under a shingle, may cause the roof to leak.

3 Remove damaged flashing. Remove damaged or worn flashing, if it is exposed, such as flashing around roof vents. Metal flashing in valleys, or *open valley* flashing, may be left in place if it is in sound condition. If it shows signs of corrosion or any other damage, then replace it.

Removing Shingle Roofing

Difficulty Level: 🔨

Required Tools:

❑ **Basic tools: drop cloths, extension ladder, hammer, pry bar, work gloves**

❑ **Special tools: dumpster, flat shovel**

Removing shingle roofing is hard physical work, but careful planning can make the job less difficult. For one thing, you must plan on having

Pro Tip   **Roof Venting**

If roofing has worn prematurely, check the attic rafters and insulation for signs of moisture. Moisture damage may indicate that the roof needs venting. Gable roofs must be vented with louvers at each end, near the ridge, and continuous screen venting in the soffits. Hip roofs must be vented at the eaves and the ridge. Net vent area must equal $1/300$ of the attic floor area. Multiply this area by 1.25 for #8 screen, or by 2.00 for #16 screen.

to dispose of a mountain of debris. Rent a dumpster so that the refuse can be carted away after the job is done. Place the dumpster as near to the work as feasible, and use drop cloths to cover areas where debris is likely to fall. Nails, broken shingles, and other roofing materials can easily damage your lawn mower.

1 Start at the ridge. Tear off shingles or shakes by sliding a pry bar or flat shovel under the roofing material and prying upward. Begin at the ridge of the roof, and continue to work your way downward. This is

1. With a pry bar or a flat shovel, begin removing shingles along the ridge of the roof, and then continue working down toward the eaves.

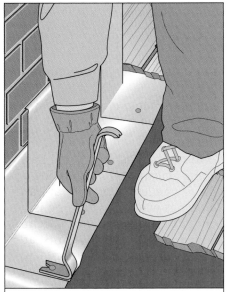

2. Carefully remove the existing flashing so that it can be used as a template for cutting the new flashing.

3. Inspect the plywood sheathing or solid wood decking for any kind of damage. Replace the damaged or rotten wood.

Underlayment and Flashing

Applying Underlayment

Difficulty Level: 𝕋

❑ **Basic tools:** extension ladder, hammer or hammer tacker, utility knife

❑ **Special materials:** felt paper, roofing nails or staples

especially important with wood shingles, where debris may fall down through open sheathing.

2 Remove old flashing. Remove the existing flashing very carefully so that it can be used as a template for cutting the replacement flashing. If it is not too badly damaged, some flashing may be salvaged. Around chimneys and at wall-to-roof joints, if the upper edge of the flashing is embedded in

mortar, try bending it out of the way, rather than removing it altogether.

3 Inspect the sheathing. Once the existing shingles have been removed, inspect the plywood sheathing or solid-wood decking for damage. Replace damaged and rotting wood with new material. If the old sheathing is thicker than what is commercially available, then use felt paper or roofing material to make up the difference, or shim the sheathing.

1 Lay down the felt paper. A roof stripped down to sheathing must receive an underlayment before you can reshingle it. Read the instructions on shingles to determine the weight of felt paper needed. Wood shingles and shakes generally require 30-pound felt; asphalt and fiberglass require 15-pound felt on steep roofs, but two layers on slopes between 2 and 4 inches per foot; and for clay tile, 45-pound felt is recommended. Eave flashing is recommended where ice dams are likely. This usually consists of 50-pound smooth surfaced roll roofing extended along the eaves over the underlayment to a point 3 feet inside the interior wall line.

Be sure the deck is dry before laying down felt paper. Extensive nailing won't be necessary, unless the underlayment will remain exposed to windy conditions. (The shingle nails will hold the felt paper down permanently.) Secure the felt paper with roofing nails or $\frac{1}{4}$- to $\frac{5}{16}$-inch staples. Be sure that the nails or

Composite shingle removal must be done if there are already too many shingle layers on a roof. This difficult job will be easier if you spread drop cloths and have a dumpster handy for debris.

1. Working toward the ridge from the bottom edge of the roof, install the felt paper. Be sure to hammer in fasteners completely.

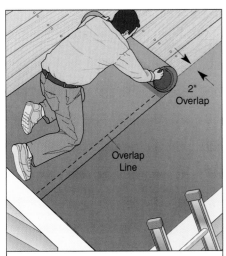

2. Overlap courses of underlayment by at least 2 in. on top laps and 4 in. on side laps. Overlap hips and ridges by 6 in.

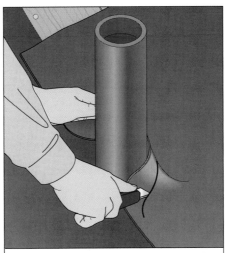

3. Trim the underlayment away from roof penetrations so that it will not buckle, and then apply the metal flashing.

staples are hammered in completely. Because exposure to sun can cause felt paper to buckle, the roofing should be applied as soon as possible.

2 Overlap the underlayment. Overlap the felt paper by 2 inches along the top edge, by 4 inches along the side edges, and by 6 inches at the hips and ridges.

3 Trim around roof penetrations. Before installing flashing, you must trim the underlayment around roof penetrations so that it will not buckle against roof vents. Use the removed flashing as a template for cutting the new flashing.

Installing Metal Flashing

Difficulty Level: 🔧

Required Tools:

❏ **Basic tools:** C-clamps, caulking gun, hammer, aviation snips, utility knife, work gloves

❏ **Special materials:** metal flashing, roofing cement, roofing nails, straight boards

Galvanized sheet metal, aluminum, or copper flashing must be applied wherever roofing materials alone cannot prevent leaks. Typically,

flashing is applied around vent pipes, chimneys, and skylights, and it is also used in valleys, at roof-to-wall joints, and on roof edges. Roofing cement is used under and between layers of flashing to seal them. Be sure to use nails made of material similar to the flashing to prevent electrolytic corrosion.

1 Bend the flashing. Metal flashing is usually 8 inches wide or wider. In valleys, it must be at least 11 inches wide. The flashing is bent to the angle of the joint being flashed. At roof-to-wall joints, at least 4 inches of flashing must lap up the wall. Preferably, 6 inches of flashing should extend over the roof. Bend flashing neatly over a board, or rent a sheet-metal brake.

2 Attach the flashing. At roof-to-wall joints, the last course of shingles must be at least 8 inches wide. Slip the top half of the flashing up behind the siding. It is not necessary to nail it to the wall. Attach the last course of shingles to the roof, and then coat the top 4 inches of the course (above the tab cuts) with roofing cement. Bed the bottom half of the flashing into the roofing cement, on top of the shingles.

3 Cover the flashing. Cut apart the tabs on as many shingles as are needed to run one shingle

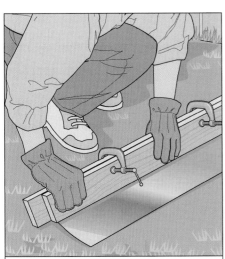

1. Use clamped pieces of straight lumber, or rent a sheet-metal brake to bend flashing to the angle of the joint being flashed.

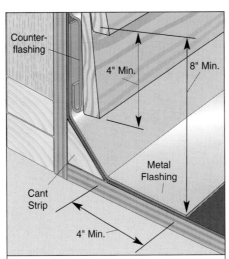

2. Slip the top of the flashing up and under the siding. Bed the lower part in roofing cement, atop the last shingle course.

3. Apply roofing cement over the exposed flashing. Cut tabs off several shingles, and then bed them in the roofing cement.

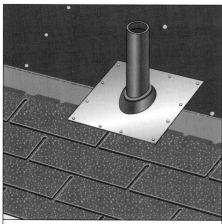

4. Shingle around the base of roof vents. Then apply roofing cement to the shingles. Embed the vent sleeve into the cement.

5. Coat the vent sleeve with roof cement. Lap the upper half of the sleeve with shingles, embedded into the roofing cement.

Shingle Replacement

Installing Composite Shingles

Difficulty Level: 🔨

- ❑ **Basic tools:** extension ladder, hammer or hammer tacker, roof brackets, utility knife

- ❑ **Special materials:** roofing nails or staples, shingles

Because shingle courses overlap, they effectively cover a roof with two layers of shingles. At the eaves, a starter strip is applied under the first course of shingles. The perimeter is protected by drip edging that keeps moisture from getting under the shingles, safeguards the fascia, and provides a straight edge.

F.Y.I.

Drip Edging

Drip Edging directs water into a gutter or away from a house. Wraparound end-cap flashing (A) covers edges of old roofing; flush end-caps (B) keep water and ice from backing up under shingles; canted drip edges (C) carry water away from the fascia, and conventional drip-cap flashing (D) overlaps the top edge of the gutter.

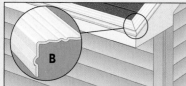

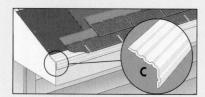

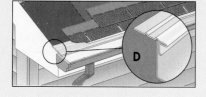

course across the length of the roof. Using a caulking gun, coat the bedded flashing with roofing cement, and then press the tabs down firmly into the cement. Do not nail down the tabs. Leave side gaps between the tabs equal to those on full shingles.

4 **Shingle around the roof vents.** Roof vents are typically covered with metal sleeves. A flap at the base of the sleeve creates a waterproof seal. Install shingles right up to the base of the roof vent, and then apply roofing cement at the base. Slip the sleeve over the vent and embed it into the cement.

5 **Flash the roof vents.** Overlap the upper half of the vent sleeve with shingles. Cut the overlapping courses around the stack, leaving a ½-inch gap, and then cement the tabs to the sleeve.

1 **Attach the drip edging.** If the roof is bare, attach drip edging along the eaves before—and along the rakes after—applying underlayment. For reroofing, nail the drip edge directly over the old shingles at 8 inches on center. Do not nail the edging into the fascia board.

2 **Install the starter course.** If old roofing has been removed, apply the starter course directly over the new roofing felt. (For reroofing, omit the starter-course.) Reverse the starter shingles so that the tabs point upward. Trim the first starter-

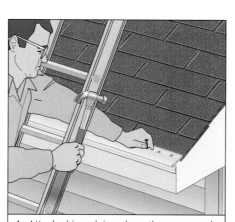

1. Attach drip edging along the eaves and along the rakes. For reroofing, apply the edging directly over the existing shingles.

2. Install starter courses with tabs facing upward. Allow shingles to overhang the roof ¼ to ³⁄₈ in. if there is no drip edge.

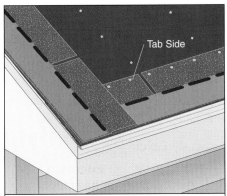

3. If rake shingles are deteriorated, apply a border of shingles, tab side in, along the rake. Nail the shingles at 12 in. on-center.

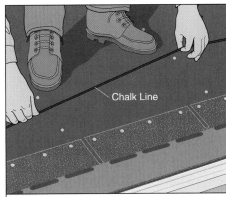

4. Align the first shingle course with the drip edge. Snap a chalk line, and then temporarily tack the new shingle into position.

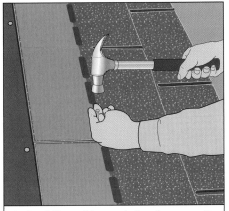

5. Carefully position and align the opposite end of the shingle, and then tack it temporarily into position.

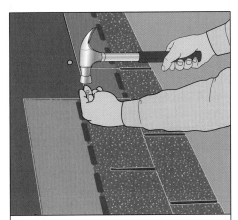

6. Double-check the shingle alignment. Realign nails, if needed, to eliminate buckling, and then finish nailing in the shingles.

course shingle so that the tabs will be offset from those of the first top course. Install starter shingles flush with the drip edge. If there is no drip edge, let the shingles overhang the roof edge by ¼ to ⅜ inch.

3 Apply the rake course. If the rake edge has worn, add a border of shingles, tab side in, along the edge. Nail the shingles every 12 inches on center vertically, at approximately 3 inches in from the edge. Allow a ¼- to ⅜-inch overhang.

4 Align the shingles. The first course of shingles must be aligned correctly. Align the edge of a new shingle with the drip edge. Snap a chalk line, and then tack one end of the new shingle in place.

5 Tack the shingle. Position and align the opposite end of the shingle, and then tack it into place.

6 Double-check the alignment. Double-check the shingle alignment, and then finish nailing the shingle. Realign nails, if necessary, to eliminate any buckling. Install the remaining shingles in a stair-step pattern, starting along an eave. This will permit the installation of a greater number of shingles before the ladders and roof brackets must be moved.

Six-Inch Method. A common way to align shingles is the *six-inch method.* Each shingle course is offset 6 inches to the side of the previous one, resulting in neatly aligned coursing. Each tab line is centered between two tab lines of the shingle directly above or below it.

Shingling Around Dormers

Pro Tip

If you have shingled the roof and valley up to one side of a dormer, continue the upper shingle course to the other side of the dormer ridge. Snap a chalk line to extend the course several feet. Check the accuracy of the line by measuring down from the main roof ridge at the beginning and end of the line. These distances should be equal. Continue the course across the roof, nailing it at the top only so that the next lower course can be slipped under it. When you have extended the course 10 feet, snap chalk lines parallel to it at 36-inch intervals down the roof. With these as a guide, align the valley cuts to match those on the other side of the dormer. If needed, make small adjustments over several courses of shingles so that they won't be noticeable.

Six-Inch Method. Align shingle courses using the 6-in. method, offsetting each course by 6 in. from the previous one.

Roofing an Open Valley

Difficulty Level:

❏ **Basic tools:** chalk-line box, extension ladder, hammer or hammer tacker, roof brackets, utility knife with hook blades, work gloves

❏ **Special materials:** planks, roll roofing, roofing cement, roof nails or staples, shingles

Though difficult, roofing a valley is crucial to a successful roofing application. A valley is the most vulnerable section of a roof, especially during a storm when water may be driven under the shingles to either side of the valley, causing a leaky roof. Because valleys form the junction where two angled planes of a roof come together, they must be able to shed a great deal of water.

There are two types of valley roofing. An *open valley* is covered with metal flashing or roofing membrane, forming an open flume to drain rainwater from the roof. A *closed valley* is one completely covered with interwoven shingles and does not form an open channel. An open valley is described below.

1 Apply roll roofing. Roll out a 36-inch-wide length of roofing, and cut it into two 18-inch-wide halves. Roll the two halves again, and carry them up to the roof.

Coat the valley with roofing cement, and then line it with an 18-inch-wide section of roll roofing. Lay the roofing granule-side down. Nail one vertical edge 12 inches on center. Press the piece into the valley, freeing it of any bubbles, bulges, or wrinkles, and then nail down the other edge.

Next, center a full 36-inch-wide length of roll roofing over the valley, with the granules facing down, as before. Split the roofing above the ridge and below the eave, so that it will lay flat. Trim the lower edge flush with the eaves, cutting

Nesting

F.Y.I. New shingles that are being applied over an existing layer of shingles can be "nested" into the old roofing. This preserves the current exposure dimension and provides a quick and easy way to align the new layer of shingles. Nesting is accomplished by first trimming the tabs off full shingles, to make a starter course. This course will fit snugly between the edge of the roof eave and the bottom edge of the second course of existing shingles. The top edge of each successive course of new shingles will be nested against the bottom edge of the existing course above it. Be sure to offset the new tab cutouts from the old ones by 3 inches to obtain a uniform, leak-free roofing installation.

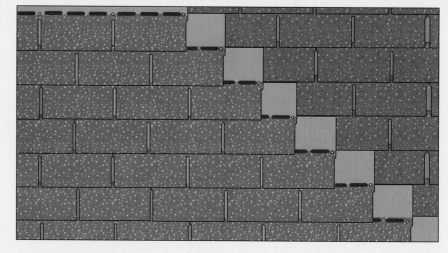

out at the appropriate angle from the center of the valley at the intersection of the eaves.

2 Apply the shingles. Using a chalk-line box, mark the center of the roof valley. Finish applying the shingles on each roof plane to within 3 inches of the centerline, and then strike guidelines for trimming the shingles. The guidelines should begin about 6 inches apart at the ridge, and then widen approximately ⅛ inch per foot as they proceed down toward the eaves.

3 Trim the shingles. To prevent the blade from cutting into the

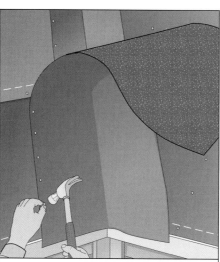

1. Apply 18-in.-wide roll roofing to the valley, granule-side down. Over this, apply 36-in.-wide roll roofing in the same way.

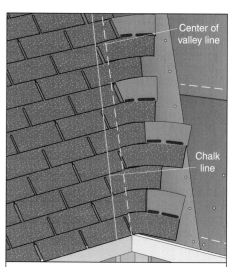

2. Mark the center of the valley with a chalk line. Trim the shingles from the ridge down to within 3 in. of the center line.

3. With a hook-bladed utility knife, trim the upper inside corner of each valley shingle, and then cut along the chalk guideline.

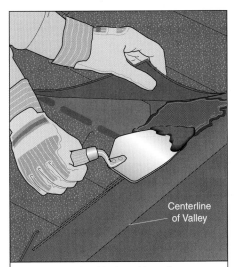

4. Seal down the shingles with roofing cement, and then nail them in place at least 4 in. in from the trimmed edge.

applied roll roofing, slip a scrap of the roofing material beneath the valley shingles, and then trim them with a hook-bladed utility knife. Trim the uppermost inside corner of each shingle, to prevent the corner from blocking the path of draining water and drawing it beneath the shingles. After you've completely trimmed one side of the valley, then work down the other side.

4 Seal and nail the shingles. Apply roofing cement as a seal to hold down the new shingles along the valley. Then nail down the shingles at least 4 inches in from the trimmed roofing edge.

Roofing a Ridge

Difficulty Level:

❑ **Basic tools:** chalk-line box, hammer, straightedge, utility knife, work gloves

❑ **Special materials:** planks, roof brackets, roofing cement, roofing nails, shingle tabs

1 Cut the tabs. Ridge shingles are made by separating the tabs on a full shingle. Use a straightedge to guide your cutting. Taper the cuts slightly, as shown in the illustration. After cutting one shingle, use it as a template to cut as many as needed.

2 Trim the final course. Overlap the ridgeline with one ridge shingle to determine whether or not it will adequately overlap the last course of full shingles on each slope. The last course of shingles should reach to within 3 inches (or less) of the ridgeline.

3 Snap a chalk line. Center one shingle tab over the ridgeline, and then use the horizontal tab edges as a guide for snapping a chalk line. Seal the shingle, and then nail one nail on each side of the ridgeline, plus one just in front of the sealant line.

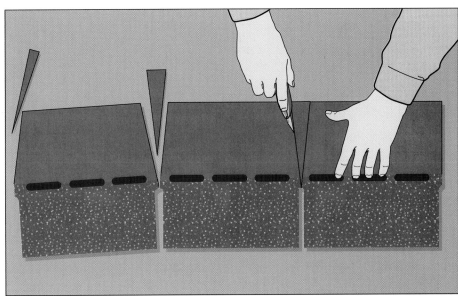

1. Ridge shingles are made by cutting apart the tabs on a full shingle. Use a straightedge as a guide to cut the first shingle. Then use the cut shingle as a template. Taper the cuts as shown.

2. Trim the last course of shingles on each slope to within 3 in. (or less) of the ridge line.

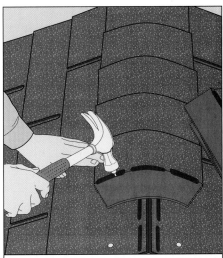

3. Center a tab on the ridge, as a guide for your chalk line. Install the tabs to the line.

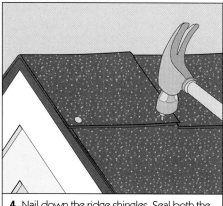

4. Nail down the ridge shingles. Seal both the shingles and the nails with roofing cement.

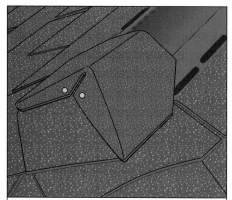

5. Where hip ridges join, miter adjacent tabs, and cover the joint with an end cap.

4 **Seal the nails.** Install the ridge shingles, and then thoroughly seal the shingles and the nails with roofing cement.

5 **Cut the hip ridge shingles.** If there are hip ridges, cut the bottom of the first tab so that, when it is bent over the ridgeline, the bottom edge will be parallel to the eaves line on both sides of the ridge. Use this as a template to cut successive ridge shingles from the eaves to the peak, so that it will match the shingle line on each side of the ridgeline. At the top of the roof, where the hip ridges join, miter the adjacent tabs, and cover the joint with a tab, that has been cut and folded into an edge cap.

Sealing and Trimming

Difficulty Level: 🔨

❑ **Basic tools:** caulking gun, chalk-line box, utility knife

❑ **Special materials:** tube of roofing cement

1 **Seal the bracket holes.** Use a caulking gun loaded with roofing cement to seal shingle holes left by roof brackets or gutter hanger nails, to coat bolts that secure antennas and other equipment to the roof, and to glue down tabs that have curled at the edges.

2 **Trim the rake shingles.** Snap a chalk line on the shingles that overhang the rake. The line should be about $1/4$ to $3/8$ inch out from the rake edge. Using a utility knife, trim the shingles along the chalk line.

1. Use a caulking gun with roofing cement to seal the holes made by roof brackets.

2. With a utility knife, trim the rake shingles to overlap the roof edge by $1/4$ to $3/8$ in.

Chalk line

Gutters and leaders must be maintained well to prevent water damage to your home.

Gutters and Leaders

Gutters and leaders are crucial to roof drainage. If they are clogged, missing, or damaged, then leaks, rotting, and other building damage may result. If gutters and leaders are reparable, fix them; if they are badly broken or corroded, replace them immediately.

Repairing Gutters

Difficulty Level: 🔩

❑ **Basic tools:** chalk-line box, machine screws with washers and nuts, pliers, pop riveter, putty knife, rag, screwdriver

❑ **Special materials:** epoxy body filler, fiberglass cloth, hanger straps, paint thinner

1 **Replace damaged hangers.** Gutters often sag because hanger straps break or become loose. Use a machine screw, washer, and nut to replace a broken or loose rivet. If the hanger is split, replace it or splice in a new hanger using a pop riveter. Snap a chalk line from one end of the gutter to the other to guide realignment of the hanger.

2 **Adjust the slope.** A dip or sag in a gutter will likely cause water to spill over the edge and down the surface of the wall. Adjust the strap by lifting up on the gutter, and then

1. Use a machine screw, washer, and nut to replace a loose or missing hanger rivet.

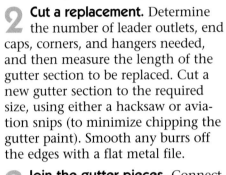

2. To adjust a strap, bend it with a pair of pliers while lifting up slightly on the gutter.

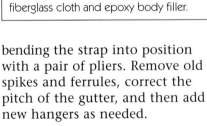

3. To repair a gutter hole, patch it with fiberglass cloth and epoxy body filler.

bending the strap into position with a pair of pliers. Remove old spikes and ferrules, correct the pitch of the gutter, and then add new hangers as needed.

3 Patch the holes. Metal gutter holes can be patched with an epoxy automotive body filler. First eliminate any dirt or corrosion around the hole, and then wipe the surface clean with a rag dipped in paint thinner. When the surface is thoroughly dried, cut a section of fiberglass cloth about 1 inch larger than the hole. Mix a small amount of the epoxy, apply it liberally around the hole, and then embed the cloth into the epoxy. Spread more epoxy smoothly over the patch to finish it.

Replacing Gutters

Difficulty Level: 🕇🕇

❑ **Basic tools:** caulking gun and mastic, flat file, hacksaw, pliers, rope, safety goggles, scrap wood, work gloves

❑ **Special tools:** angle gauge, aviation snips

1 Remove the damaged gutter. Mark the angle of incline on the fascia, but do not yet remove the old gutter. Gutters typically slope 1 inch for every 20 feet of length. Use an angle gauge to mark a square cut line on the gutter section to be removed. Secure the damaged section with a rope until it can be lowered. Wedge scrap wood between the

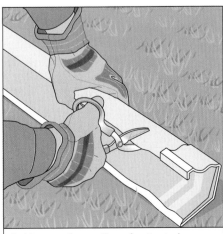

2. Measure the section of gutter to be replaced. Cut a new piece with a hacksaw or aviation snips. File the burred edges.

gutter and fascia to protect the roof edge from saw damage, and then place a 2x4 scrap piece in the gutter to prevent the saw from binding. Wearing safety goggles, cut through the gutter with a hacksaw. Finish the cut with aviation snips, and then lower the gutter to the ground.

2 Cut a replacement. Determine the number of leader outlets, end caps, corners, and hangers needed, and then measure the length of the gutter section to be replaced. Cut a new gutter section to the required size, using either a hacksaw or aviation snips (to minimize chipping the gutter paint). Smooth any burrs off the edges with a flat metal file.

3 Join the gutter pieces. Connect the end caps, corners, and drop

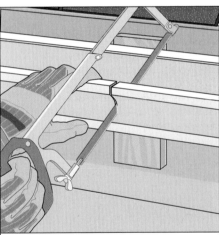

1. Protect the roof edge with a scrap of wood, and then cut away the damaged section of the gutter with a hacksaw.

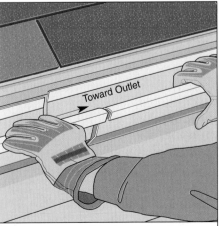

Toward Outlet

3. For lap joints, slide the section farthest from the drop outlet into the end of the one that's closer. Lap them by 6 in.

outlets with mastic, as needed. Where possible, preassemble the gutter sections on the ground. Use a slip joint, lap joint, or rivets to join gutter sections. Apply mastic to the joints, and then connect the gutter sections by pressing them together.

For slip joints, bend the rear tip inward, and crimp it with pliers. For lap joints, the section of gutter farthest from a leader outlet goes inside the section closer to the drop outlet. Allow a 6-inch minimum overlap. If necessary, trim the inside gutter lip to permit the full overlap, and then slide the joint apart. Apply a 6-inch band of sealant to the bottom of the outer gutter section. Connect the sections, and press them together firmly to seal the joints.

To install a new gutter section, tip the back edge of the gutter into the brackets, and then tilt the section toward you. Finally, slide the piece into the expansion joint.

Maintaining Gutters

Difficulty Level: 🔧

- ❑ **Basic tools:** dustpan, garden hose, plumber's snake, whisk broom, work gloves

- ❑ **Special materials:** leaf strainers or gutter screens

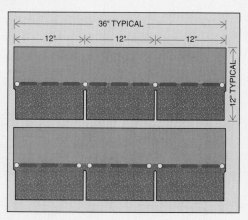

Nailing Shingles

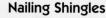
F.Y.I. Shingles are typically fastened with four nails — one at each end of the shingle, and one above each tab slot. In windy areas use six nails to affix the shingles, placing one on each side of the tab slots. Position the nails just beneath the adhesive patch but above the tab slots. Roofing nails should be long enough to penetrate sheathing by $\frac{3}{4}$ inch, whether shingling over or replacing existing roofing.

1 Unclog the downspouts.
Remove as much debris as possible from inside leader outlets. Use a garden hose to flush the elbow bends. If an elbow remains blocked, run a plumber's snake down the outlet. If blockage persists, remove the splash block elbow and try working from the bottom. Once the downspout is clear, flush it again, and then equip the leader inlet with a leaf strainer, or screen the gutter to prevent any more clogging.

2 Flush the gutters. Starting at the high end of a gutter run and working toward the downspout, remove accumulated leaves and debris. Using a garden hose and a whisk broom, brush and flush out the remaining dirt and debris.

3 Manage the runoff. Prevent water from seeping through basement walls, hydrostatic pressure under basement slabs, and soil erosion around the foundation by directing drainage away from the house. Use splash blocks, perforated drain tile (pipe), or dry wells if necessary. Slope the grade and the drains to carry water away from the foundation.

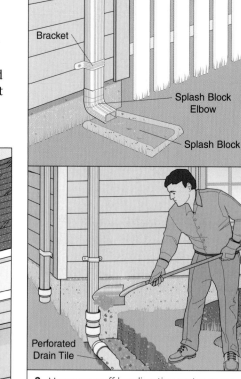

3. Manage runoff by directing water away from the foundation using splash blocks or perforated subsurface drain tiles.

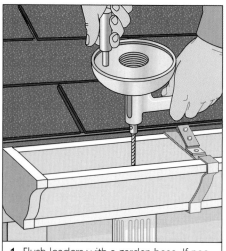

1. Flush leaders with a garden hose. If necessary, clear them with a plumber's snake.

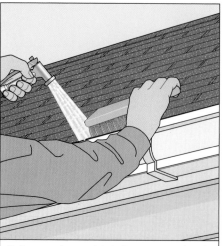

2. Remove loose debris from gutters, brush them out, and then flush them with water.

Chapter 6
Exterior Painting

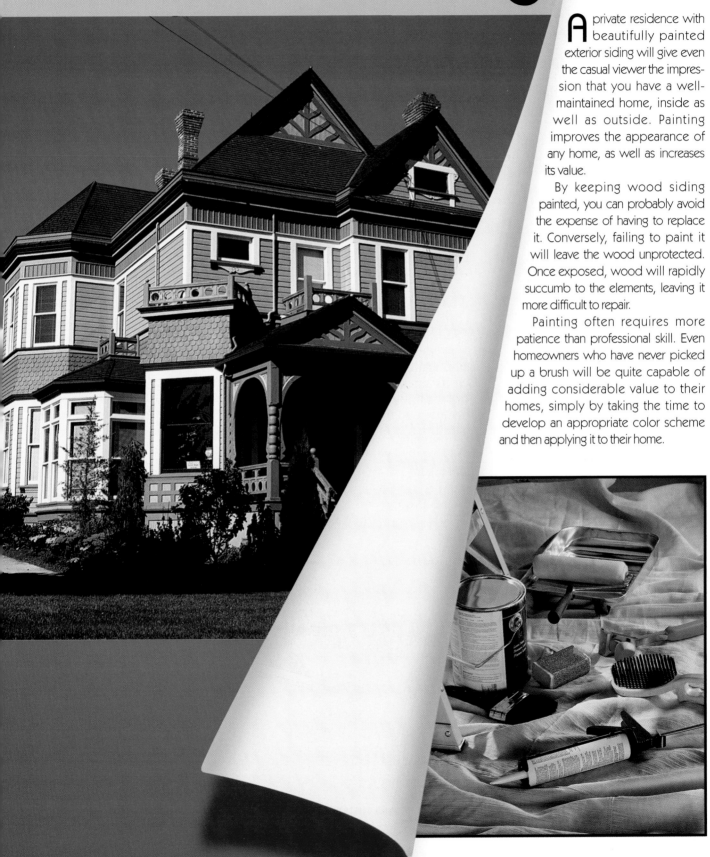

A private residence with beautifully painted exterior siding will give even the casual viewer the impression that you have a well-maintained home, inside as well as outside. Painting improves the appearance of any home, as well as increases its value.

By keeping wood siding painted, you can probably avoid the expense of having to replace it. Conversely, failing to paint it will leave the wood unprotected. Once exposed, wood will rapidly succumb to the elements, leaving it more difficult to repair.

Painting often requires more patience than professional skill. Even homeowners who have never picked up a brush will be quite capable of adding considerable value to their homes, simply by taking the time to develop an appropriate color scheme and then applying it to their home.

IN THIS CHAPTER

Paints and Stains

Latex Paints 78

Solvent-based Paints 79

Paint Sheen 79

Primers/Sealers 79

Stains 79

Painting Tools

Paintbrushes 79

Paint Rollers 80

Paint Scrapers 81

Sanders 81

Ladders and Scaffolding

Stepladders 82

Extension Ladders 82

Ladder-Jack Scaffolding 83

Preparation

Removing Paint 84

Repairing Damaged Wood 85

Caulking 86

Paint Colors

Color Schemes 87

Painting

Painting Sequence
and the Weather 89

Painting Wood Siding 89

Painting Masonry 90

TODAY'S TRENDS

Restoration of Original Color Schemes

Accenting Decorative Trim

Multicolor Schemes

Paints and Stains

Paint is composed of a solid pigment, a liquid medium, and additives—all of which affect the flow and drying characteristics of the paint. For latex paint, the medium is a water-based emulsion. For solvent-based paint, the medium is either a natural or a synthetic (alkyd) oil. A third, new type of paint is latex paint that contains some alkyd resins.

The first rule of buying paint is to select from the top of the line brands—cheap paint is no bargain if you have to do the job twice. To save money, choose from the manufacturer's premixed color palette. Premixed colors are generally a few dollars less per gallon than custom-mixed shades.

Latex Paints

Although some experts claim that latex paints do not *flow* off the brush as smoothly or dry as hard as solvent-based paints, latex is the preferred paint for most home painting tasks.

A majority of homeowners and professional painters prefer latex paints because they dry in just a few hours, making it possible to apply two coats in the same day. In addition, cleanup is a snap. When the job is done, everything can be cleaned using soap and warm water.

Latex paints are environmentally safer than solvent-based paints because, in contrast, they emit relatively lower levels of volatile organic compounds (VOCs), which have been virtually outlawed in some states. Latex paint is easier on the eyes, nose, lungs, and skin, too. Also, latex paint does not require toxic solvents, such as mineral spirits, for cleanup.

There are a few situations where you might not want to use latex. Latex paint should not be used over solvent paints, unless you carefully sand or chemically *degloss* the surface. On the other hand, it is perfectly okay to use a solvent-based *primer* under latex paint. Solvent-based primers will soak into unpainted surfaces, more so than latex primers. Latex paint is not recommended for painting in extremely hot or cold temperatures.

F.Y.I.

LEAD IN PAINT

Prior to the 1970s most paint contained lead, which is toxic to humans. Lead poisoning symptoms include headaches, fatigue, disorientation, and in extreme cases brain damage. Lead in paint has been banned, but many buildings still contain lead paint. Lead-paint-testing kits are available in many home centers. If you detect lead paint in your home, you should remove it. Because preparation for new painting work involves sanding and scraping, dangerous lead-laced chips and dust can be spread through the air and into your lungs. You should take the following common-sense precautions:

◆ Use drop cloths to catch paint chips, and then dispose of the chips. Vacuum and damp-mop the floor at the end of each workday.

◆ Wear a mask designed to filter out lead dust.

◆ Remove and wash work clothes every day. Shower and change before eating.

◆ Children and fetuses are particularly susceptible to lead poisoning. You should keep children and pregnant women away from the work area until the work is completed. Have your children tested for lead levels, whether or not you are working with lead paint.

Solvent-Based Paints

If you are painting over an existing solvent-based paint or want the look of gloss enamel, then the best choice is traditional solvent-based paint.

If you choose to use a solvent-based paint, then you'll need mineral spirits or turpentine to clean the brushes and roller covers, as well as yourself. These solvents are somewhat expensive, especially compared with water, and they emit strong fumes that can be irritating to eyes, nose, lungs, and skin. After tools and your skin have been cleaned with mineral spirits, a final cleanup with soap and water is still needed.

Usually you have to wait a day before recoating solvent-based paints. This can be inconvenient, especially if you can work only on weekends. If the first coat isn't dry on Sunday, you'll wind up waiting a week to finish the job.

In addition, some localities have rules governing the disposal of solvents and solvent-based paints, which means you may be stuck with half-empty containers or have to pay to dispose of the excess materials.

Paint Sheen

In addition to choosing the colors—and latex or solvent-based paint—you will need to specify a suitable degree of luster (sheen), ranging from flat to gloss. Most sheens are available in interior or exterior paints, in either latex- or solvent-based formulations.

Flat, or Matte. A low-gloss finish hides surface flaws and flaws in pre-paint preparation. But because the paint is slightly rough, flat paints do not take scrubbing as well as glossier finishes do. Scrubbing flat paint tends to smear the dirt, making a larger dirty spot.

Eggshell and Satin. An eggshell finish is glossier than a flat finish and has slightly better abrasion resistance. A satin finish is glossier than an eggshell finish.

Semigloss. Glossier than satin, these paints take scrubbing moderately well.

Gloss. This is the highest gloss classification. It is highest in resin and lowest in absorption. Gloss paints take scrubbing well and are easiest to clean. However, the glossier the paint, the more obvious the flaws.

Enamel. Once this term was synonymous with solvent-based paint. Today it is a loose term that refers to the glossiness of paint. The term is reliable only in that you can be reasonably sure that a paint labeled *enamel* is a semigloss or gloss paint. One manufacturer's enamel may be glossier than another's.

Primers/Sealers

Primer is the paint applied before the undercoat and the finish coat. Often it makes the difference between a high-quality result and a poor result. Primers are available in both solvent-based and water-based formulations. In general, experts prefer solvent-based primer for exterior wood and latex primer for interior plaster and drywall.

Stains

Exterior stain is essentially paint with a reduced amount of pigment suspended in oils and resins of various types. Because stains are thinner than paint, they tend to soak into wood and form a thinner film. As a result, stain doesn't peel the way paint does, and new layers can be added through the years without buildup. Another advantage to stain is that it doesn't require a primer. There are two types of exterior stains; semitransparent penetrating stains, which add color yet reveal the grain, and opaque stains, which obscure the grain but are thinner than paint.

There is a downside to reduced pigment in stains. Pigment plays a big part in resisting the weather and sunlight, which break down paint. Homes painted with semitranspar-ent penetrating stains must be recoated more frequently than homes coated with opaque stains. However, opaque stains form a surface coating that may peel later. All stained houses must be recoated more frequently than painted houses. The more severe the regional weather conditions, the less suitable exterior stain becomes for a home.

Painting Tools

Most painting can be handled with brushes and rollers. Brushes are good for both narrow edges and broad surfaces and can be fit into tight spots. Rollers are excellent for coating large surface areas. When used correctly, a roller can mimic the texture of a brush stroke.

Paintbrushes

It makes little sense to pinch pennies on tools and equipment, especially brushes. Quality brushes have thicker, softer bristles, which means that they hold a lot of paint, produce a high-quality finish, and withstand years of hard use. The extra cost is worth it.

Flat (Wall) Brush. If you could buy only one brush, a 3- or 4-inch flat wall brush with a chiseled edge would be the best choice for handling almost any painting task. It covers large areas quickly, and its tapered edge can paint a crisp line.

Sash Brush. This brush has angled bristles that are ideal for making crisp lines on trim, moldings, and window muntins.

Stain Brush. The bristle area on this brush is shorter and wider than a paintbrush, to counteract the tendency stain has to drip into the brush ferrule.

Foam Brush. This cheap and disposable brush is really just a foam pad on a stick. Foam brushes are good for applying stain and painting window muntins.

TESTING A BRUSH

Tug gently on the bristles. If more than a few fall out, then do not buy the brush.

Bounce and wiggle the bristles in your palm. A good brush has bristles that feel soft and springy and that bounce back into shape quickly when you let go.

The bristles should be thick and plentiful. Fold back the bristles with your hand, and look where they connect to the handle. If you see a lot of handle between a few plugs of bristles, you have an inferior brush. Good brushes have bristles that are at least 2 inches long. A good 3-inch brush has bristles that are about 4 inches long.

Check the metal ferrule that holds the bristles to the handle. It must be substantial (not flimsy) and firmly attached to the handle. Make sure it does not rock when you twist the bristles back and forth.

Paint Pad. This is a rectangular foam pad with a fiber pile or nap, useful for painting rough surfaces such as striated wood shingles.

Paint Rollers

The two parts of a paint roller include the handle (frame) and the cover (sleeve). As with brushes, the first rule in choosing a roller is to buy the best. Poor-quality roller handles bend under pressure. Similarly, it makes sense to buy high-quality roller covers. The nap on a good roller cover won't have bumpy or flat spots. To test a roller, gently tug at the nap; if fuzz comes off, find a better cover.

Nylon Roller Covers. These covers are suitable for most paint jobs. The advantages of nylon roller covers are that they're inexpensive, and they can be stored wet during a painting job. A short-napped roller cover can apply a smooth finish on very flat surfaces. A medium-napped cover is a good choice for walls and ceilings, and a long-napped cover is designed for painting concrete or other rough surfaces.

Lamb's Wool Covers. These high-quality roller covers are considerably more expensive than nylon covers, but they can be reused time and time again. A lamb's wool cover will produce a slightly stippled textural effect. Regardless of which type roller cover you use, be sure to test the finish in an inconspicuous spot before painting the entire room.

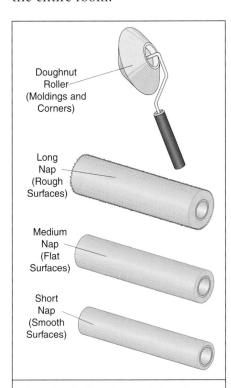

Doughnut Roller (Moldings and Corners)

Long Nap (Rough Surfaces)

Medium Nap (Flat Surfaces)

Short Nap (Smooth Surfaces)

Choosing Rollers Covers. When buying a roller cover, be sure to select one with a nap that is appropriate for the surface being painted.

BRUSH BRISTLES

Flat (Wall) Brush

Sash Brush

Handle

Bristles

Stain Brush

Ferrule

Nylon Bristles. These are most suitable for latex paint, although they can also be used with solvent-based paint.

Natural Bristles. Also called "China bristle," natural bristle brushes are preferred for use with solvent-based paints and varnishes because they tend to hold more paint and generally brush out to a smoother looking finish. Natural bristle brushes should not be used with latex paint. The water in the paint will cause the bristles to expand and ruin the brush.

Choosing Brushes. When buying a brush, check for thick, resilient bristles that are firmly held in place. Be sure, also, to get the proper type brush for the job.

Doughnut Rollers. These small, one-piece foam rollers are particularly good for painting moldings and wall corners. Some painters find them indispensable, while others prefer to work with brushes and a standard 9-inch roller.

Foam Rollers. These super-smooth rollers are useful for painting cabinets and vanities because they leave a surface as smooth as a brush finish in a fraction of the time. Foam rollers are not suitable, however, for painting textured or irregular surfaces, such as drywall.

Paint Scrapers

Peeling and cracking paint must be completely removed before either a prime coat or a new finish coat of paint can be applied to a home. There are many ways to remove failed paint from a house. The extent of paint failure, the type and quality of available tools, and your skill level and disposition will determine the best way to resolve paint problems.

Whichever method you choose, when scraping, sanding, or stripping paint, remember this important time-saving rule: If the paint is adhered well enough to resist removal, then it is not likely to fall off anytime soon. So leave it alone.

Scraping Paint. Scraping is the easiest, least toxic, and lowest-tech way to remove problem paint. This method is labor intensive but simple for the homeowner, fairly tidy, and definitely the best way to proceed for most paint removal.

The best tool for the job is a pull, or *hook,* scraper, which has a wide blade end and removable blades. Be sure to buy plenty of replacement blades if you have a lot of scraping to do. The blades dull quickly, and you will change them fairly often. When using a pull scraper, be sure to keep the blade flat on the surface. If you rotate the scraper, the edge of the blade will dig into the wood and cause scarring.

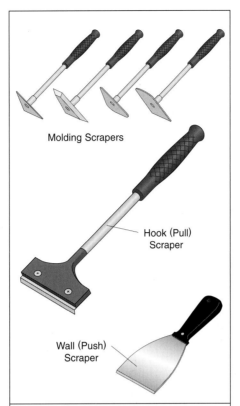

Molding Scrapers

Hook (Pull) Scraper

Wall (Push) Scraper

Scrapers. Wall, hook, and molding scrapers have many specific uses. Be sure to use the appropriate scraper for the work you are doing.

Because you cannot exert enough downward pressure on a push type, or *wall,* scraper it tends to remove less paint than a pull scraper. However, it is handy when using a heat gun because it requires only one hand. You can run the heat gun just ahead of the scraper, which will easily lift off the softened paint. It might be good to have a push scraper on hand just to give your pulling muscles an occasional break. Another advantage to using push scrapers is that they are more likely to send paint chips flying away from rather than toward you.

If your house has highly detailed architectural moldings, such as dentils, egg-and-dart trim, or highly ornate window and door casings, you will need to have *molding* scrapers. Molding scrapers come in a variety of shapes and sizes that match common molding profiles, and they are usually available at well-stocked paint stores and home-improvement centers.

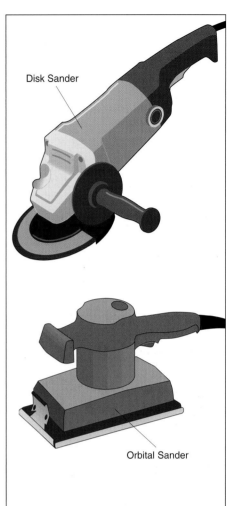

Disk Sander

Orbital Sander

Finishing Sanders. For sanding large surfaces, use a professional-quality heavy-duty disk or orbital sander.

Sanders

If the siding has large areas of peeled, alligatored, or blistered paint or many layers of paint that must be removed, sanding may be the best option. Sanding is the most effective way to take shingles or clapboard down to bare wood. Do not attempt to do this job with a sanding attachment on a power drill. Use a professional-quality rotary *disk sander*, sometimes called a *disk grinder*. This is a heavy-duty, two-handed machine. Use paper or fiber-backed sanding disks. Both the sander and the disks can be purchased at paint stores and home-improvement centers.

Although effective, sanding is difficult and dirty work. Dust is the main problem, even with drop cloths laid down, because the dust will still swirl and blow around in the wind. Some sanders come with collection bags. If you use one of these, be wary of striking a nailhead. A stray spark can ignite wood dust and cause a flash fire. Always wear goggles and a dust mask when sanding.

Most sanding work must be done twice. Begin with 16-grit disks for heavy-duty paint removal, and then give the surface a light pass with 60-grit sandpaper to smooth it enough for painting. Powerful sanders can leave permanent marks on a wood surface. To prevent this, keep the sander moving. If it remains in one area for too long, the sander will make ruts in the wood. Also, avoid turning the sander at an angle to the siding. Although this will take the paint off faster, it will gouge the wood. Always keep the sanding disk parallel to the surface.

Ladders and Scaffolding

Multistory homes or homes with high eaves require the use of extension ladders or scaffolding. For a two-story home, a 28-foot-long extension ladder is recommended. An older home may need an even longer ladder. If an extension ladder is needed, consider whether you want to do the work yourself or hire a contractor to do it for you. Working high up on a ladder is not for everyone, considering the potential for injury. The same is true for scaffolding. At the very least, you might want to have a contractor assemble the scaffolding and disassemble it when the work is completed.

Stepladders

Stepladders are available in several heights, ranging from 36-inch step stools to tall ladders used for specialized jobs such as tree trimming. An 8-foot stepladder is adequate for most homeowners.

Stepladders are also constructed from a variety of materials, including aluminum, fiberglass, and wood. Aluminum ladders are the lightest, while fiberglass ladders are somewhat heavier, and wood ladders are the heaviest. Aluminum or fiberglass ladders are superior to wood ladders because wood has a tendency to deteriorate when exposed to weather. Fiberglass ladders have the further advantage of being nonconductive, which provides some protection if the ladder accidentally brushes against a live electrical wire. Extreme caution must nevertheless be exercised around live wires. A fiberglass ladder is no guarantee against an electric shock.

Be sure that stepladder legs are level and stable. If necessary, place stabilizing blocks under ladder legs that don't reach the ground, or dig the ground out from under legs that are too long. Take care to open the ladder completely, and make certain that the hinged support frame is locked. If the ladder bends or twists, get off it immediately, and check to see if it is level. If twisting persists, the ladder may be defective.

Extension Ladders

The standard extension ladder is 16 feet long, which is long enough to reach to the roof of most one-story homes. Many people are not comfortable on ladders that extend higher than 24 to 28 feet. Moving a ladder much longer than this often requires more than one person.

To determine the ladder size needed, calculate approximately 10 feet for each story of the house, add the height of the foundation, and then add the height from the attic floor to the roof ridge. The ladder should extend about 4 feet higher than the maximum height to be reached.

Carrying an Extension Ladder. The safest way to transport an extension ladder is to grasp it at the center, hold it at waist height, and carry it like a briefcase. If the ladder is longer than 16 feet, you might need an assistant to help you carry it.

70° angle

Extension Ladders. The top rails of an extension ladder ride in the track of the bottom rails, and are extended by means of a rope and pulley system. The ideal ladder angle is 70 deg., or about 1 ft. away from the wall for every 4 ft. of vertical extension.

Raising an extension ladder may take some practice.

Protecting Exterior Siding. Before positioning a ladder, wrap upper rail ends with old socks, or tape some foam padding on them to prevent them from damaging the siding.

Checking a Ladder for Stability. Before climbing up a ladder, make certain that its legs are level. Use bricks, solid-wood chock blocks, or built-in leveling attachments to stabilize the ladder legs. Be sure that chock blocks are set securely on the ground. Do not climb on windy days. Wind can move a ladder, even with a person standing on it.

Positioning a Ladder. Secure the legs of a ladder firmly on the ground, and then walk the ladder toward the

Ladder Stability. Before climbing up a ladder, always confirm that its legs are level. Use blocking or built-in leveling devices for stability.

house, moving your hands down the rungs as you proceed.

Keeping a Ladder Vertical. Once a ladder is raised, take care to keep it vertical. If the top leans significantly to one side, you may not be able to keep the ladder from tumbling over.

Lowering an Extension Ladder. With an assistant *footing* the ladder to stabilize it, lower the ladder sideways, keeping one hand on the ladder at all times.

Positioning to Catch a Ladder. While an assistant balances it, move back to *catch* the ladder at its mid-point as it is lowered.

Catching a Ladder. Using your free hand, catch a rung near the top of the ladder. Again, use both arms to stabilize the ladder at waist height while you are carrying it.

Ladder-Jack Scaffolding

A ladder-jack scaffold is constructed from two ladders, a set of ladder jacks, and a scaffolding plank. Ladder jacks are brackets that are used to support a scaffolding plank between two ladders. Ladder jacks can provide easily assembled scaffolding. However, because of their

small scale, painting while standing on this type of scaffolding requires concentration. You cannot forget that you are standing on a 12-inch-wide platform.

Ladder jacks are useful when you must work in one spot for an extended period of time or when work must be done where a single ladder cannot be supported, such as the center of a second-floor window.

Never attempt to construct ladder jack scaffolding without assistance, and always use genuine *scaffolding planks* (typically of aluminum) between ladder jacks. Scrap lumber cannot be trusted to safely carry the load of a worker. Planks and ladder jacks can be purchased or rented at most home improvement centers or equipment rental stores.

Setting Up Ladder Jacks. Carry each ladder jack up a ladder and secure it properly. Be sure the jacks are secured at the same height on both ladders.

Bringing Up an End. Bring an end of the plank up one of the ladders, while your assistant remains on the ground to support the other end.

Bringing Up the Other End. Rest one end of the scaffolding plank on a ladder jack, and then hold it in place while your assistant brings up the other end.

Securing the Plank. Flip the plank into position. Make sure it is securely held by the ladder jacks and that it extends at least 12 inches beyond the end of each jack.

Preparation

The quality of a finished paint job depends almost entirely upon the quality of the surface preparation that precedes it. Look carefully over the surface of your home, and make a list of items that need replacing, such as siding and trim that are damaged or weatherbeaten. When paint on the siding or fascia boards fails because of moisture penetration,

Using Ladder Jacks. Ladder jacks provide simple, portable scaffolding for one or two people.

this often indicates the presence of more serious problems. You must trace such problems back to their origins and fix them before any painting can begin. Eliminate water leaks, replace rotted wood, and caulk all areas where moisture may penetrate.

Next, you must clean the outside of the house thoroughly to remove dirt, grease, and chalking before priming and painting. This is a job that can be done quickly with a pressure washer. However, pressure washers are capable of blowing out mortar, driving water into and through walls, and sweeping workers off ladders. If you decide on pressure washing, it is best to have it done by an insured professional contractor.

The simplest and safest way to clean the outside of your house is to wash the walls by hand. Use a solution of trisodium phosphate (TSP), available at paint stores. Put on rubber gloves and goggles, and with a scrub brush attached to a pole, wash down the exterior surfaces. Use a garden hose to rinse the house. Be sure to cover plants to prevent them from being burned by the TSP solution.

READING THE PAINT

Problem	Appearance	What It's Telling You	The Solution
Blistering and Bubbling	Raised paint pulling away from the surface	Wood contains moisture or was painted in the hot sun.	Scrape, sand, and repaint. Prime back of new wood.
Alligatoring	Surface checking and cracking	Surface was improperly prepared or not primed first.	Scrape, sand, prime, and then repaint.
Peeling	Flaking and curling strips of paint on the surface	Paint has been applied over dirt, grease, or glossy paint.	Scrape, sand, apply a sealer, and then repaint.
Bleeding	Wood knots or imperfections showing through	There is pitch or resin in the wood, preventing bonding.	Scrape, sand, seal with shellac, and then repaint.
Chalking	Surface that looks powdery and chalky	The pigment is breaking down from age and exposure.	Wash and/or sand, and then repaint.
Staining	Rust colored drips, lines, and spots	Nails or screws are rusting from corrosion.	Replace the fasteners with galvanized or stainless steel.

Removing Paint

Difficulty Level:

Required Tools:

☐ **Basic tools: dropcloths, hook scraper, hose, sanding block, sandpaper, wall scraper**

Preparing to Prime. Wearing eye protection and rubber gloves, wash the dirt and grit off the house with a solution of TSP and water. Scrub the surface with a pole brush.

☐ **Special tools: heat gun, molding scrapers, paint remover, power sander, pressure washer**

Scraping paint with hand tools is simple and effective, but it has two serious disadvantages: It is labor-intensive work, and it can do severe damage to wood. Pull scrapers have a tendency to dig into wood, making deep gouge marks, and push scrapers easily split off the edges of wood trim. Scrapers are, however, useful with heat guns. Running a heat gun just ahead of a scraper will soften the paint, making it easier to remove.

1 Scrape the siding. Close the windows on the side of the house to be scraped. Lay down heavy drop cloths to catch most of the paint chips and dust. Keep the scraper flat on the surface, and scrape parallel to the wood grain.

2 Scrape the molding. For decorative molding and difficult-to-reach areas, use a molding scraper. Molding scrapers come in a variety of shapes and sizes to match common molding profiles.

3 Sand the surface of the siding. Once failed paint has been scraped loose, use a power sander to finish the job. Keep the sander moving horizontally while applying a light, constant pressure. Work from side to side as far as you can easily reach.

Pro Tip

SAFETY FIRST

For scraping and sanding work, take safety precautions to protect yourself from flying debris and sharp tools. Protect your arms and hands by wearing a **long-sleeved shirt** and **heavy gloves**. Wear **safety glasses** or **goggles** to keep paint chips and dust from getting into your eyes. A paper **dust mask** rated for nuisance dust is sufficient to keep dust particles out of your lungs. However, houses painted before the mid-1970s are likely to have some lead-based paint. If you have much scraping to do on an older house, use a **respirator** that is rated for lead-laced dust.

4 Sand the bottom edge of the siding. If there are many layers of built-up paint, the bottom edge of the clapboards will probably also need to be sanded. Turn the sander at a 90-degree angle to the siding and, using a light hand, sand the bottom edges of the siding. Because an electric sander is so powerful, be careful not to chew off a chunk of siding without realizing it. If the sander cannot reach into the joints where siding boards meet vertical or horizontal trim, remove this paint with a molding scraper or hand-held sandpaper. If there is any dried caulking between the siding and the trim, scrape it out, also.

1 Hold a hook scraper parallel to the grain of the siding boards, and then pull the scraper toward you.

2. Use a molding scraper to remove paint in places where a power sander is not able to reach.

3. Keep power sanders moving side to side across the surface of the siding. Work from top to bottom.

4. Hold the sander with the disk facing up to sand the bottom edge of the clapboard or shingles.

Repairing Damaged Wood

Difficulty Level: 𝕋

Required Tools:

❑ **Basic tools:** mixing board, putty knife, rubber gloves, sandpaper or chisel

❑ **Special materials:** two-part epoxy mixture

Repairing damaged wood is an important part of any preparation work. No paint will look good applied over damaged wood. More importantly, if wood is damaged by water, paint will not adhere properly to the wood surface.

Before repairing water-damaged wood, locate the source of the water problem and eliminate it. Leaky gutters and downspouts are frequent sources of water damage. Some wood components, such as window sills and moldings, are available in stock sizes and can be replaced more readily than they can be repaired.

Damaged wood can be repaired in place by filling. Many exterior wood fillers are available, including various kinds of exterior wood putty. One of the best systems for filling severely damaged wood involves a two-step process using a proprietary compound. Such compounds usually consist of a thin liquid preparation coat, poured onto the damaged wood to harden it, followed by a two-part epoxy filler. Once it is cured, the filler can be sanded, drilled and worked with power tools. Epoxy fillers are stronger than natural wood, and can be primed and painted just like wood.

1 Mix the epoxy. Mix the epoxy components on a board, according to the manufacturer's instructions—typically one part resin to one part hardener. Epoxy works by a heat reaction. Do not mix too much of it in a small container, or the heat may build up to a point where it will harden the epoxy before you can get a chance to use it.

2 **Apply the epoxy.** Using a putty knife, apply the epoxy filler to the damaged area of the wood. Work quickly, because once the epoxy begins hardening, you will no longer be able to spread it. Use a putty knife to shape the epoxy until it matches the form of the original wood. When it begins to harden, stop working. After the epoxy has completely cured, sand it to shape. If necessary, you can use a chisel to shave the cured epoxy.

1. Use an old putty knife to mix epoxy, according to the directions on the can.

2. Epoxy does not take long to set, so work it quickly into the damaged areas.

Caulking

Caulking is an essential part of the preparation work that must be done before painting the exterior of a home. Aside from preventing air infiltration around windows, doors, and construction joints, caulking also prevents water penetration. Silicone caulking is expensive, but it withstands temperature and humidity changes better than other types. One disadvantage to using silicone caulking is that it is not always paintable. However, silicone caulking is available with color tinting. As an alternative to silicone, either a latex or an acrylic caulking may be used. These types of caulking are less expensive than silicone caulking, they work almost as well, and they are paintable.

Paint Colors

What color should you paint your home? Should you choose colors that reflect your taste, or play it safe and go with white? First, consider what colors work well with similar homes in your area. For example, certain architectural styles traditionally favor particular color schemes. The color scheme for an ornate three-story Victorian, for example, will not work on a simple one-story bungalow. Varying too much from such accepted norms will almost certainly diminish the beauty and value of your home.

One way to take the guesswork out of choosing a color scheme is to look at quality homes in your area to see what is currently in style. Consider asking a local paint retailer or interior designer what colors are suitable for your home.

In addition, you can try experimenting with color schemes without picking up a brush. To do this, simply take a picture of your house and enlarge the photo to at least 8x10 inches. Lay a sheet of tracing paper over the enlargement, and trace the outline of the house onto the paper. Include the doors, win-

Caulking. Seal joints with paintable caulk. Allow it to cure before painting.

dows, trim, and trees. Then make a dozen photocopies of the drawing. Use crayons, felt-tip pens, or watercolors to highlight the house and trim in different color schemes. As you do this, be sure to include colors of foliage and structures, such as flowers, patios, and even neighboring homes. Try several schemes until you find one that you like.

$ **Value Tip**

Color Choices

◆ Earth tones are easy to decorate with because they are neutral colors. Use neutral or muted tones, such as light grays, browns, or greens with either lighter or darker shades for accenting.

◆ Use bright colors sparingly, to catch the eye. Painting the front door a bright color creates a cheerful entryway.

◆ Investigate home shows, magazines, and houses in your area for color ideas. Paint suppliers can also give you valuable tips on appropriate color schemes.

◆ Colors that look just right on a color card may need to be toned down for painting large areas. If in doubt, buy a quart of paint and test it.

Color Schemes

Once you have selected a color scheme for your home, it will be necessary to decide what color to assign to a particular architectural element. Usually, the siding will be done in one color, but if there is decorative molding above the first floor, you might choose a second siding color to add interest. The casings around windows and doors, however, should all be painted the same color; otherwise the color scheme will seem too busy. To accent highlights on decorative trim and molding, two or more colors are fine if the pattern is repeated around the entire house.

Here are some tips for other architectural features:

Front Entrance. Create a striking effect by spotlighting this important element of your home. For example, a white house with a door painted a bright color, such as red or green, draws attention to the door, making the entrance seem more inviting.

Frieze. An historically appropriate treatment for the frieze is to use the trim color. Let the trim color be dominant to distinguish it from the top of the siding. Be careful not

A paint scheme can be made more interesting by using contrasting or complementary colors on architectural detailing, such as the frieze, corner brackets, railings, and posts.

to introduce too many colors, or you may end up with an effect that is too distracting.

Corner Brackets. Simple brackets should be considered part of the overall structure and painted so that they do not appear to *float free* of the structure. Use the principal trim color.

Sandwich brackets consist of more than one layer and are more complex than simple corner brackets. For that reason it is better to use several colors. Paint the exterior layers to match the trim and frieze, and paint the center layer another color to show off the scroll work.

Posts. Simple rectangular posts should be painted to match either the overall trim or the body paint of the house. However, if the posts have custom millwork, such as a chamfer on a square post or a ring on a turned post, it is perfectly acceptable to highlight these decorations with a flourish of color.

Rails. The rails are essentially extensions of the posts and are usually painted in the same color.

Balusters. Paint the balusters a lighter color than the railings, or if the posts and rails have been painted in the main body color, use a trim color to make the balusters

F.Y.I. COLOR CARDS

Choosing specific colors in a multicolor scheme can be a daunting task. To make this process easier, paint manufacturers have created color cards to help the homeowner to select coordinated base and trim colors. Many color cards are also prearranged in color groups that match the typical color schemes of various historical periods. Be aware, however, that colors on sample cards can be deceiving because of their limited size or the light in which you view them. Colors tend to look more intense when applied to a home than they do on the card. When in doubt, choose the next lighter shade.

Exterior Color Schemes. Choose exterior colors that are appropriate to the style of your home and in keeping with its natural and man-made context. Trim colors should carry over to fencing and other landscape features to establish a sense of unified design.

stand out. Even if you have elaborately worked balusters, don't use too many colors to highlight your handiwork. Aside from the amount of time involved in detailing each baluster, the result will look fussy.

Floors and Ceilings. Porches are painted certain colors not only for decoration but also for reasons of practicality. Light-colored ceilings maintain a sense of airiness and brightness. Painting porch ceilings blue is a technique that has been used for centuries to suggest the sky

overhead. If the undersides of porch ceiling rafters are exposed, paint them with a combination of body and trim colors. A somewhat darker color on a porch floor is practical, because it will show dirt much less readily than a lighter color.

Steps and Risers. The risers of wooden steps are typically painted the same color as the trim work. The treads, however, carry the surface of the porch or deck to the ground and should therefore be painted the same color as the floorboards.

Handrails and balusters on steps should be painted to match the color scheme used for the porch rail and balusters.

Masonry Foundations. Many homes have a partially exposed brick or concrete-block foundation. While it is acceptable to paint this band the same color as the siding, a darker color will make the house appear firmly rooted to its site and will also hide dirt and mud. Basement window trim is generally painted the same color to de-emphasize it.

Pro Tip

PAINTING TIPS

As with any skill, there is a right and a wrong way to paint. There is a right way to hold a brush, a right way to maneuver a roller, a right way to spray a wall, etc. Follow these basic professional tips:

Brushing vs. Rolling. Some painters insist that only a brush-painted job looks right. However, most painters will "cut in" the edges with a brush, and then finish the main body of a wall or ceiling using a roller. Brushing alone can be time-consuming, and it is typically reserved for architectural woodwork.

Using the Right Brush. Use the largest brush that you are comfortable with. Professional painters seldom pick up anything smaller than a 4-inch brush. Most homeowners will achieve good results using a 4-inch brush for "cutting in" and for large surfaces, and an angled 2½- to 3-inch sash brush for trim around windows and doors. Be sure, also, to use brushes that are appropriate for the type of paint being applied. Oil-based paints require a natural bristle (also called "China bristles"), while water-based paints are applied with a synthetic bristle brush.

Handling a Brush. Many people grip a paintbrush as if they were shaking someone's hand. It is better to grip a brush more like a pencil, with the fingers and thumb wrapped around the metal ferrule. This grip provides the hand and wrist with a wider range of motion and therefore greater speed and precision. If your hand cramps, switch hands or switch temporarily to the handshake grip.

Wiping Rags. Before you begin painting, put a dust rag in your pocket. This is helpful for clearing away cobwebs and dust before painting. It is also handy for wiping off paint drips before they have a chance to dry.

Paint Hooks. When working on a ladder, use a good-quality paint hook to secure the paint bucket to your ladder. Avoid makeshift hooks made with wire or coat hangers. Paint hooks are inexpensive and available at virtually all paint and hardware stores.

Painting

Applying the finish coat of paint is the most rewarding part of the job. The paint spreads more easily than the prime coat, and the end result looks great. But the best part of all is knowing that you won't have to repeat this again for at least another few years.

Painting Sequence and the Weather

There are a number of different factors to consider when painting a house. Depending upon your preference, you may wish to work from right to left or left to right, for example. However, the weather is also an important consideration. On sunny days, you may want to develop a strategy to keep yourself out of the sun. In the winter, though, try to work in a pattern that will keep you in the warmth and light of the sun as much as possible. Also, work from the top down so that the more difficult work will be done first, before fatigue sets in, and so that drippings can be removed as the work proceeds. Work horizontally across the building, to a logical stopping point such as a window surround or the end of a wall. And plan the workday so that you will reach a break point before quitting time.

When painting, start with the siding first, and then paint the trim. Try to get doors and windows painted early in the day, so that they will be dry by the end of the day and you can reinstall the hardware. This will allow the first-floor windows and doors to be locked up for the night.

Be especially aware of the weather if you are using latex paints, which are much less tolerant of temperature extremes than oil-based paints. Because water is the solvent for latex, rain can also wash away the paint if it hasn't had adequate time to dry.

Painting in Hot Weather. The hotter the weather, the quicker latex paint

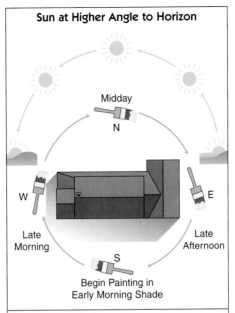

Painting in Hot Weather. If paint dries too quickly it will not adhere properly. In warmer weather (over 70° F) time the job so that you may avoid direct sunlight.

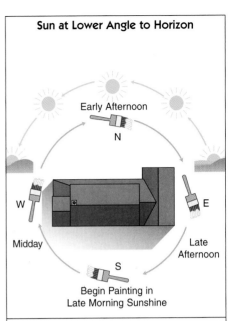

Painting in Cold Weather. When painting a house in cooler weather (55-70° F), follow the movement of the sun, to quicken the drying time.

will dry. Nevertheless, excessively hot weather can cause a host of problems: Brushes and rollers may gum up; paint may fail to bond properly with the surface underneath it; and glossy patches may be caused by uneven drying.

The ideal painting temperature is around 70 degrees Fahrenheit, although you can do a perfectly good job when the temperature is in the 90s. If the temperature is between 55 and 70 degrees, plan your work so that you are in the sun. If the weather is warmer, stay out of direct sunlight. During hot weather, avoid painting on a breezy day, because wind will accelerate drying even more.

Painting in Cold Weather. Latex paint will not set at temperatures below 45 degrees Fahrenheit. That is why manufacturers' specifications always call for latex paint to be applied at temperatures no lower than 50 degrees and rising. It is best to plan paint jobs for spring, summer, or early fall. Do not paint when the mercury falls below 50 degrees. There are few things more discouraging than watching paint bubble and peel off a wall.

Checking for Moisture. It is okay to apply latex paint to a surface that is slightly damp (cool to the touch) but not wet. Let wet surfaces dry out before painting. If rain or dew gets on latex paint before it is dry, symptoms range from nothing, to mottling, to blistering, to washing off entirely. If the paint bubbles, you must scrape or sand it off and repaint the surface.

Painting Wood Siding

Difficulty Level: 🔨

Required Tools:

❑ **Basic tools: caulking gun, drop cloths, 4-in.-wide flat paint brush, extension ladder, ladder jacks or scaffolding, paint hooks, putty knife, sash brush, scrapers, sanding block and sandpaper, wiping rags**

❑ **Special materials: thinners (if using oil-based paints)**

Use as large a brush as you can comfortably handle. A 4-inch-wide flat brush is a good choice.

1 Painting bottom ridges.
Beginning with the bottom edges of the siding, apply the paint, and then brush it out thoroughly.

2 Painting the face. Apply paint to the face of the siding, brushing as large an area as you can before the paint begins to pull. Brush on the paint with long, smooth strokes running parallel to the grain of the wood. Keep a wet edge, and work to a logical stopping point (the end of a wall or a window or door frame). Drips often form on the bottom edges of siding, so be sure to check the work from time to time to pick up any drips, runs, or *holidays* (spots that were missed).

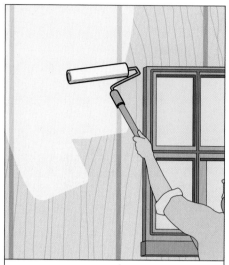

Painting Plywood Siding. To paint plywood and panel siding, first use a roller, and then brush in missed spots.

Painting Stucco. Use a thick, long-napped roller or an airless spray gun to apply finish paint on stucco.

1. Start painting at the bottom edge of a wood siding course.

2. Paint with the wood grain, horizontally on clapboard, vertically on shingles.

Painting Plywood and Panel Siding.
Paint Texture 1-11 (T1-11) plywood siding with a long-napped roller, and then use a brush for cutting in and painting areas where the roller is not able reach or where there will be a sharply defined color change. Keep the brush handy as you apply the paint. Switch to the brush as needed, pushing paint evenly into the vertical grooves.

Painting Masonry

Painting Brick. Do not paint brick unless it has already been painted. Unlike wood, brick does not need to be painted to survive the weather, unless it has been sandblasted. In this case, the brick is painted with latex to prevent water from seeping into the walls. Brick survives best unpainted because the hard face of the brick is tougher than paint, and peeling paint tends to trap moisture in the mortar. Once brick is painted, it must continue to be painted.

If the brick is dirty, have it cleaned. Cleaning brick often costs less than it would to paint it, and cleaned brick will require less maintenance than painted brick.

Before painting brick, have the mortar joints *repointed*. Apply latex paint with a long-napped roller,

using a brush to work paint into the mortar joints. Check the work frequently, and pick up drips or runs.

Painting Stucco. Stucco and wood have very different material properties. Wood expands and contracts with changing weather, while stucco does not. This rigidity frequently causes stucco to develop cracks. Cracks are not only an eyesore, but they also let in moisture, which can lead to structural problems.

While standard latex paint will fill hairline cracks, *elastomeric* paints are needed for more serious problems. These paints are flexible and generally outlast other paints. The durability and elasticity are due in part to the paint's thickness. A coat of elastomeric paint may be 10 times thicker than a coat of latex paint.

Stucco is usually painted with latex paint applied with a long-napped roller. However, unlike siding and other surfaces with plane changes, stucco is an ideal surface for spraying. Simply cut in the corners with a brush, and then use an airless spray gun to finish the surface. Whether spraying or rolling, be sure to repair cracks and bulges in the stucco with stucco patch or paintable caulking before painting. Prime the stucco with a latex primer, and then finish it.

Chapter 7
Kitchens

It has often been said that the kitchen is the heart of a home. During informal gatherings, your family and friends will naturally gravitate toward the kitchen. If it is well-designed and thoughtfully arranged, they will feel comfortably at home. However, if the kitchen looks dated, or poorly laid out, your guests may not be so favorably impressed.

Considering the high cost of a major kitchen renovation, it is no wonder that this is a job most homeowners would rather avoid. Fortunately, it is possible to upgrade a kitchen by turning it into a warm, inviting space, without spending a fortune. A modest sum of money and a little time and effort can achieve dramatic results. A whole new look can be created simply by refinishing, refacing, or replacing kitchen cabinets, and/or by installing new color-coordinated appliances.

IN THIS CHAPTER

Kitchen Cabinet Improvements

Refinishing Cabinets 92

Refacing Cabinets 94

Kitchen Cabinet Replacements

Installing Base Cabinets 95

Installing Wall Cabinets 97

Kitchen Countertops

Installing a
Prefabricated Countertop 97

Installing a Custom Countertop . .99

Fixtures and Appliances

Installing a Sink 100

Replacing a Faucet 101

Installing a Range 103

Installing a
Built-in Dishwasher 105

Installing a
Waste-Disposal Unit 107

TODAY'S TRENDS

Eat-in Kitchens

Custom Cabinets

Built-in Storage

Islands and Peninsulas

Energy-efficient Appliances

Kitchen Cabinet Improvements

Cabinets are the most visible element in a kitchen. If they are in reasonably good condition, you can upgrade them by either refinishing them or by refacing the cases. Adding new hinges and pulls will give the refurbished cabinets a whole new look. If the cabinetry is not in good shape, however, it must be entirely replaced.

Refinishing Cabinets

Difficulty Level: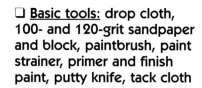

Required Tools:

❑ **Basic tools: drop cloth, 100- and 120-grit sandpaper and block, paintbrush, paint strainer, primer and finish paint, putty knife, tack cloth**

❑ **Special tools and materials: airless sprayer, electric sander, trisodium phosphate (TSP)**

Kitchen cabinets can be refinished with either paint, transparent stain, or opaque stain, depending upon the original finish. Avoid using latex paints over solvent paints or stains. Unless a stain is opaque, it must be applied to bare wood, which will require stripping off the old finish. Be sure to read the manufacturer's label on the container for special precautions or recommendations.

1 Prepare the surface. A first-rate refinishing job begins with good preparation. Remove the hardware, drawers, and adjustable shelving, and then scrub down the cabinets using a trisodium phosphate (TSP) and water solution to dissolve grease. Sand the cabinets after they have dried. If they are in good shape, scuff-sand the surface with 120-grit sandpaper. If the surface is chipped or rough, use 100-grit sandpaper. Vacuum up the wood dust, and wipe the surface clean with a tack cloth.

Refinishing kitchen cabinets can provide them with an entirely different look.

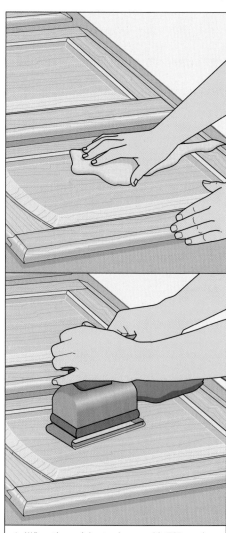

1. Wipe the cabinets down with TSP, and then sand them with 120-grit sandpaper. For rough surfaces use 100-grit sandpaper.

2. Prime all of the cabinets first with a 50:50 mixture of primer and finish paint, and then paint the inside of the cabinets. Paint the cabinet frame next, and then finish by painting the face of the cabinet drawers and doors.

Value Tip

Plan First, Install Later

✦ **Make a plan.** Invest time in planning your kitchen. Work on graph paper, or use an inexpensive computer software program to develop an idea of what your finished kitchen will look like. On-screen changes cost nothing, but a change during construction may be devastating. If you don't wish to do design work, consult a kitchen designer. Either way, try to plan around the existing plumbing, electrical, and heating systems, as well as door and window openings. Even minor structural changes can be costly.

✦ **Use neutral colors.** Trendy colors may quickly date a kitchen, so use neutral colors instead, and then add color with furnishings and decorative elements. The lighter colors will also make the kitchen appear more spacious.

✦ **Buy standard appliances.** Save money by purchasing *better* than average quality fixtures and appliances rather than the top-of-the-line *best* products, but don't buy cheap economy-type products.

✦ **"Let there be light."** Lighting can have a dramatic effect on a kitchen design. Plan extra outlets and task lighting to brighten the space and make it a pleasant place in which to work. Also, consider skylighting to bring in natural light.

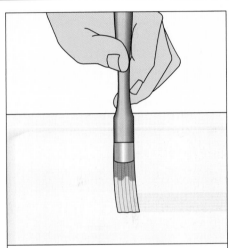

3. Tip off the finish by dragging the tip of a brush lightly through the paint in the direction of the wood grain.

2 Prime the cabinets. For the first coat use a *split mix* of equal parts primer and finish paint. Strain the paint, and then paint the cabinets as shown. Repair chips and holes with wood putty after the split coat dries. Lightly scuff the surface with 220-grit sandpaper, and then apply a second split coat.

3 Apply the finish coat. The finish coat should be perfect. A glossy finish will magnify drips, dust flecks, brush marks, and other imperfections. A semigloss paint may be less of a problem. After applying the last coat, *tip off* the finish by dragging the tip of a brush lightly through the paint in the direction of the wood grain.

Refacing Cabinets

Difficulty Level: 🔩

Required Tools:

❑ <u>Basic tools:</u> **flathead screwdriver, handsaw, paintbrushes, paint scraper, Phillips screwdriver, putty knife, sandpaper, utility knife**

❑ <u>Special tools:</u> **laminate roller, 1-in. wood screws, power drill and bits, spring or C-clamps, stenciling brush, wood putty**

Refacing cabinets with wood veneer or plastic laminate may improve the appearance of many kitchens. If the cabinets are basically sound, refacing them is an easy way to give the kitchen an entirely new look. Refacing simply means replacing the existing cabinet doors and drawer fronts. Although this is more expensive than refinishing the existing cabinets, the material cost is still much less than the price of new cabinetry.

The decision to reface cabinets also provides the opportunity to add features such as glass, new hardware, or matching fronts for appliances.

1 Strip the cabinets. Remove the doors, drawers, and hinges from the existing cabinets, and then remove the hardware from the drawer fronts. Scrape and sand off the old finish on the cabinet sides and face frames. Fill holes, gouges, and scratches with wood putty. After the putty has dried, sand the filled areas with 150-grit sandpaper. If desired, paint the cabinet interiors.

2 Apply the veneer. Lay out the veneer on a smooth surface. Measure an area to be covered, adding ¼ inch to each dimension. Mark the veneer accordingly, and then cut it using a utility knife; use a steel straightedge as a guide. Remove the paper backing, and apply the veneer first to the sides of the cabinets, then to the front vertical frames, and lastly to the front horizontal frames. Carefully trim the veneer with a razor knife, and sand

1. Remove hardware, doors, and drawers from the wall and base cabinets.

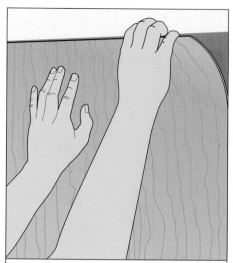

2. Apply the veneer to the sides of the cabinets first and then to the face.

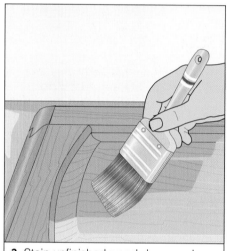

3. Stain unfinished wood doors and drawer fronts. Stain the veneer on the cabinet sides and frames to match.

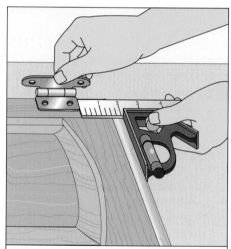

4. Attach one door hinge 2 in. down from the top edge and another 2 in. up from the bottom edge on each door.

the rough edges after each application. Roll all the veneered surfaces using a laminate or wallpaper roller.

3 Apply the new finish. Stain the new doors and drawer fronts. When the stain has dried, cover it with three coats of clear polyurethane. If you want the look of natural wood, omit the stain and use only the polyurethane. Sand lightly between each finish coat. Be sure to finish the sides and face frames to match the doors.

4 Attach the door hinges. Lay the doors on a smooth surface. Attach the new hinges, setting one 2 inches down from the top edge of each door and another up 2 inches

from the bottom edge of each door. Mark the location of the screw holes. If the hinges will be concealed, lay the doors face down. If the hinges will be visible, lay the doors face up. Drill pilot holes *partway* into the wood, and then align and screw the hinges onto the doors. Hold each door in the appropriate opening, and then mark the hinge locations on the cabinet face frame. Be sure each door overlaps its opening by an equal distance on all four sides. Leave approximately ⅛ inch between doors covering a single opening. Drill the pilot holes in the face frame, and then hang the doors. Lastly, install the door handles, drawer pulls, and other selected hardware.

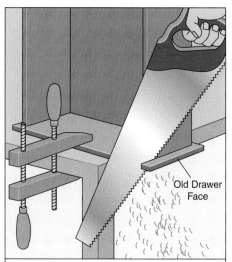

5. Clamp a drawer box to a work surface to trim off any face overhangs.

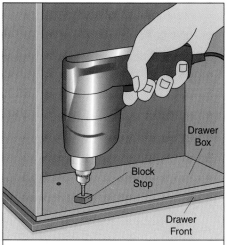

6. Drill pilot holes from the inside of each drawer box, and then screw each box into a new drawer face panel.

5. Prepare the drawer fronts. Clamp the existing drawer boxes face down on a worktable to cut off any overhanging edges. If the drawers have false fronts, simply remove and discard them.

6. Attach the new drawer fronts. Lay a new drawer front face down on the worktable, and then center a trimmed drawer box over it. Be sure that the overlap is even all the way around the perimeter of the box front. Drill pilot holes through the drawer box and partway into the back of the new face panel. Be careful not to drill through the drawer face. Then screw the panel and box together. Attach pulls or handles to the new face panel to complete the installation.

Kitchen Cabinet Replacements

Refacing kitchen cabinets may be adequate in many instances, but some kitchens may have been so poorly planned that a complete redesign is needed. Aside from giving the kitchen a fresh look, the replacement cabinets can be arranged in a different, more efficient layout. Furthermore, you can remove boxed soffits to create additional cabinet height and therefore more storage space.

Installing Base Cabinets
Difficulty Level: 🔨🔨🔨

Required Tools:

❏ **Basic tools:** flathead screwdriver, handsaw, measuring tape, Phillips screwdriver, spirit level, stud finder, utility knife, wood chisel

❏ **Special tools and materials:** C-clamps, construction adhesive or contact cement, 1x2 ledger material, power drill and bits, quarter-round molding, 2-, 2½-, 3-, and 3½-in. wood screws, vinyl or wood base moldings, wood shims

1. Check whether the floor is level. If it isn't, find the high spot. From here, measure the cabinet height on the wall.

Before installing new kitchen cabinets, be sure that the walls are plumb. Even minor imperfections can lead to misaligned cabinets. Fortunately, you can readily accommodate such imperfections during the cabinet installation.

1 Scribe a level line. Using a spirit level, find the high spot in the floor along the proposed cabinet wall as follows: Check the floor to see whether it is level. If it is not, slide the level along the floor, parallel to the wall, until the bubble shifts over from one end of the glass tube to the opposite end. Mark this location as the high point of the floor. Measuring up the wall from this point, mark the cabinet height on the wall. Using the spirit level as a guide, scribe a reference line on the wall the full length of the cabinets.

2 Install the cabinets. Slide the first cabinet against the wall. Using wood shims at the base of the cabinet sides, level it to the reference line. Shim at the back or front to plumb it. Once the cabinet is level and plumb, screw the mounting rails into the studs using 3½-inch screws, and then trim the shims using a utility knife or a wood chisel.

3 Install filler strips. If a cabinet run requires filler strips, carefully measure and rip-cut each strip to

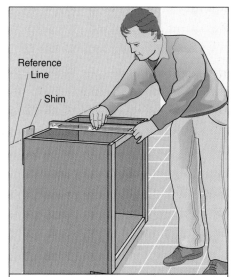

2. Place the cabinet against the wall, and then use shims to level it to the reference line and to plumb it.

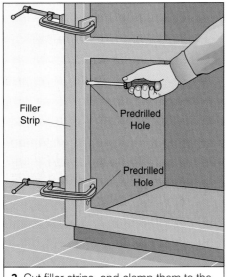

3. Cut filler strips, and clamp them to the cabinet stiles. Fasten them using screws.

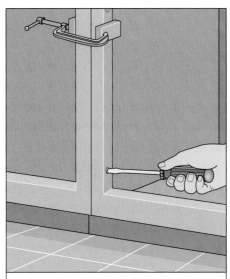

4. Screw adjoining cabinets together through the stiles. Keep the faces flush.

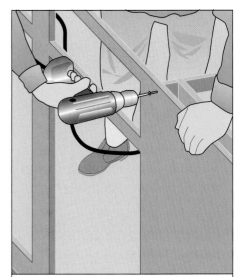

5. At corners, install one cabinet, attach a filler, and then connect the other cabinet.

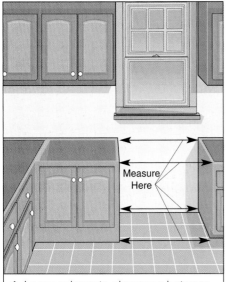

6. Leave adequate clearance between cabinets for built-in appliances.

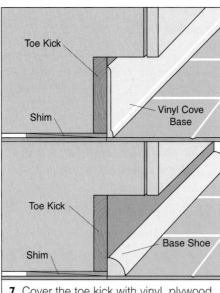

7. Cover the toe kick with vinyl, plywood or quarter-round molding.

literature for this dimension. Measure the opening at the front and rear and at the top and bottom.

7 Install the toe kick. There are several ways to conceal the shim space between the base cabinets and the floor. One way is with vinyl base molding. You can attach this type of molding with either construction adhesive or contact cement. It is flexible enough to be easily pressed into place, and then it can be neatly trimmed using a utility knife. You can also use traditional wood base-board molding, cut cabinet-grade plywood, or quarter-round molding to trim a toe kick.

fit. Pull out the end cabinet, clamp the strip to the stile of the adjoining cabinet, and then drill pilot holes for the screws through the edge of each stile and into the filler. Counter-sink the holes so that the screwheads will not project above the surface. Fasten the screws, slide the cabinet back into position, and then level it once again.

4 Join the cabinets. Connect the cabinets by screwing them together through their stiles. Drill and countersink holes for two #8x2½-inch wood screws at each joint. Be sure that face frames

remain square and on the same plane as you tighten the screws.

5 How to turn a corner. At corner joints a filler strip will be needed. Install one of the cabinets, and then screw the filler strip to the other one. Butt the two cabinets together, and then drive screws into the filler from the first cabinet, off-setting them from the other screws.

6 Leave space for appliances. Wherever there will be a dish-washer, range, or other built-in appliance, provide an opening the exact width required for clear-ance. Check the manufacturer's

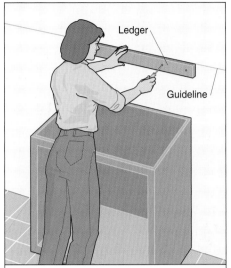

1. Draw a level line at the correct height, and attach a temporary ledger.

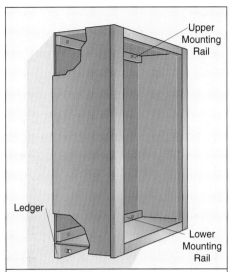

2. Set the cabinet on the ledger; then fasten it through the mounting rails.

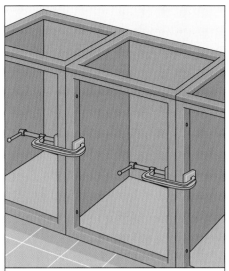

3. Connect two cabinets through the stiles with screws top and bottom.

Installing Wall Cabinets

Difficulty Level: ⚊⚊⚊

Required Tools:

❑ **Basic tools:** flathead screwdriver, handsaw, measuring tape, Phillips screwdriver, spirit level, stud finder, utility knife, wood chisel

❑ **Special tools and materials:** C-clamps, construction adhesive or contact cement, 1x2 ledger material, power drill and bits, quarter-round molding, 2-, 2½-, 3-, and 3½-in. wood screws, vinyl or wood base moldings, wood shims

Wall cabinets require more effort to install than base cabinets. Because they are wall-hung, positioning them can be difficult. The best way to temporarily support wall cabinets during installation is to nail or screw a ledger along the guideline for the lower edge of the cabinets.

1 Install the ledger. Using a spirit level as a guide, draw a pencil line on the wall to mark the bottom edge of the cabinets. Using screws or double-headed nails, secure a temporary ledger on the line. Be sure to fasten it into the stud framing for solid support, and

check to be sure the ledger is level before proceeding further.

2 Hang the cabinets. Begin the cabinet installation with an end or corner unit. The first cabinet installed will determine the alignment for the entire run, so be sure to level and shim it carefully. Lift the next cabinet onto the ledger and position it, and then screw two 3-inch screws through the upper mounting rail into the stud framing. Check whether the cabinet is plumb, and then tighten the screws adequately enough to

hold the cabinet firmly in place. Next, screw the lower mounting rail into the studs.

3 Connect the cabinets. After you have installed two or more adjacent cabinets, clamp them together at the face frames. Drill horizontal pilot holes through the stiles with a ³⁄₃₂-inch bit, and screw the frames together with #6x2½-inch wood screws at both the top and bottom. After the cabinets are installed, remove the ledger. Conceal any gaps between the cabinets and the wall using quarter-round molding.

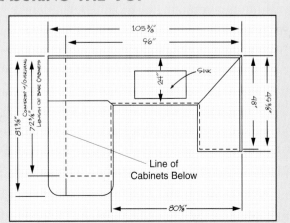

MEASURING THE TOP

F.Y.I. Custom cabinet-makers will sometimes come to your house to measure for a countertop, but home centers and kitchen stores may require that you come to them with the dimensions already in hand. Be sure to double-check measurements carefully. Being off by only ½ in. can be quite upsetting.

To ensure accuracy, sketch out the countertop on a sheet of graph paper. Include all the essential dimensions. To be on the safe side, have someone else double-check your numbers.

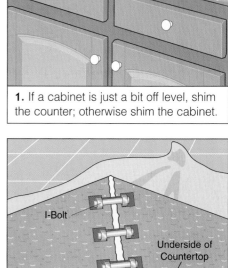

1. If a cabinet is just a bit off level, shim the counter; otherwise shim the cabinet.

I-Bolt

Underside of Countertop

2. Turn the countertop over, and secure the joint with several I-bolts.

A new countertop is one way to transform the appearance of your kitchen without having to replace the cabinetry. A change in material, color, and texture can alter the style of your kitchen. Add new curtains and a coat of paint to complement the change.

Countertops

A new kitchen countertop can transform the appearance of any kitchen, yet installing one is relatively simple and economical. A countertop may be either standard stock or custom-made. Though custom-made countertops are more expensive, they have the advantage of giving you a greater choice in color, material, and style. Plastic laminates are the most commonly used and least expensive countertop material. In addition to laminates, there are also solid-surface materials, such as Corian and Gibraltar. These are quite popular, but also very expensive. Other countertop materials include butcher block, ceramic tile, and—most expensive—granite.

Installing a Prefabricated Countertop

Difficulty Level: 🔨🔨

Required Tools:

❑ **Basic tools:** caulking gun, file, 4-ft. spirit level, sanding block, sandpaper, shims

❑ **Special tools and materials:** adhesive caulk, power drill and assorted bits, tub and tile caulk, wood screws

1 Check whether the cabinets are level. If you have installed new base cabinets in accordance with the instructions above, then the cabinets should be level. Existing cabinets, however, may be out of alignment.

Place a spirit level at several points along the front, rear, and side edges of the base cabinets to see whether or not they need to be adjusted.

2 Assemble the corner miters. Precut laminate tops usually come with mitered corner joints. Lay perpendicular pieces together, upside down, on a cushioned surface. Apply adhesive caulking to the mitered ends, and then press the pieces tightly together. Slip I-bolts into the joinery slots, and tighten them only partway. Be sure the pieces are properly aligned, tighten the bolts, and wipe away excess adhesive.

3 Lift the countertop into place. With an assistant, set the assembled countertop into position. Push

3. Maneuver unwieldy countertops carefully to avoid damaging either the counter or the cabinets. Enlist the aid of a helper or two for moving large pieces.

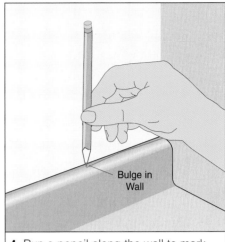

4. Run a pencil along the wall to mark bulges on the backsplash. Sand or rasp the back of the splash at these points.

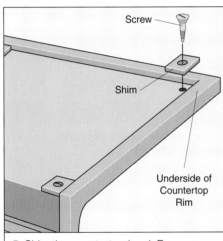

5. Shim the countertop level. Be sure the underside of the countertop rim is at least 34½ in. above the finished floor.

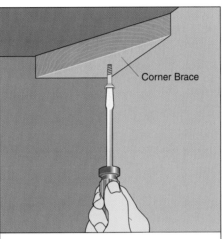

6. Screw through the corner braces to secure the countertop. Be sure to level it before tightening the screws.

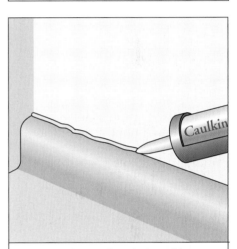

7. Apply an even bead of caulking along the top joint of the backsplash, and smooth it in with a wet finger.

the backsplash snugly to the wall, and shim the counter, if necessary.

4 Check the fit at the wall. Any bulge on the wall surface will create a gap between the wall and the backsplash. To locate these points, hold a pencil tightly against the wall, with the point on the backsplash. Pull the pencil along the length of the counter to scribe a line on the top of the backsplash. At any point where the line curves out, you will need to sand or rasp the backsplash to bring it flush with the wall.

5 Level the countertop. If the countertop is not level, shim beneath it over the corner braces of the base cabinet. Be sure that the

underside of the countertop is at least 34½ inches above the finished floor. This is the minimum rough-opening height for under-counter kitchen appliances.

6 Screw in the countertop. While an assistant holds the countertop firmly against the wall, drill pilot holes up through the corner braces of the cabinet and into the underside of the countertop. Be especially careful not to drill the pilot holes any deeper than two-thirds of the way through the countertop, to prevent the screw tips from protruding through the surface. Insert #10 wood screws through the braces to fasten the countertop in place.

7 Caulk the backsplash. After securing the countertop, caulk the joint between the backsplash and the wall to keep moisture from getting behind the counter.

Installing a Custom Countertop

Install butcher block, synthetic marble, or other solid-surface materials in the same way as laminates. These alternative materials are often butt jointed at the corners rather than mitered; as with laminate countertops, they come with I-bolts or turnbuckles for securing the joints. Most kitchen suppliers will make the necessary countertop cutouts for you.

Fixtures and Appliances

When replacing a kitchen fixture or appliance, avoid purchasing a premium-grade model. You should also avoid bottom-of-the-line models because they tend to break down and require frequent maintenance. It is most economical to select a mid-grade fixture or appliance made by a well-known manufacturer. These will hold up well and are likely to come with a warranty.

A **double-bowl sink** with a cutting board that fits over one bowl provides extra counter space. The smaller bowl can serve as an ideal location for a garbage disposal unit.

Installing a Sink

Difficulty Level: 🔨 🔨

Required Tools:

❑ **Basic tools: adjustable wrench, caulking gun, masking tape, power drill (with assorted bits), rope, saber saw, screwdriver, silicone caulk, utility knife**

1 **Position the basin.** Make a line on the countertop indicating the centerline of where the sink will be positioned. If the basin is self-rimming, place it upside down and centered on the reference line. Trace the outline of the sink onto the countertop, and then remove the basin. Draw a cutting line offset to the inside of the outline. To find the offset dimension for the cutout, read the manufacturer's literature.

If the basin has a metal rim, lay the rim on the counter, and use it as a template to trace the cutout. Drill ¼-inch holes at the corners to create an outline of the cutout on the reverse side of the countertop.

2 **Add supports.** If the countertop consists of two layers of ¾-inch plywood or solid-surface material, bracing may not be necessary. If braces are necessary, install them beneath the countertop along the side edges of the sink.

3 **Cut the opening.** Cut the openings for the sink using either a saber saw or a keyhole saw. For a ceramic-tile finish, be sure to cut the opening before setting the tiles on the countertop.

4 **Install the sink.** If the sink is self-rimming, it can be installed on any countertop. Once the opening has been cut (see Step 1, above), place a bead of silicone caulk on the countertop where the rim will go.

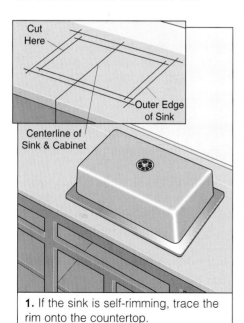

1. If the sink is self-rimming, trace the rim onto the countertop.

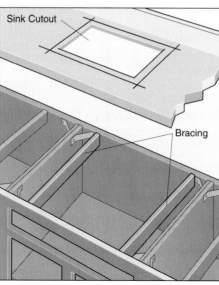

2. For support, add bracing beneath the side edges of the sink cutout.

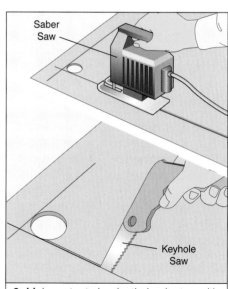

3. Make cutouts in plastic laminates with either a saber saw or a keyhole saw.

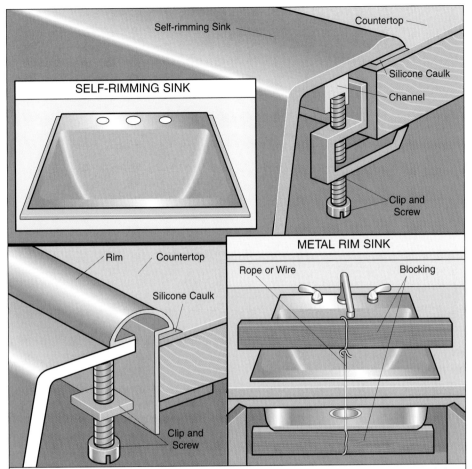

4. Self-rimming sinks are set into caulk and held in place with clips (top). A metal-rim sink is pushed up against the counter and supported from below (bottom left). If you are working alone, support the sink with wood blocking and rope (bottom right).

Replacing a Faucet

Difficulty Level: ⟍⟍

Required Tools:

❏ **Basic tools:** adjustable wrench, basin wrench, caulking gun, flashlight, putty knife, spud wrench

❏ **Special materials:** braided stainless-steel supply risers, plumber's putty or silicone sealant

If your existing kitchen faucet looks worn, stained, or simply outdated, then replace it with a new one. It is best to shop for a mid-priced model to get the greatest value. A quality faucet will have solid brass fittings and a cast body and will come with a warranty.

1 **Close the shutoff valves.**
Close the shutoff valves for the hot- and cold-water-supply pipes. If there are no shutoff valves for the sink, then shut off the main water valve.

Position the sink carefully over the opening, and press it firmly down into the sealant. Insert the metal clips provided under the sink, and then tighten each clip screw part of the way. Gradually tighten them enough to hold the sink securely in place. Run a wet finger along the rim to shape the caulking. Afterward, remove any excess sealant from the countertop.

If the sink is metal-rimmed, place a bead of silicone caulk around the cutout, and then set the rim into it. While someone pushes the sink up from below, tighten the clips. If you're working alone, suspend the sink with 2x4s. Lay one 2x4 across the sink opening. Tie a short rope around it, and thread the rope down the sink drain. Tie the loose end around another 2x4, bridging the underside of the sink. Before tightening the rope, place a bead of caulk

between the sink edge and the metal rim. Tighten the rope, twisting it with a screwdriver, to pull the sink to the rim. Finally, tighten the clips below and wipe away excess caulk.

Value Tip

Getting a Steal on Steel

When buying a stainless-steel sink, get the most value for your money. Consider the following:

Gauge. Thickness is indicated by gauge. The smaller the gauge, the thicker the steel. High-grade steel will be 18 gauge or less.

Magnetism. A magnet will not stick to high-grade stainless steel.

Sound. Better-grade sinks will have a noise-reducing coating on the underside.

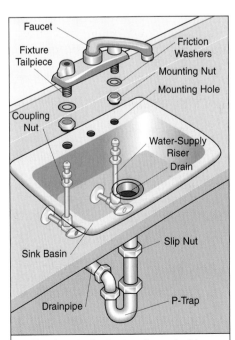

1. This is a typical setup for a dual-lever faucet set. To begin disassembly, close the water-shutoff valves below the sink.

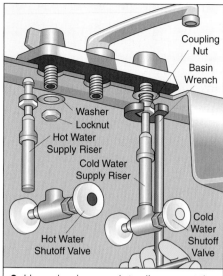

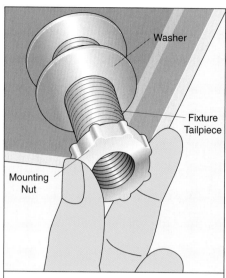

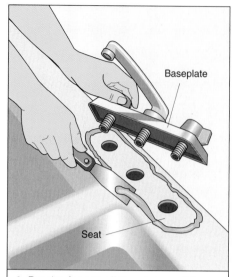

2. Use a basin wrench to disconnect the faucet tailpieces from the supply risers.

3. Turn faucet mounting nuts counter-clockwise to remove them.

4. Pry the faucet off the sink, and then clean the baseplate seat.

2 Disconnect the tailpieces from the risers. If the valves are in a vanity, use a flashlight to see under the sink. With a basin wrench, disconnect the faucet tailpieces from the water-supply risers.

3 Remove nuts and washers. For single-lever faucets, the supply risers converge at the center of the baseplate. The faucet baseplate is held in place with mounting nuts. Using an adjustable wrench, turn the faucet-mounting nuts counterclockwise to remove them.

4 Loosen the baseplate. If the faucet won't come loose, pry it up by inserting a putty knife under the baseplate. Then use the putty knife to remove any caulk or adhesive from the baseplate seat.

5 Install the gasket or sealant. After cleaning the baseplate seat, install the gasket. If the faucet set did not come with a gasket, apply a bed of silicone sealant or plumber's putty to the faucet baseplate. Insert the faucet tailpieces through the mounting holes of the basin, and

press the faucet baseplate firmly onto the surface. Once the faucet set is positioned properly, wipe off excess sealant with a rag.

6 Attach the mounting nuts. Attach the washers and mounting nuts to the faucet tailpieces, and then tighten the nuts. Be careful not to overtighten them.

7 Connect the risers. Connect braided stainless-steel risers between the faucet and the water-shutoff valves. This type of tubing is flexible, and easier to adjust than chrome-plated copper tubing. Secure the risers, again taking care not to overtighten the nuts.

8 Install the drain fittings. After you have installed the sink and faucet, hook up the drainage system, which consists primarily of the P-trap and the drainpipe. Place the basket strainer into the sink, and tighten the locknut. Connect the tailpiece to the strainer with a slip nut, and then install the P-trap. The long end of the P-trap goes over the tailpiece. Finally, tighten the slip nuts at each end of the trap.

When you've assembled all the parts, turn on the supply valves, and check all the connections for leaks. If a connection leaks, turn the nut a little at a time until the leak stops.

A new faucet set can give your kitchen a whole new look, simply and inexpensively.

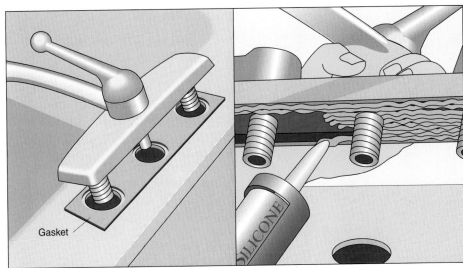

5. If the faucet comes with a gasket, clean the baseplate seat, and position the gasket on the sink as shown (above, left); if the faucet does not come with a gasket, then apply silicone sealant directly to the faucet baseplate as shown (above, right).

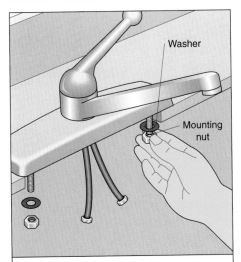

6. Attach the washers and mounting nuts to the faucet tailpieces, and then tighten them securely.

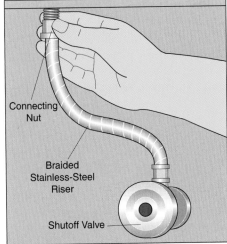

7. Connect the supply risers between the faucet and the shutoff valves, and then tighten the compression nuts.

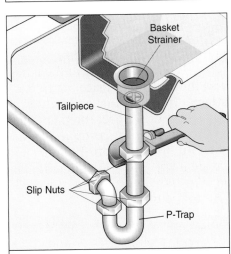

8. After installing the sink and faucet, install the basket strainer and drainpipe.

Installing a Range

Difficulty Level: 🔨

Required Tools:

❏ **Basic tools:** adjustable wrenches, 24-in. spirit level, 2-in. brush

❏ **Special materials:** pipe fittings as needed, pipe joint compound or plumber's tape

Replacing an old range may simply require disconnecting the old one and connecting the new one. If, however, you wish to change from a built-in range to a freestanding

model or vice versa, this will involve removing or adding kitchen cabinetry. If you are installing a new built-in cabinet, this also means getting a stock or custom-made cabinet to match the existing cabinets.

An electric range requires a special type of electrical wall receptacle. A gas range, on the other hand, will require a gas line for the gas burners and oven and a 120-volt receptacle to bring power to the clock, lights, and electronic ignition devices.

Check local codes before hooking up either a gas or an electric range. The code will specify the type and length of appliance cord required for an electric range or the type of piping required on a gas-line shut-off for a natural-gas or liquid-propane range. Some codes permit flexible brass tubing, and others require rigid iron gas pipe, commonly known as *black iron pipe*.

Electric Ranges:

1 **Attach the appliance cord.** For an electric range, typical 120/240 volt installations require four connections. Check the manufacturer's

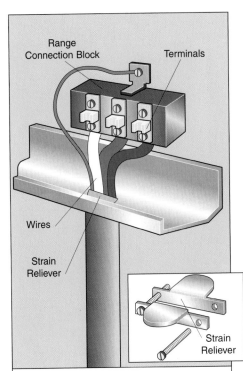

1. Attach the wires to the terminals on the range connection block. Use a strain reliever to take stress off the cord.

Electric Range
Outlet

2. Position the range, and then plug it in or connect the wires as required. Test the range to be sure it is getting power.

Level

Locknut

3. Place a spirit level across the top of the unit to see whether it is level. If necessary, adjust the leveling legs.

Gas Ranges:

1 **Install the gas connector.** For a gas range, if a flexible connector is permissible, purchase one slightly longer than required. Do not run the line through walls, cabinets, or anyplace else where it might be inaccessible. Coat the threads on the shutoff-valve connection with pipe joint compound, or wrap them with plumber's tape, and then attach the flexible connector nut to the shutoff valve. Hand-tighten the nut, and then tighten it about a quarter turn more using one wrench to hold the shutoff valve and another to turn the connector nut.

Caution: Overtightening may crack brass fittings, causing a gas leak.

instruction manual. There are separate terminals for black and red hot wires, the white neutral wire, and the green ground wire. Remove the cover and knockout from the range connection block. Secure the wires to the terminals as specified, and then replace the cover. (Note that some ranges must be hard-wired directly to a junction box.)

2 **Plug in the range.** Plug the range into the special receptacle, or wire it directly to a junction box, as required, and then slide the unit carefully into place.

3 **Level the range.** If the top of the range is not even with adjacent cabinets, adjust the leveling legs beneath the appliance. Place a 24-inch spirit level across the top of the range to determine whether or not it is level. Once you've leveled the range, use a wrench to tighten the locknuts on the legs.

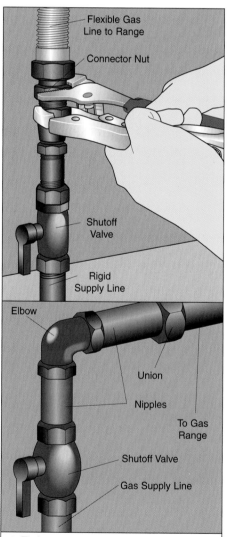

Flexible Gas
Line to Range

Connector Nut

Shutoff
Valve

Rigid
Supply Line

Elbow

Union

Nipples

To Gas
Range

Shutoff Valve

Gas Supply Line

1. Tighten the nut on the gas connector (above). If black iron pipe is used, be sure to seal the connections (below).

A built-in range can be selected to accommodate any kitchen style. Such appliances not only save space but can be a part of the overall design, rather than an add-on.

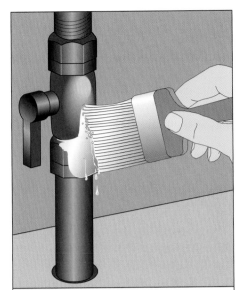

2. After installing the gas connectors, test for leaks. Brush the connections with soapy water. If bubbles appear, there is a leak. Tighten the connection and retest it.

If your local code requires rigid black iron pipe, purchase a couple of short threaded lengths, called *nipples*; elbow and union fittings; and enough pipe to reach the gas inlet on the range. Before connecting them, be sure to seal all the gas connections with pipe joint compound or plumber's tape.

2 **Hook up the gas range.** Level the range. (See Step 3, above, under "Electric Ranges.") Then secure the flexible connector or black iron pipe to the gas range inlet, and plug in the power cord. With the burner jets and oven turned off, turn on the gas, and test all the connections by brushing them with soapy water. If the solution bubbles, this indicates leaking gas; tighten the connection a bit and retest it.

Other Range Types:

Installing drop-in units and wall ovens. Follow the same procedures as for built-in cooking units. Check the manufacturer's literature to see whether or not the appliance needs to be wired directly to an electrical junction box. Many codes do not allow plug-in connections for range types that are considered more permanent than slide-in units.

Installing cooktops. Cooktops also require permanent electrical connections. Cooktop units attach to kitchen countertops in much the same way that kitchen sinks do.

Installing a Built-in Dishwasher

Difficulty Level: 🔩 🔩

Required Tools:

- ❏ **Basic tools:** adjustable wrench, bucket, electrical tape, insulated screwdrivers, 1-in. wood screws

- ❏ **Special tools and materials:** compression T-fitting and shutoff valve, copper tubing (³⁄₈-in. or larger), hose clamps, rubber or plastic drain line, tubing cutter, 12-ga. electric cable, wire connectors

These days, almost everyone has an automatic dishwasher. If you don't have one, installing one can be relatively easy. Built-in dishwashers are generally designed to fit in a 24-inch wide space beneath a kitchen counter. Hookups for hot water, wastewater, and electricity are required for installation.

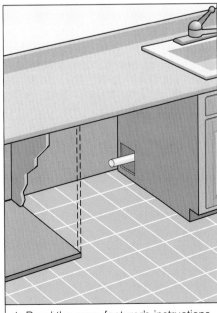

1. Read the manufacturer's instructions to determine the required rough opening dimensions for the dishwasher.

1 **Prepare the opening.** If all new cabinets are being installed, leave space for the dishwasher as near to the sink as possible. Continue the countertop over the dishwasher space. If the dishwasher is being installed in an existing kitchen, you'll have to cut out a 24-inch section of base cabinet. Test-fit the dishwasher in the cutout space, and make adjustments as needed. Then remove the dishwasher, and cut a hole in the base cabinet wall between the dishwasher and the undersink compartment. This opening must be large enough to accommodate the water-supply risers and the drain hose.

2 **Connect the hot-water line.** Ideally, you should locate a dishwasher near the kitchen sink. This is usually the most convenient place to tap into a hot-water line. However, it is also possible to run a line up from the basement or in the stud wall behind the dishwasher location. Regardless of where you tap into a hot-water line, you will need a T-fitting, a shutoff valve, and a piece of copper tubing long enough to reach from the riser connection to the dishwasher connection. These connections will require compression fittings. The installation manual for the dishwasher should specify

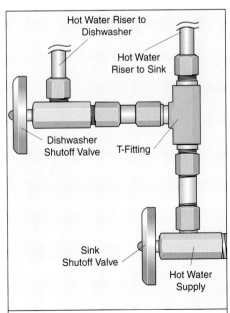

2. Turn off the water, and install a T-fitting and shutoff valve. Hook up the water supply with compression fittings.

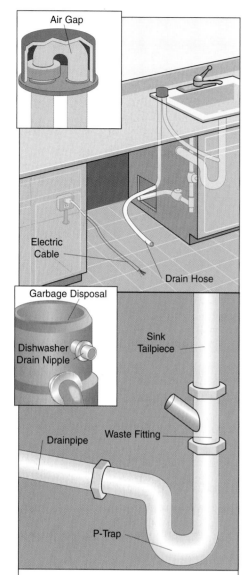

3. Dishwasher connections include a power cable, a water-supply line, and a drain hose. An air gap prevents waste-water from backing up into the dish-washer. Connect the drain hose from the dishwasher to either a sink drain pipe or to a garbage disposal drain nipple.

the tubing size needed (usually ⅜ inch).

Before making the plumbing connections, shut off the house water main, and drain the hot-water-supply line. Cut the line where the tap-in will be located, and then connect the T-fitting. Secure the fitting with compression nuts and rings. Tighten the connectors by hand; then give them an additional one-quarter turn with a wrench. Be careful not to overtighten the compression nuts. Overtightening may deform the compression

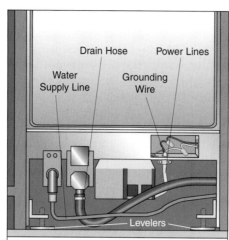

4. Shown, left to right, are typical connections for water supply, drainage, and power lines. The wire attached to the screw is the grounding wire.

ring or the copper tubing, causing a leak. Connect the shutoff valve for the dishwasher to the T-fitting, and then run a water line to the front of the dishwasher compartment.

Place a bucket beneath the hot-water-supply line, turn on the water main, and then check all the connections for leaks. If necessary, tighten the connections further.

3 Provide a drain hose. The drain hose should be a rubber or plastic hose that is resistant to high temperatures. Extend this hose through the hole cut earlier in the base-cabinet wall between the sink and the dishwasher.

Local plumbing codes may or may not require an air gap. In either case, it is a good idea to provide one. If the sink drain becomes obstructed, this will prevent dirty water from backing up into the dishwasher. Either use a commercially available prefabricated air-gap device, or loop the hose by hand. The loop should be as high up under the sink cabinet as possible so that any wastewater will be prevented from backing up.

Be sure all drain line connections are secured with hose clamps. If there is a waste-disposal unit, it should have a drain nipple for the dishwater drain hose. If it does not have one, then purchase a waste T-fitting, and install it above the sink trap.

4 Connect the power, and finish the installation. A dishwasher requires its own 20-amp grounded circuit. Switch off the appropriate circuit breaker at the electric panel, and run a cable from a convenient junction box to the dishwasher. Remove the front panel at the bottom of the dishwasher, and slide the unit into place. There should be adequate space beneath the dishwasher to provide clearance for water, waste, and power lines.

Level the dishwasher by adjusting the leg levelers beneath the unit. Fasten the dishwasher to the kitchen counter with wood screws.

Use wire connectors to make the electrical connections from the circuit wire to the dishwasher. Be sure to connect the circuit's black wire to black, white wire to white, and green ground wire to the grounding screw. When the electrical connections are made, attach the water line to the fill connection inside the dishwasher. Do not overtighten the compression fittings. Next, attach the drain line to the waste connection with a hose clamp. Turn on the water and the electricity, and run

A built-in automatic dishwasher is a real convenience—and a value-adding feature—in any kitchen.

the washer through one cycle. Check for leaks; then reinstall the kickplate cover to the bottom of the unit.

Installing a Waste-Disposal Unit

Difficulty Level: 🔨 🔨

Required Tools:

- ❑ **Basic tools:** adjustable wrench, flathead screwdrivers, Phillips screwdrivers, pliers

- ❑ **Special tools:** plastic wire nuts, plumber's putty

In addition to installing a dishwasher, another good way to enhance the value of a kitchen is by installing a waste-disposal unit. If you are planning to remodel your kitchen anyway, it would make sense to include this contemporary convenience in your plans. Even if you already have a disposal unit, replacing an older one with a newer, more energy-efficient model will not only add value to your home, but will also save on maintenance and operating costs in the long run.

1 **Install the switch and receptacle.** If a new waste-disposal unit will be installed, it will be necessary to install a switch and receptacle box. The unit should be connected to a switch located above the kitchen counter and near the sink. Snake 12/2 Romex cable through the stud wall, and connect it to the new switch and receptacle.

2 **Prepare the sink opening.** Apply a bead of plumber's putty on the underside of the sink flange, and slip the disposal unit's sleeve into the sink drain. Press firmly on the sink flange to be sure it is well seated.

3 **Attach the mounting assembly.** Slip the fiber gasket and metal mounting ring over the sink sleeve, and push them up to cover the sink flange. Place the backup ring over the sink sleeve, push it firmly up to the mounting ring, and then pop

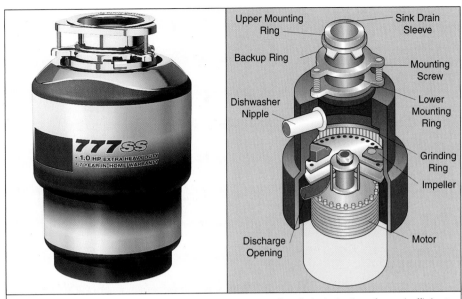

A **batch-feed waste-disposal unit**, controlled by a wall switch, is both safe and efficient. This type of unit comes with installation hardware that includes a sink flange, a gasket, and mounting rings. It is connected to the sink drainpipe through a discharge tube.

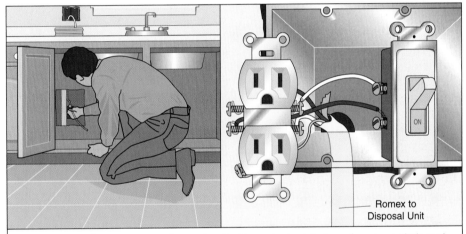

1. Installation of a new waste-disposal unit will require installation of a new switch and receptacle box, as well. The disposal unit should be connected to a switch located above the counter and near the sink, for both convenience and safety.

2. Apply a bead of plumber's putty to the underside of the sink flange, and slip the disposal unit's sleeve into the sink drain.

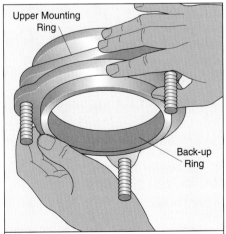

3. Place the gasket and the metal back-up ring over the sink sleeve, and then set the mounting ring over the sleeve.

the snap ring into the groove of the sink sleeve. Make sure that the mounting assembly is firmly and evenly seated, and then tighten the assembly screws.

4 **Connect the wiring.** Carefully remove the electrical cover plate from the waste-disposal unit, and locate the black and white wires. Connect the white wire from the appliance cord to the white wire on the disposal unit, and then connect the black wire from the appliance cord to the black wire on the disposal unit. Use wire connectors to secure the connections. Finally, attach the ground wire on the appliance cord to the ground screw on the disposal unit. Replace the electrical cover plate.

5 **Connect the disposal unit and the mounting assembly.** If you are also installing a dishwasher, place the disposal unit on its side, and remove the drain plug from the dishwasher nipple. Lift the disposal unit into position, and line it up with the mounting screws on the sink assembly. Turn the lower mounting ring on the disposal unit to the right until the flanges on the upper mounting ring are engaged.

6 **Attach the discharge pipe and drain trap.** Screw the discharge pipe into the waste-disposal unit, securing it with the metal flange and rubber gasket. Rotate the unit so that it aligns with the P-trap. Slip the drainpipe nut and washer onto the discharge pipe, attach the P-trap, and tighten the slip nut. If you are installing a dishwasher, attach the drain hose to the dishwasher nipple on the waste-disposal unit.

7 **Secure the unit.** Insert a screwdriver into one of the lugs on the disposal unit. Turn the lug counterclockwise until the unit is engaged in the locking notch. Fill the sink with water, and then let it drain. Carefully observe the drain connections to be sure that they are not leaking.

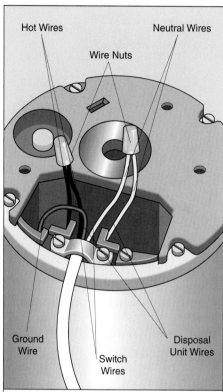

4. Locate the electrical wires on the waste-disposal unit, and connect them to the wires on the appliance cord; white to white and black to black.

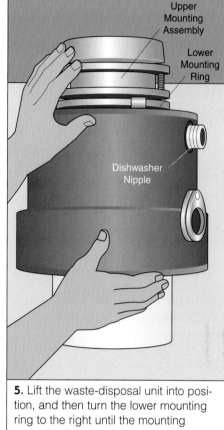

5. Lift the waste-disposal unit into position, and then turn the lower mounting ring to the right until the mounting assembly is properly engaged.

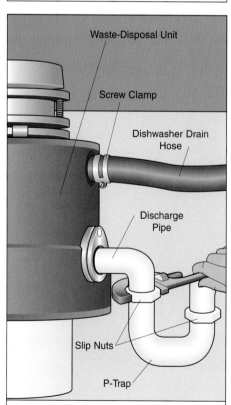

6. Screw the discharge pipe into the disposal unit. Attach the drainpipe slip nut to the discharge pipe, insert the P-trap, and then tighten the slip nut.

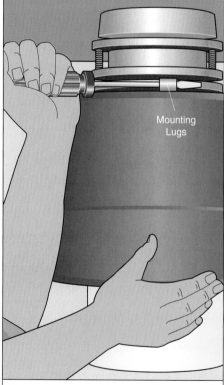

7. Insert a screwdriver into the lug, and turn it until the disposal unit is fully engaged in the locking notch. Fill the sink with water, and test the unit for leaks.

Chapter 8
Bathrooms

Bathroom styles have changed radically during the twentieth century, and no doubt will continue to change as we progress into the twenty-first century. For one thing, as people seek greater comfort in life, they drive development of new technologies and products, in turn driving changes in style. Another driving force is the simple desire to replace old fixtures, broken tiles, or dingy wall finishes. For these reasons, the bathroom is frequently chosen for upgrading by the average homeowner. Whether it is a replacement for a faucet, sink, or toilet; a new shower; or a change in bathroom accessories, even a simple improvement can make any bathroom a more pleasant place to be and can thus increase the value of a home. The variety of fixture styles available limits the quality and extent of any bathroom renovation only to one's imagination.

In This Chapter

Lavatories

Installing a Prefab Vanity 110

Installing a Pedestal Sink 111

Selecting a New Faucet 114

Removing the Old Faucet 114

Installing the New Faucet 115

Bathroom Accessories

Installing a Recessed
Medicine Cabinet 116

Hanging a Wall Mirror 117

Toilets

Removing an
Old Toilet 119

Installing a
New Toilet 119

Shower Enclosures

Installing a
Shower Enclosure 121

Today's Trends

Vanities with
His & Her Lavatories

Shallow-Trap Water Closets

Tiled Vanity Countertops

Steam Showers

Flow Controls

Saunas

Lavatories

Installing a new vanity is a quick way to upgrade the appearance of a bathroom. An old vanity that is in good shape may only need a new faucet, lavatory, or countertop. Today, home centers everywhere carry a variety of prefabricated units. They may come as a base unit only, as a base unit combined with an integral lavatory/countertop, or as a base unit with a countertop cut for a separate lavatory.

The steps below describe how to install a prefabricated vanity that has an integral countertop with a backsplash and a cutout for a separate basin. Be sure to plan and complete any necessary alterations to wall surfaces and floors before attempting to install a new vanity.

Installing a Prefab Vanity

Difficulty Level: 🔨

Required Tools:

❏ **Basic tools: caulking gun, hole saw, power drill, spirit level, wood plane, wrenches**

❏ **Special materials: construction adhesive, paint or sealer, masking tape, plumber's putty, wood screws (1¼-in. and 2½-in.), wood shims**

1 Plan the location. Minimize plumbing work by situating the vanity so that the lavatory will align with the existing plumbing chase. Outline the openings for the water shutoff valves and the drainpipe on the back panel of the vanity. Disconnect the valves and drain, and then use a hole saw to cut the openings. Set the vanity in place against the wall, and connect the pipes.

2 Level the vanity. Placing a carpenter's level on top of the vanity, check to see whether it is level from front to back and from side to side. If it is not, insert some wood shims under the base, tapping them into place gently, until the vanity is level in both directions.

3 Secure the vanity. Determine the stud locations behind the wall where the vanity will be located. Using 2½-inch wood screws through the back mounting rail, secure the vanity to the wall. Be sure to fasten the screws into the

Add brightness and comfort to a bathroom with sparkling new fixtures and bath accessories, or add a wall mirror to create the illusion of spaciousness.

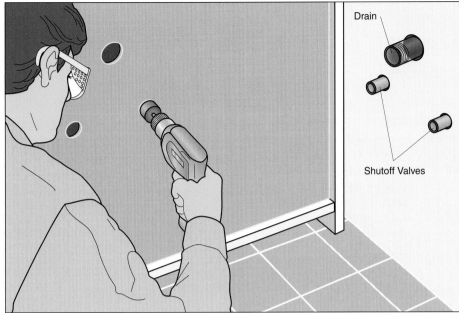

1. Outline the location of the shutoff valves and drainpipe on the back of the vanity, and then use a hole saw attachment on a power drill to cut the openings.

2. Using a carpenter's level as a guide, level the vanity with wood shims.

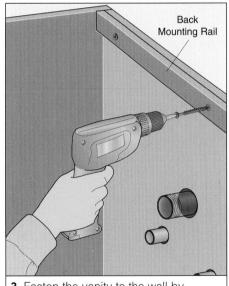

3. Fasten the vanity to the wall by driving screws through the back mounting rails and into the wall studs.

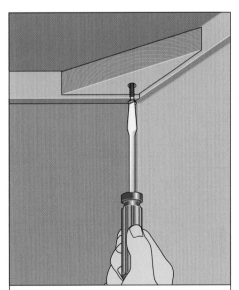

4. With an assistant bracing the countertop, drill pilot holes from below, and screw the countertop onto the vanity.

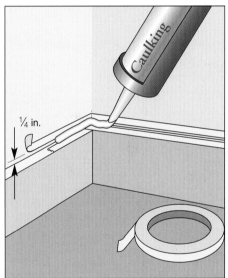

5. Mask the wall and the backsplash, offsetting the tape ¼ in. from the joint, and then apply silicone caulking.

studs that are nearest to each end of the vanity.

4 Attach the countertop. With the help of another person, hold the vanity countertop down and firmly against the wall. Next, drill pilot holes through the corner braces and then up into the countertop above. Finally, drive 1¼-inch wood screws through the pre-drilled holes in the corner braces to secure the countertop to the vanity base unit below.

5 Caulk the backsplash. After you've secured the countertop, apply a strip of masking tape along the wall, ¼ inch above the back-splash. Apply another strip along the top of the backsplash, ¼ inch out from the wall. Run a bead of silicone caulking in the joint between the backsplash and the wall between the two strips of masking tape. Smooth the caulking to a concave profile with your finger, and then carefully remove the masking tape.

Installing a Pedestal Sink

Difficulty Level: 🔨🔨

Required Tools:

❑ **Basic tools: caulking gun, drywall saw, hacksaw, level, measuring tape, utility knife**

❑ **Special tools: carbide bit, drill, propane torch, soldering gun, stud finder, tubing cutter**

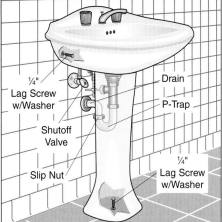

Pedestal Sink. For those who don't need storage space or who are designing a period style bathroom, a pedestal sink is an elegant choice.

Compared with a vanity unit, a pedestal sink takes up little floor and wall space, which helps make a small bathroom seem larger.

Installing a pedestal sink may involve more than simply replacing an old lavatory with a new one. If a vanity unit is being replaced by the pedestal sink, it will probably be necessary to move existing water supply lines, repair damaged drywall, and perhaps finish areas on the wall or floor that were previously left unfinished. Rather than trying to match old colors and patterns, this may be an opportune time to

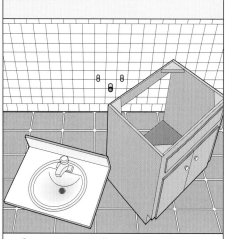

1. Close the shutoff valves under the lavatory. If there are none, then shut the main water valve. Lastly, remove the existing lavatory and vanity cabinet.

replace old bathroom flooring and wallcovering and improve the overall quality of your home.

Although basin sizes and pedestal heights may vary slightly, the steps for installing a pedestal sink are fairly universal. Nevertheless, refer to the manufacturer's instruction manual for specific installation details.

1 Remove the existing fixture. If the old lavatory has shutoff valves on the water-supply lines, turn them off. Next, shut off the water at the main valve because you will be moving the valves once the lavatory is out of the way. Disconnect the water-supply lines, drain arm, and trap from the basin. Try to lift out the basin and countertop as a single unit. Next, remove the vanity cabinet.

2 Install the backer board. You will need to get into the wall behind the sink to install a backer board. The backer board will serve as a support for the hanger bracket and mounting bolts for the sink. Cut back the drywall, making the opening slightly wider than the space between wall studs. (Expose a ¾-inch lip on each stud for securing a new section of drywall.) Cut a length of 2x8 lumber to fit between the wall studs as the backer board, spanning the space between the studs. Check

2. Cut the drywall behind the lavatory, exposing half of a stud on each side of the opening, and then nail a 2x8 backer board between the studs.

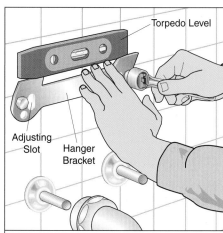

3. Screw the hanger bracket into the new backer board at the appropriate height for the new pedestal sink.

the pedestal sink instructions for the correct installation height.

The instructions for the lavatory should specify the location for the new shutoff valves. As soon as the valve stubouts are in place, solder a pipe cap over the end of each one. This will allow you to turn the water on for the rest of the house.

Once the stubouts are in place, patch the opening with a piece of drywall, and then repair any damage done to the wall and floor finishes.

3 Install the lavatory support. Secure the hanger bracket to the wall using ¼-inch diameter lag screws screwed into the backer board.

The mounting holes are slotted so that minor adjustments can be made.

4 Install shutoff valves. Place the escutcheon plate over the stubout and against the wall. Next, measure a distance out from the plate along the stubout enough to allow room for the valve, including the nut and collar. Mark the length, turn the water off, and then cut each stubout with a tube cutter.

The valve compression nut and the brass compression ring should be installed next. Simply slide the valve as far onto the stubout as it will go, and then screw the compression nut onto the threads of the valve collar. As the nut is tightened, it will force the compression ring onto the copper supply pipe and against the inside of the valve collar, creating a leak-free joint.

Have someone turn the water on while you check the valves for leaks. If necessary, tighten the compression nuts further.

5 Mount the faucet and drain. Turn the lavatory upside down and install the faucet handle(s) through the mounting holes. Apply the gaskets supplied with the sink, or some plumber's putty, and then tighten the mounting nut. Bend the supply tubes for a proper fit.

Attach the supply tubes (risers) next. Smooth chrome risers look best, but they must be bent using a spring tubing bender. Flexible braided metal supply tubes are easier to work with, although they cannot be cut.

6 Hang the lavatory. Lift the lavatory onto the hanger bracket, and then check the alignment of the drain, trap, and supply tubes. If necessary, cut the drain tailpiece to length with a hacksaw or bend the supply tubes and then rehang the lavatory.

With the lavatory on the hanger bracket, tighten the compression nuts that connect the water supply risers to the shutoff valves. Put the P-trap into position, and tighten the slip nuts connecting it to the sink tailpiece and drain arm in the wall.

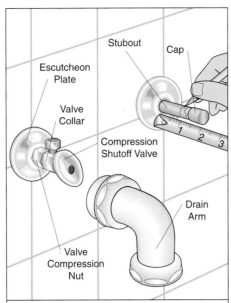

4. Measuring from the escutcheon plate, mark the stubout, allowing enough room for the nut and collar of the shutoff valve.

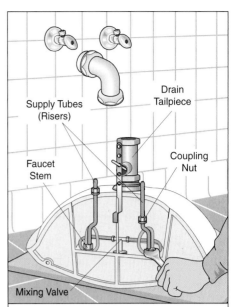

5. With the lavatory turned upside down, install the handles through the mounting holes, and attach the supply tubes.

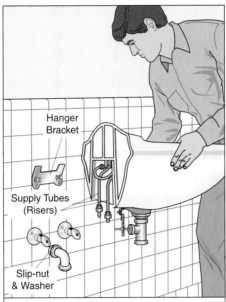

6. Lift the lavatory onto the hanger bracket, aligning the supply tubes, drain, and trap. Cut or bend the piping to fit.

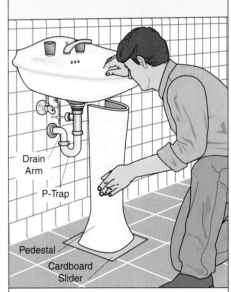

7. Raising the lavatory slightly, slide the pedestal underneath it, and insert the lag screw into the pedestal base.

7 Install the pedestal. Slide the pedestal under the lavatory, protecting the floor with a thin piece of cardboard. Carefully raise the lavatory. You should only be able to raise it about 1/8 inch—just enough to move the pedestal into position. Pedestals are typically fastened in place with a lag screw driven through a hole in the base. Mark the center of the hole, remove the pedestal, and then drill the pilot hole for the screw.

Do not attempt to drill the hole with the pedestal in position; the maneuvering area is limited, and you will risk cracking the base. After making the hole, position the base, and then tighten the lag screw.

To finish, apply a bead of silicone caulk along the edge of the lavatory where it joins the wall and along the pedestal edge at the floor. Turn on the valves to check for leaks.

Selecting a New Faucet

There is a great variety of faucet styles available. In addition to traditional dual-lever faucets with replaceable washers, there are also single-lever styles. Spouts and bases

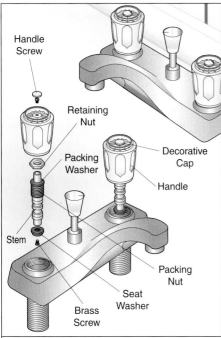

Compression faucet. A compression faucet relies on neoprene washers or a diaphragm to control the flow of water.

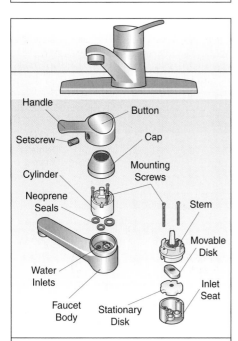

Disk faucet. Disk faucets contain a pair of plastic or ceramic disks that move up and down to regulate flow and rotate to control water temperature.

also vary and may come in polished or matte finishes, in chrome, brass, nickel, and even enameled metal.

First, choose whether you want a dual- or single-lever faucet. Either is available with, or without, drain-control levers. A faucet may control water flow in different ways. A compression faucet depends on neoprene washers or diaphragms to start or stop the flow of water. Newer style faucets may control the flow of water with cartridges, balls, or disks. Cartridge faucets regulate water flow with a movable cartridge and neoprene O-rings. Ball faucets use a slotted plastic or brass ball atop a pair of spring-loaded neoprene seats. The single lever rotates the ball to adjust water temperature as well as flow. Disk faucets contain a pair of plastic or ceramic disks that move up and down to regulate flow volume and rotate to control water temperature.

After selecting the type of faucet to install, be sure to measure the offset (the distance, center to center, between the hot and cold taps) before making a purchase. The offset of the faucet set must match the hole spacing of the lavatory.

Removing the Old Faucet

Difficulty Level: 🔧

Required Tools:

❑ **Basic tools: adjustable wrenches or pliers, flashlight, putty knife**

❑ **Special tools: basin wrench**

1 **Close the shutoff valves.** Begin by shutting off the valves in the hot and cold supply pipes below the lavatory. If there are no valves, shut off the water supply at the house water main, which is usually located in the basement.

2 **Disconnect the tailpieces.** Set a flashlight to shine on the pipes

under the lavatory. Use a basin wrench to disconnect the faucet tailpieces from the water-supply risers.

3 **Remove the drain controls.** If the faucet contains a drain control, it must be removed before you can remove the faucet. Using adjustable pliers, loosen the clevis screw and free the lift rod. Next, free

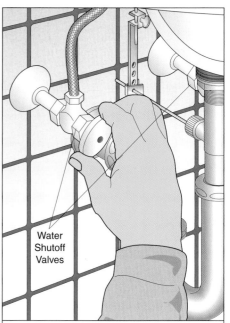

1. Before removing a faucet, always shut off either the water shutoff valves beneath the lavatory or the house water main.

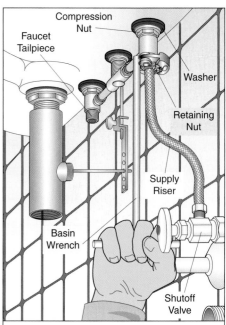

2. With a basin or adjustable wrench, disconnect the water-supply risers, using penetrating oil if they are rusted in place.

the pivot rod from the drain. Lastly, disconnect the pivot rod from the pop-up plug, and remove them both. The new faucet set should come with drain replacement parts.

4 **Remove the mounting nuts and washers.** Using an adjustable wrench or a basin wrench, remove the faucet-

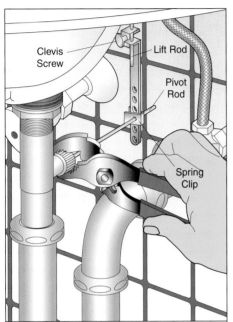

3. Loosen the clevis screw and free the lift rod. Next, free the pivot rod from the drain and the pop-up plug.

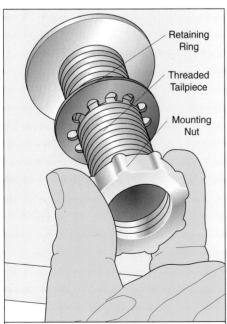

4. Remove mounting nuts and washers, loosen any adhesive under the baseplate, and then pry up the old faucet.

mounting nuts and washers by turning them counterclockwise. On single-lever faucets, the supply pipes converge at the center. The unit is held in place by mounting nuts on the sides and a nut and retaining ring at the center. If the faucet is difficult to remove, even after unscrewing the mounting nuts, then loosen the caulk or adhesive under the baseplate using a putty knife.

Installing the New Faucet

Difficulty Level: 🔨

Required Tools:

❏ **Basic tools: adjustable wrenches or pliers, caulking gun, flashlight, putty knife**

❏ **Special tools: basin wrench, pipe wrench, plumber's putty, silicone sealant**

1 **Install the gasket or sealant.** Clean the surface of the lavatory where the new faucet set will be positioned, and then install the gasket. If the faucet set did not come with a gasket, apply a layer of silicone sealant or plumber's putty to the faucet baseplate. Insert the faucet tailpieces into the mounting holes of the lavatory, and then press the faucet firmly into place. Wipe off any excess sealant.

2 **Tighten the mounting nuts.** Put the washers and mounting nuts onto the tailpieces, taking care not to thread the nuts too tightly.

3 **Attach the risers.** Attach braided stainless-steel risers to the faucet and to the water shutoff valves. Unlike chrome-plated copper, this type of tubing is flexible and easier to adjust when making connections. Thread the nuts, but not too tightly.

4 **Install the drain fittings.** Insert the lift rod control through the top of the faucet. Attach the lift rod to the clevis. Insert the pop-up stopper into the drain hole, and

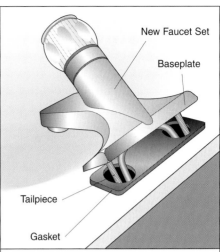

1. Install a new gasket or seal around the lip of the new faucet baseplate, and then press the faucet firmly into position.

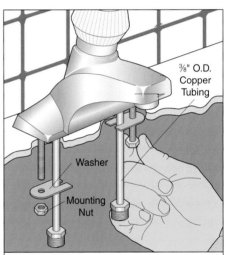

2. Tighten the washers and mounting nuts on the faucet tailpieces, taking care not to thread them too tightly.

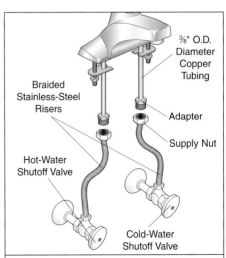

3. Connect the water-supply lines between the faucet tailpieces and shutoff valves, and then tighten the supply nuts.

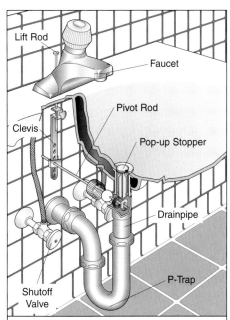

4. Insert the lift rod control through the faucet, and attach it to the clevis. Insert the pop-up stopper into the drain hole, engage it with the pivot rod, and then attach the spring clip.

then engage it with the pivot rod. Adjust the elevation of the stopper by selecting the appropriate hole in the clevis for the pivot rod, and attach the spring clip.

When all the parts are properly assembled, turn on the shutoff valves, and then check all the connections for leaks. If a connection is leaking, turn the nut a little bit at a time until the leak stops.

Bathroom Accessories

A recessed medicine cabinet is an accessory that few bathrooms should be without. Cutting a recess in a stud wall covered with drywall is a relatively simple task, and although tile and plaster walls offer more of a challenge, even these can be overcome with average skills.

A large wall-sized mirror is another bathroom accessory that many people find not only a convenience but a necessity. For most homeowners, installing one should not be particularly difficult.

Installing a Recessed Medicine Cabinet

Difficulty Level: ⏛⏛

Required Tools:

❏ **Basic tools:** backsaw, drywall knife, drywall saw, hammer, power drill with screwdriver bit, spirit level, stud finder, utility knife, wood chisel

❏ **Special Materials:** drywall, drywall tape, joint compound, screws, 6d and 10d common nails

1 Locate and mark wall studs. Shut off the circuit breakers that control power and lighting to the bathroom, as well as to wires running through the wall that is to be opened. Using a stud finder, locate the studs in the wall where the new medicine cabinet will be installed. Using a spirit level, mark the top line of the cabinet opening on the wall. Generally, this is 72 inches above the floor, plus the header height. Measure down the height of the recessed cabinet plus 3 inches for the header and sill plate. Mark a horizontal reference line at this point. Locate the vertical studs and mark the cabinet width, using a spirit level as your guide.

2 Remove the wall finish. Drill a pilot hole at least ¾ inch in

Lavatory accessories. A recessed medicine cabinet can be an aesthetically pleasing, as well as a practical, solution to your bathroom storage needs.

diameter at each corner of the cutout. Next, cut the wall finish, using a utility knife or drywall saw. If the wall is faced with ceramic tile, strip off the tile before cutting through either drywall or plaster substrate.

3 Remove the studs. After the studs have been exposed, decide which ones need to be cut. But first, determine whether or not the wall is load-bearing. If it is, you will need to provide jack studs and a header across the opening. Use a backsaw to cut through the studs.

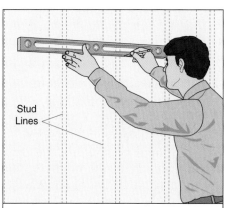

1. Mark guidelines on the wall for the upper and lower edges of the cabinet. Using a stud finder, locate and mark the position of the nearest studs outside cabinet dimensions.

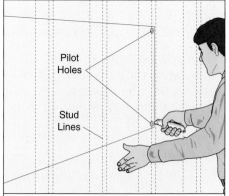

2. After marking the opening for the cabinet header and sill plate, drill pilot holes to mark the inside corners of the outline. Cut out the drywall with a utility knife or drywall saw.

3. Cut the exposed studs in the opening with a backsaw. (If the wall is load-bearing, install a double-2x8-header with a ½ plywood filler over the opening.)

4. Nail a 2x4 (or 2x6 for a 2x6 wall), on flat, onto the cut studs at the head and the sill of the opening, toenailing them into the uncut studs at the sides.

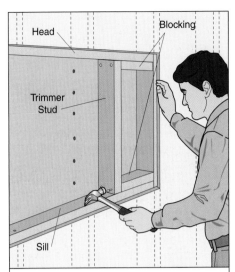

5. If the cabinet is narrower than the opening, adjust the opening to fit the cabinet by installing trimmer studs between the head and the sill.

6. Any wall area that will not be covered by the medicine cabinet must be recovered with drywall and then taped, spackled, sanded, and refinished.

7. If the cabinet comes with a light, connect the wiring, and then place the cabinet into the recess. Screw the cabinet into the studs at each side.

Install the head and sill. Measure the horizontal distance between the edge studs, and cut 2x4s or 2x6s to this dimension for the head and sill. Nail the head and sill into the cut ends of the wall studs with 10d nails. Toenail the head and sill to the edge studs using 8d nails.

Install trimmer studs. If it is necessary, cut 2x4 trimmers to reduce one or both sides of the wall opening to the width required to fit the cabinet correctly. Install 2x4 blocking at the head and sill, to support the trimmer, and then nail the trimmers into the blocking.

Patch and finish the wall. Cut sections of drywall, and install them over the exposed wall studs, leaving the recess open for the cabinet. Tape and spackle the drywall joints, and then refinish the wall.

Install the cabinet. If the unit comes with a lighting fixture, complete the electrical wiring. Place the cabinet into the recess, and screw it to the edge framing through the holes provided in the sides.

Hanging a Wall Mirror

Difficulty Level:

Required Tools:

❏ **Basic tools: caulking gun, hammer**

❏ **Special Materials: drywall nails, J-channels, mastic adhesive**

Size and order the glass. Mirrors can be custom made in virtually any size or shape. Check the yellow pages of your regional telephone book for "Mirror, Retail." When buying a mirror, specify ¼-inch thick glass. Mirrors ⅛-inch thick are available, but thin glass, especially if the mirror is large, tends to be more distorting than thicker glass.

About ¼ inch of clearance will be necessary on each side of the mirror for it to be installed without the walls being scraped. Because most

---

$ Value Tip

Reflected Light

The addition of a large mirror can bring reflected light into a small bathroom, adding the illusion of space without the expense of renovation.

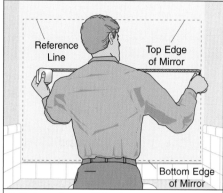

1. If the mirror will be in a tight space, measure the space in at least three places. The width of the mirror should be less than the smallest measurement.

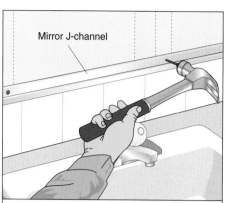

2. If the mirror will be supported by J-channels, secure one channel into the studs at the bottom and another ¼ in. higher than the top edge of the mirror.

to be used to install mirrors. It will not chemically damage the silver coating on the back of a mirror. For this reason, do not use common construction adhesives, because they will react with the silvering and ruin the finish on the mirror.

To apply the mirror to the wall, squeeze one glob of mastic on the back of the mirror for each square foot of its size. Take extreme care to ensure that the mastic does not ooze out along the edges. Once you have placed the mirror in the correct position, press it firmly against the entire surface to spread the mastic. If any slight adjustments are needed, make them immediately. Once the mastic is set, you cannot move the mirror without causing damage.

Toilets

Older toilets, or water closets, are replaced for several good reasons. For one, more contemporary designs are available to meet the needs of today's homeowner. For another, older vitreous china fixtures are often chipped, stained, or dysfunctional. And, lastly, older toilets waste water.

3. If the mirror is to be installed with mastic, use an adhesive formulated for use on the back of a mirror. Squeeze a glob of the mastic on each square foot of the mirror's back, and then press the mirror firmly against the surface of the wall.

A modern toilet will not only add beauty to your bathroom but also save on bills by conserving water.

walls aren't plumb, measure the width of the opening in at least three places, top, bottom and center. Order the mirror about ½ inch narrower than the smallest measurement.

2 Install the J-channels. All mirror manufacturers require that their mirrors be attached to a wall using two different methods. One must be *mechanical*, the other *adhesive*. Aluminum J-channels are mechanical supports that have a nice appearance, and they are easy to install. Simply cut the channels equal to the length of the mirror, and then secure

them to the wall studs using 1½-inch drywall nails or screws. If the mirror is going to be positioned over a lavatory, the bottom channel is typically installed over the top edge of the backsplash. The top channel is installed next, typically with the top edge about ¼ inch higher than the height of the mirror. This will permit the mirror to be raised into the upper J-channel and then released into the lower J-channel.

3 Apply adhesive mastic, and install the mirror. Adhesive mirror mastic is specifically formulated

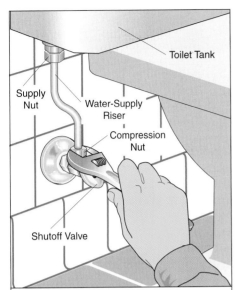

1. Before removing a water closet, shut off the house water main. Then disconnect the risers and remove the shutoff valves and their escutcheon plates.

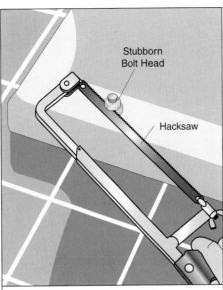

2. Using a wrench, remove the bolts holding the old water closet to the floor. If necessary, cut off stubborn bolt heads using a hacksaw.

The newer ones conserve water, and this is an attractive feature for today's environmentally conscientious homeowner.

Installing a new toilet involves removing the older one and then mounting and connecting the new one. If the toilet will be installed in a new location, the existing plumbing will need modification.

Removing an Old Toilet

Difficulty Level: 🔨

Required Tools:

❏ **Basic tools:** adjustable wrench, hacksaw

1 Disconnect the riser. Shut the water off at the house water main, even if the water closet has a separate shutoff, because you will be removing the old valve. Drain the fixture, and then disconnect the riser. Using an adjustable wrench, remove the shutoff valve and the escutcheon plate.

2 Disconnect the toilet. Remove the protective caps (if any) from the bolts holding the toilet to the

3. Rock the water closet slowly back and forth to free it from the adhesive holding it in place, and then remove it.

floor, and then unscrew the nuts with a wrench. If the bolts are too corroded to come loose, cut them with a hacksaw.

3 Remove the toilet. Rock the bowl back and forth to loosen it from the floor, and then lift it straight up off the drain. Next, stuff the drain hole with rags in order to keep the sewer gases from rising into the house. Scrape the residue remaining from the wax ring seal off both the floor and the drain.

Installing a New Toilet

Difficulty Level: 🔨🔨

Required Tools:

❏ **Basic tools:** adjustable wrench, hacksaw, measuring tape, power drill, spirit level

❏ **Special tools:** spud wrench, tubing cutter

Required Materials:

❏ **Basic materials:** plumber's putty, Teflon tape

❏ **Special materials:** braided stainless-steel riser, closet-bend flange (transition piece between soil stack and water closet), coupling nut and compression ring (if needed for chromed copper piping), extension piping and fittings for water supply, extension piping for drain, spud washer, threaded compression union (if needed to join steel pipes), wax ring seal

1 Attach the mounting bolts to the flange. Slip the heads of the floor mounting bolts into the adjusting slots on the toilet flange.

2 Seal the base. With the water closet turned on its side or upside down, press the wax ring seal over the horn (the lip around the

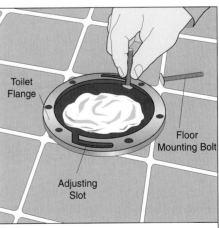

1. Attach the mounting bolts to the flange by slipping the bolt heads into the adjusting slots on the flange.

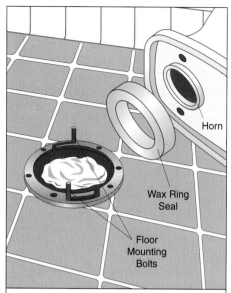

2. Turn the water closet on its side, and then press the wax ring seal over the horn (lip of the drain opening) on the water closet.

Labels in image: Horn, Wax Ring Seal, Floor Mounting Bolts

3. Turn the water closet right-side up, and align the bolt holes over the floor mounting bolts. Position the bowl, twisting it slightly to seal the wax ring.

4. If the water closet has a tank, place the neoprene spud washer over the drain opening and set the tank over it. Then tighten the washers and nuts.

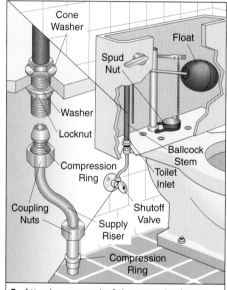

5. Attach one end of the supply riser to the tank and the other to the shutoff valve, and then turn on the water to check for any leaks.

Labels in image: Cone Washer, Spud Nut, Float, Washer, Locknut, Compression Ring, Coupling Nuts, Supply Riser, Shutoff Valve, Ballcock Stem, Toilet Inlet, Compression Ring

tank over it. Attach the tank to the bowl rim with washers and nuts from below.

5 Connect the tank to the shut-off valve. A properly sized braided stainless-steel riser is preferable, but a chromed copper riser can also be used. The diameter of the pipe must conform to the recommendations of the toilet manufacturer. If you use a braided riser, fit one end into the shutoff valve and the other into the threaded inlet of the tank. Hand-tighten the nuts, and then tighten them further with an adjustable wrench. For chromed copper pipes, measure the distance from the toilet connection to the shutoff valve, allowing extra length for the fittings, and then cut the pipe with a tube cutter. Slip a coupling nut and compression ring over both ends of the pipe before inserting it into the shutoff valve and toilet inlet. Next, tighten the nuts, taking care not to put a bend or kink in the copper tubing. Lastly, turn on the water supply, and check for leaks. To stop a leak, drain the tank, disconnect the riser, and then apply plumber's putty or Teflon tape to the threads.

Shower Enclosures

Replacing an outdated shower or bathtub is a worthwhile investment. It not only increases the value of a home but, if done well, adds beauty and convenience. Further, replacing an existing fixture usually doesn't involve extensive renovation work. Installing a *new* shower, however, will likely involve opening walls and floors to replace or reroute plumbing or to install new plumbing.

Prefabricated enclosures come with instructions to guide a homeowner through a shower installation. If you're considering a one-piece shower enclosure, be sure it fits through an existing doorway or window. If you can't easily get a one-piece unit into your home, select a unit that comes disassembled.

drain opening at the base of the water closet).

3 Position the toilet. Remove the rags from the drain opening. Turning the toilet right side up, lift it into position, aligning the bolt holes at the base with the bolts in the flange. Lower the bowl, slowly coaxing it into position, and then twist it slightly to seal the wax ring. Place a level across the rim to ensure

that it is plumb. Pour water into the bowl next to see if it leaks. Remold the wax ring if necessary. When it's set, place the washers and nuts on the bolts. Do not overtighten the nuts, or you may crack the bowl.

4 Install the new tank. If the tank is separate from the bowl, place the spud washer (a large neoprene ring) over the drain opening in the lower section, and then place the

Prefabricated shower enclosures have their own watertight walls, eliminating the need for special wall substrates like cement board. Nevertheless, you must check for leaks in the plumbing before putting up wall panels and finishing the floor. If a problem arises later, fixing it will be more difficult.

Installing a Shower Enclosure

Difficulty Level: ⫯ ⫯ ⫯

Required Tools:

❑ **Basic tools:** adjustable wrenches, caulking gun, combination square, hacksaw, hammer, measuring tape, power drill, saber saw, spirit level, utility knife

Required Materials:

❑ **Basic materials:** adhesive caulking, plumber's putty, silicone sealant, 2x4s

❑ **Special materials:** shower stall components (kit)

1 Cut an opening for the control valve. If the side panel of the shower enclosure does not have a precut opening for the control valve, then you must make one. To do this, first drill a pilot hole, and then use a saber saw with a fine-toothed blade to cut an opening large enough for the control valve.

2 Check the match between the drain opening and base. Attach the drain fittings to the shower base, and then temporarily place the base into position on the subflooring. Be certain that the drain opening is appropriately matched up with the floor drain nipple.

3 Check the wall panels for fit. With the shower base in place, slide the wall panels into position. Be sure that they fit plumb and square to the walls and that they are aligned with each other. Trace the cutouts for the control valve and

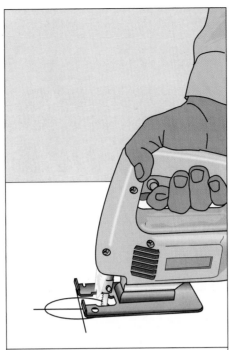

1. If there is no precut opening in the panel for a control valve, drill a pilot hole, and cut an opening using a saber saw.

2. Attach the drain to the shower base, and then temporarily place the base into position to check for proper alignment.

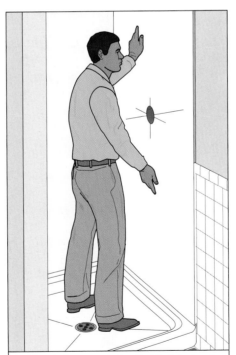

3. Check the panels for fit. Mark holes for the valve and showerhead on the wall, remove the panels, and cut the holes.

4. Apply adhesive evenly, on both the floor and the wall substrates, following the manufacturer's instructions.

showerhead onto the wall. Move the shower panels and base aside, and then cut the wall openings.

4 Apply the adhesive. Spread the adhesive evenly on both the floor and the wall substrates, following the manufacturer's instructions. Then place the base into position, being certain that the drain opening is fitted and centered properly over the drain.

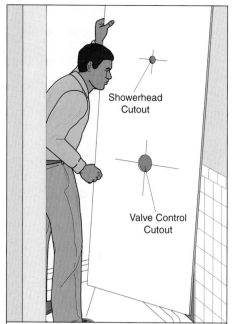

5. Next, slide the wall panels into position and press them firmly against the adhesive. Check whether they are plumb. If necessary, shim the panels to square them.

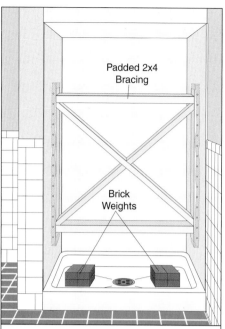

6. Prop the side panels tightly against the wall using a 2x4 brace padded with soft cloth or carpet scraps to protect the finish on the wall panels.

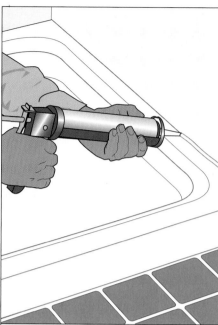

7. Carefully seal around all the perimeter joints of the wall panels and the joint between the floor and the shower base to prevent water damage.

5 **Position the side panels.** Slide the shower enclosure wall panels into position, and then press them firmly into place against the adhesive. Check to see that they are plumb, and insert shims, wherever needed, to square up the side panels.

6 **Brace the side panels and the shower base.** Brace the floor and wall panels tightly to the subflooring and to the walls. While the adhesive is setting, the shower enclosure base should be weighed down with bricks or some other heavy material. The side panels should be propped against the backer walls with 2x4s, padded with soft cloth or carpeting scraps,

to protect the finish on the shower enclosure. If the shower unit comes with a glass door, rather than a rod for a curtain, follow the manufacturer's instructions for assembling the components of the door.

7 **Seal the joints.** Thoroughly seal around the shower-door jambs

and around the perimeter of the shower base with silicone sealant. This step is very important because, if water works its way behind the wall panels or beneath the shower base, the result may be extensive water damage to the walls and floor or even to the ceiling below, leading to expensive repair work.

Period-style fixtures that are damaged beyond repair may be replaced with similar fixtures salvaged from older homes or with replicas available through specialty suppliers.

Chapter 9
Walls and Ceilings

Walls provide more than a support system for ceilings and roofs. Walls are the principal, though not the exclusive, means by which habitable space is delineated. More importantly, walls and ceilings provide a canvas upon which the creative homeowner can mirror his or her tastes. Walls and ceilings, freshly painted with bright, cheery colors, can create a welcoming atmosphere. Walls that are cracked, dirty, or painted with out-of-date colors may produce a feeling of dreariness. Giving the interior of your home a fresh coat of paint or new wall-covering is a worthwhile investment. The simple addition of an accent color to a neutral space may be an economical yet dramatic change. The variety of wall treatments from which to choose is as limitless as one's imagination.

IN THIS CHAPTER

Repairing Walls

Repairing Drywall 124

Repairing Plaster Cracks 125

Overlaying a Wall 126

Repairing Ceilings

Overlaying a Ceiling 127

Texturing a Ceiling 127

Painting Walls and Ceilings

Tools and Materials 128

Surface Preparation 129

Painting a Room 129

Wallcovering

Wallcovering Basics 131

Wall Tiling

Tile Layout 135

Installing Tile 136

Cutting Tile 137

Grouting 138

TODAY'S TRENDS

Decorative
Window & Ceiling Moldings

Ceramic Tile Between
Countertops & Wall Cabinets

Faux Finishes & Textured
Surfaces

Chair Rails

Repairing Walls

Before you begin to decorate walls and ceilings, be sure that they are clean and in the best possible condition to receive paint or new wallcovering. Holes, chips, water damage, and other surface problems must be corrected prior to painting and decorating in order to achieve desirable results.

This section covers drywall and plaster repairs that might be undertaken by the average homeowner. However, if you wish to preserve the original plaster and lath, it might be more sensible to hire a professional plasterer to handle the work.

Repairing Drywall

Difficulty Level: ⏚

Required Tools:

❑ **Basic tools: drywall knife, hammer, drywall saw, nails, sandpaper, utility knife**

❑ **Special tools: drywall screws, power screwdriver**

1 Conceal popped nails.
Sometimes drywall nailheads pop out and show through wallcovering or paint. Most popped nails are caused by wood shrinkage. Over time, studs shrink as the wood loses its moisture content. However, the nails remain in place. The drywall pulls away from the nails, causing the nailheads to appear raised. Repair these "popped" nails by either removing them or hammering them back into the wall. To ensure that they do not pop again, drive in another nail or drywall screw slightly above or below the one that was popped. Exert pressure on the drywall to be sure that it is firmly secured to the stud. More than one nail or screw may be needed to adequately fasten the drywall to the studs. Cover all exposed fasteners with joint compound; then smooth the repair.

Damaged drywall is easy to repair, requiring only drywall tape, joint compound, and careful sanding.

2 Cut out damaged drywall. To replace a piece of drywall, draw a rectangle around the damaged area. If you keep the edges straight and the corners square, it will be easier to fit the replacement piece. Drill starter holes within diagonally opposed corners of the rectangle, and then carefully cut out the damaged drywall. If the damaged area is large, use a utility knife to cut the drywall back to the center of the nearest studs.

3 Install backing blocks. Sawcut two wooden backing blocks from 1x3s or from ³⁄₄-inch thick plywood. You should cut the blocks 6 inches longer than the vertical height of the hole to be repaired. Insert one block into the opening, holding it tightly in place while securing it with at least two screws through the drywall and into the block. Secure the second block on the opposite side of the opening in the same way. If necessary, cut the drywall back to the nearest studs, and then nail 1x3 strips flush to the side of each stud, providing a surface for screwing in the drywall patch.

4 Tape and finish the patch. Cut the drywall patch to the proper size, fit it in place, and then secure it using drywall screws. Tape over the seams, and apply joint compound in feathered layers, blending it into the surrounding wall surface. When the joint compound is dry sand it

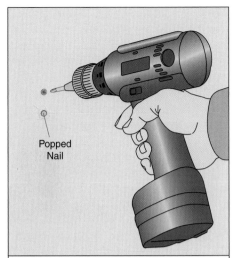

1. When nails pop out from drywall, remove them or drive them back in. Set a drywall screw a few inches above and below the nails; then patch the wall.

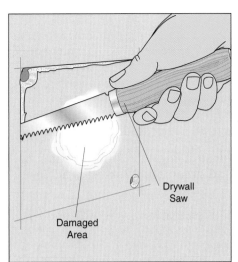

2. Damaged areas of drywall should be removed with a drywall saw. Drill holes at the corners to establish a starting point for the saw cut.

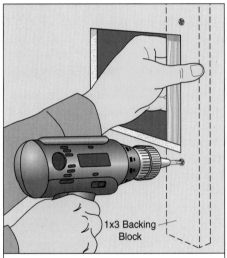

3. Brace a drywall patch with vertical backing cut from 1x3s or scrap plywood. Screw the braces in behind the opening to hold the patch in place.

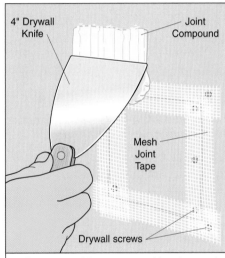

4. Cover patching seams with a layer of fiberglass mesh tape, and then finish them (and screwhead depressions) with three feathered coats of joint compound.

smooth, and then prime and paint the patched area so that it will match the adjacent wall in color and finish.

Repairing Plaster Cracks

Difficulty Level: 🔨

Required Tools:

❑ **Basic tools:** drywall knife, putty knife, sandpaper

❑ **Special materials:** patching plaster or powdered joint compound and perlited gypsum

Making minor repairs to plaster is not unlike working with joint compound. In fact, you can apply a layer or two of joint compound with a broad knife to fill small holes in plaster. Readily available peel-and-stick patches can also be used to repair holes up to 3 inches in diameter. Simply cut a patch to the size needed, press it into place, and

then apply two coats of patching plaster or joint compound. When it is dry, sand it smooth.

Hairline cracks in otherwise sound plaster are usually cosmetic. A good coat of primer, followed by a finish coat of latex paint, may be sufficient to hide such cracks. A spray-on crack filler may also be applied and then painted over. Still, hairline cracks have a habit of stubbornly reappearing, and it may be necessary to just accept them as part of the character of an old house, or you'll have to replace the plaster with drywall.

1 Enlarge the crack. Using the point of a can opener or putty knife, enlarge the crack. Undercut the edges to create a *key* with which the patch material may lock. Clean dust and debris out of the crack. If the crack is lengthy, create undercuts every few inches along the length of the crack to help anchor the plaster in place.

2 Fill the crack. Fill in the crack with high-tensile-strength patching plaster. A mixture of water, perlited gypsum, powdered joint compound, and acrylic binder may be made and used to fill larger cracks without sagging. When the filler is thoroughly dry, apply a finish coat of patching plaster, feathering it

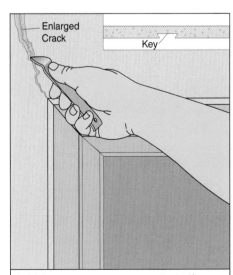

1. Using a can opener or putty knife, enlarge the crack. Undercut loose plaster into a "key" shape, which will better hold the patching plaster.

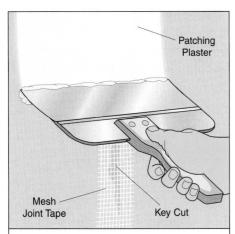

2. Cover plaster cracks with fiberglass mesh drywall tape, and then finish them with patching plaster.

onto the adjacent wall surface. Finally, sand the patched area smooth and finish as desired.

Overlaying a Wall

Difficulty Level: 🔨

Required Tools:

❑ **Basic tools: drywall knife, caulking gun, flashlight, hammer or power drill, spirit level**

❑ **Special materials: adhesive, caulking, drywall nails, joint compound, perlited gypsum**

Aside from the natural desire for perfection, how plumb and smooth a wall must be depends, to an extent, on the finish material that will be applied to it. For tile, a nearly perfect wall surface is an absolute necessity. Nothing short of professional skill as a tile setter is likely to resolve the kinds of problems that may arise during a tile installation. For the average homeowner, sheet paneling or new drywall is a more practical choice for minor wall repairs, yet even these may not hide visible bulges in a wall. Slightly out-of-plumb walls matter less if new drywall is to be applied. In any case, whether installing panels or tile, significantly out-of-plumb corners will be quite obvious.

If a wall surface is greatly deteriorated, it might be best to *skin* over it first with ¼-inch drywall, and then apply a new surface finish. This will eliminate demolition work, but the added layer of drywall may require that window and door jambs be increased in depth and some trim temporarily removed.

1 **Check the wall.** Use a spirit level at regular intervals along the length of the wall to make sure it is plumb. To check for bulges and depressions, place a long, straight board against a wall, and then flash a light under the board. Note where the light shines through behind the board, and mark these areas as low spots. Also mark bumps in the wall that cause the board to rock. A few low spots can easily be built up with joint compound or, better yet, perlited gypsum mixed with joint compound to prevent potential sagging. For deep hollows, form a new surface in successive layers. Break out high spots with a hammer. For broader areas of irregularity, attach 1x2 furring strips or 1½-inch strips of ¾-inch plywood to shim them plumb. If a wall must be unequivocally smooth and plumb, fur it out completely. Then apply new drywall or backer board.

2 **Apply the adhesive.** Using a caulking gun, apply wallboard adhesive to the back of a drywall panel just before installing it. This will reduce the number of screws or nails required to secure the panel.

3 **Hang the drywall.** Lift the drywall panel into place. Be certain that the edges are tightly abutted, and then fasten the panel in place with 1⅜-inch drywall nails or screws 16 inches on center across the field and 8 inches on center at the edges. Tape all joints, and fill nail or screw dimples with joint compound.

1. Using a 4-ft. level, check the walls for bulges and depressions. Low spots can be filled with joint compound, and high spots can be broken out.

2. Using a caulking gun, spread thin beads of adhesive on the back of the drywall panel. Keep clear of the edges so that the adhesive won't squeeze out.

3. Position the panel against the wall, abutting the seams tightly. Raise the panel flush to the ceiling, press it into place, and then fasten it with nails or screws.

Repairing Ceilings

Cracks in original plaster ceilings may occasionally be patched with some degree of success. However, such cracks may indicate that the plaster is coming loose from the lath. To determine whether this is the case, push against the surface of the ceiling. If plaster is loose in only one area, it may be relatively simple to repair the isolated damage. However, if a significant amount of plaster is loose, additional plaster will probably loosen as well. In this case, if the anticipated amount of work, dust, and debris involved in replacing a plaster ceiling seems daunting, the best solution might simply be to cover the old plaster with drywall.

Overlaying a Ceiling

As with old plaster, even drywall ceilings may need replacement. This might be necessary because of water damage or perhaps the ceiling simply has a texture or finish that is no longer desired. Removing drywall, of course, is much easier than removing plaster. Removal is not always necessary, however, especially if the drywall is not crumbling because of water or some other type of damage. Simply skin over it with new drywall, following the same procedure as for installing drywall over plaster walls. First, be certain that any sources of water damage have been eliminated.

In some ways, overlaying ceilings is easier than overlaying walls because ceilings have few, if any, moldings or openings to deal with. Further, the workload may be lightened by using ⅜-inch drywall, and much of the taping work can be omitted by installing crown molding at the wall-to-ceiling joints. Be conscious, however, of the fact that doing ceiling work is strenuous, often requiring the worker to remain in an awkward and unnatural posture while positioning and securing

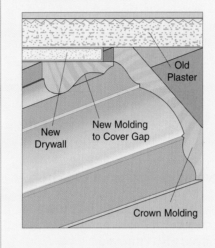

Pro Tip

CROWN MOLDING

If you are planning to overlay a ceiling that has an existing crown molding, it is better not to butt the drywall against the molding. It will never look professionally finished. Instead, stop the drywall short of the molding, and then add a new piece of molding to cover the gap, as shown below.

Old Plaster

New Drywall

New Molding to Cover Gap

Crown Molding

drywall panels. Having another person on hand to offer assistance is a virtual necessity.

Bracing drywall. Having the proper equipment on hand is also important, including at least two sturdy ladders, T-braces, and 2x4 cleats to temporarily brace drywall panels

during installation. Place ladders carefully below where the drywall will be installed. With an assistant, raise the drywall into place. While one person props the panel with the T-brace, the other aligns the panel and fastens it to the ceiling joists or furring strips with 1⅜-inch drywall nails or screws, 16 inches on center across the field and 8 inches on center along the edges.

Texturing a Ceiling

Difficulty Level: 🔨

Required Tools:

❏ **Basic tools: metal tray, 6- to 12-in.-wide drywall knife**

❏ **Special tools: joint compound, texturing brushes**

Textured finishes help to hide minor flaws, such as discolored or uneven surfaces. A simple way to texture a ceiling is with joint compound, a texturing brush, and a 10-inch wide drywall knife. Clean the knife edge on a metal tray as you *knock down* the peaks in the joint compound. This process yields dramatic results with little effort.

1 Prepare the compound. Pour two quarts of joint compound on a scrap of drywall. Coat a texture brush with the joint compound.

2x4 Cleat

T-Brace

Bracing drywall to a ceiling is much easier with the use of a T-brace, a wooden support that serves as an extra pair of hands to hold a panel in place.

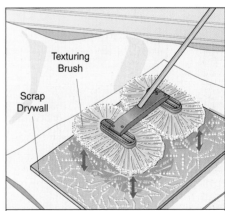

Texturing Brush

Scrap Drywall

1. Always test the consistency of a texturing compound before you apply it to a surface. The mixture should be thick enough so that it won't slump.

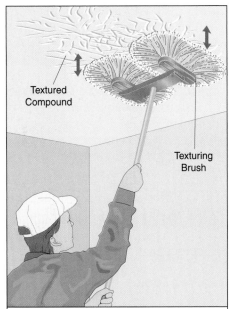

2. Coat a texturing brush with enough compound to cover about 25 sq. ft. of the ceiling, and then daub the texture randomly onto the drywall surface.

3. While the texturing compound is still wet, knock down the peaks with a 6- to 12-in. drywall knife, and then allow the compound to dry.

2 Daub the ceiling. With the loaded texture brush, randomly daub the ceiling. Coat the brush with enough joint compound to cover an area of approximately 25 square feet with each brush load.

3 Knock down the peaks. After a section of ceiling is completed, drag the drywall knife lightly over the textured joint compound to knock down excessively high ridges and to fill in the low spots.

When the entire ceiling has been completed, allow the joint compound to dry. Paint it, as desired, using a medium-napped roller cover.

Painting Walls and Ceilings

Painting is a quick, inexpensive way to freshen the appearance of a room. An average size room may be done in one weekend, with the bulk of time spent on surface preparation.

For paint to adhere properly it must be applied to a dry surface, free of dirt, dust, grease, flaking paint, wall-covering, or paste residue. Furthermore, paint will only cover surface

blemishes. Cracks, abrasions, holes, popped nails, and other surface defects will show through the paint if they are not first corrected. Time and care spent cleaning, scraping, and spackling will ensure that the end results will be worth the effort.

Painting a ceiling is backbreaking work, even with the right equipment. Be sure to pace yourself sensibly.

Tools and Materials

Types of Paint. For interior use, the most common types of paint are either water-based (latex) or solvent-based (oil or alkyd). Both are available in premixed, as well as custom-mixed, colors. The more traditional oil-based paint has mostly been replaced by alkyd paint, a mixture of a solvent like mineral spirits with a nonvolatile synthetic resin. Alkyd paint retains color and adheres well.

Because of environmental concerns, paint companies have largely focused their research on latex paints. Due to technological advances, latex paint now spreads as easily as, and has better color retention than, traditional oil-based paints. Latex paint dries quickly, cleans up easily, and is available in a variety of sheens, including flat, eggshell, and semigloss.

Synthetic-based alkyd paint adheres to a variety of surfaces. It provides a durable finish that is most suitable for baseboards, doors, and other areas that get a good deal of abuse and handling. Alkyd paint is, however, both slower-drying and more expensive than latex paint. Alkyd paints must also be removed from hands and tools with mineral spirits or other types of solvents. Be sure to provide adequate ventilation when using alkyd paints.

Other special interior finishes include texture paint, sand paint, and fire-retardant paint for covering high-heat areas, such as kitchens and furnace rooms.

Selecting Brushes. Brushes are made with either natural or synthetic bristles. Natural bristles, often labeled *china bristle*, should never be used with a water-based paint because the bristles absorb water and become bloated. The tips of natural bristles are flagged to offer more brushing surface and hold more paint. Use natural bristles for alkyd-based paints. Synthetic (nylon) bristle brushes can be used for any paint. Before buying a

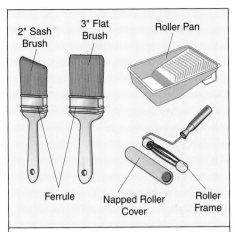

Brushes and Rollers. Even if you're an inexperienced painter, buy the best grade brushes and roller covers you can afford. Quality tools give better results.

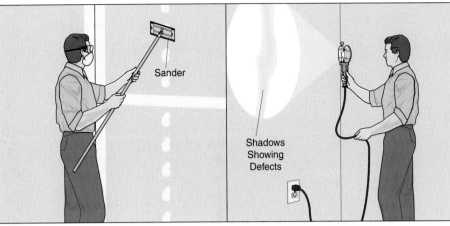

Sanding. Joint compound must be sanded perfectly flat before you begin painting, or it will show up as lumps and bumps on your walls. If you can't tell whether a surface is smooth by hand, shine a bright light on the surface at an angle. This will shadow bumps or recesses clearly.

brush, check it for thick, soft, and resilient bristles held in place by a sturdy metal ferrule. Always buy the best brush you can afford. Cheap brushes lose bristles in the paint and will not provide a smooth finish.

Most interior paint jobs can be handled with just two brushes; a 3-inch flat brush and a 2-inch angled sash brush. The 3-inch flat brush is the brush used most frequently. It has a tapered bottom that will paint a fine line, yet it is broad enough to cover large surface areas. The sash brush, on the other hand, is angled for crisp lines on trim, molding, and window parts. Avoid brushes wider than 4 inches. Use a roller instead.

Selecting Rollers and Pans. A roller consists of a cover and a frame. Covers come in several sizes and thicknesses. A standard roller is 9 inches long, available with a short, medium, or long nap. Short-napped rollers, about ¼-inch thick, are used to apply paint to smooth surfaces, such as drywall. Medium-napped rollers are used for semi-rough surfaces, such as plaster. And long-napped rollers are used for rough surfaces, such as concrete block, stucco, and brick. Most roller frames have a threaded handle that secures to an extension pole for reaching ceilings and the tops of walls. A standard mop handle may be used, but a painter's extension

pole is preferable. Roller pans should be deep, sturdy, and ribbed. Ribs enable the roller cover to pick up paint more evenly.

Surface Preparation

Scraping and Filling Defects. Cover the floor and furnishings completely before beginning work. Carefully prepare surfaces to be painted. Paint that is peeling, blistered, or alligatored must be removed entirely. Remove loose paint with a paint scraper, and then fill cracks and depressions with joint compound.

Sanding. With a fine or medium grade of sandpaper, sand the compound-filled areas and lightly rough up the remainder of the wall or ceiling surface to improve the adhesion of new paint. Use a pole sander for sanding areas that are difficult to reach. Shine an angled drop light on the wall to shadow any remaining rough spots, and then sand these smooth.

Masking. After sanding, thoroughly clean all surfaces of dust. Remove switchplates, receptacle covers, door knobs, kickplates, picture hooks, thermostat covers, etc. Remove or loosen wall and ceiling lights, and enclose them in plastic bags. Next, mask out the trimwork, using painter's masking tape.

Priming. Lastly, prime the unfinished surfaces. Primers are available for both solvent-based and water-based paints. Joint-compounded drywall seams and patched areas should be primed with latex primer or an alkyd sealer. For discolorations such as water stains, which will bleed through ordinary primers, use a white-shellac-based primer.

Painting a Room

Difficulty Level: 🖌

Required Tools (including surface preparation):

> drop cloths, drop light, drywall knife, joint compound, masking tape, paint roller with pole, paintbrushes (1–1½-in. trim, 2–2½-in. sash, 3–4-in. flat), painting edger, roller tray, sandpaper, step ladder

1 Cut-in the ceiling. With a 3-inch brush, paint the perimeter portion of the ceiling that cannot be reached with the roller. This process is called *cutting-in*. To reduce drips, dip the brush into the paint only one-third the length of its bristles. If the wall and ceiling are to be different colors, allow the lighter color to overlap the edge, and cut

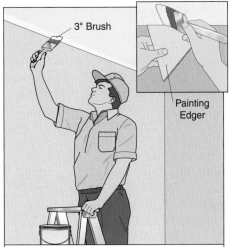

1. Using a 3-in. brush, cut-in the areas that can't be reached with the roller, such as around fixtures and at wall joints.

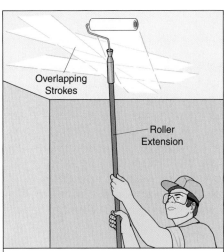

2. Roll paint onto the ceiling as close to the wall as possible. Overlap strokes to avoid leaving roller marks behind.

3. Areas on walls that can't be reached with a roller, such as ceiling and corner joints, must be cut-in with a 3-in. brush.

4. Finally, using a roller, paint the surface of the walls. Use an extension pole to reach the higher part of a wall.

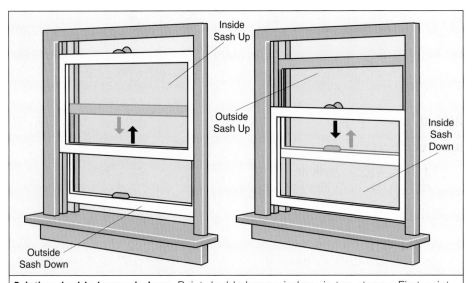

Painting double-hung windows. Paint double-hung windows in two stages: First paint the outside sash, and then paint the inside sash, shifting panes as shown.

the darker color in over it. Usually, ceiling colors are lighter than wall colors so that the ceiling color may overlap the surface of the wall. But if the ceiling will be darker than the wall, use a painting edger to obtain a crisp edge between the ceiling and wall surfaces.

2 Roll the ceiling. Push the roller along the bottom of the roller pan, where the paint should be no more than ¾ inch deep. Liberally coat the entire roller, and then apply the paint to the ceiling, rolling in one direction only. Go back over the work, rolling at a right angle to the original direction. Begin and end strokes gradually, so that roller marks will not remain on the surface. Before reloading the roller, finish each area by overlapping and feathering the roller strokes. Examine the surface carefully from several different angles, and then go over missed spots with a nearly dry roller.

3 Cut-in the walls. With a 3-inch brush, cut-in wall edges that cannot be reached with a roller, such as corners, along baseboards, and around window and door casings. Again, use a painting edger to cut-in the top of the wall, if necessary.

4 Roll the walls. Roll the walls next, being careful not to touch the ceiling with the paint roller. Apply paint in the same alternating pattern described for ceilings, and then, using a fairly dry roller, finish with up-and-down or side-to-side strokes.

Painting Double-Hung Windows. To paint a double-hung window, the top and bottom sash must be raised and lowered in sequence. Using a sash brush, first paint the outside sash as far as you can reach, and then paint the inside sash in the same way. Reverse the window sash positions, but without closing either one of them completely. After finishing the windows, paint the sill and the window casing. Use a painting edger to avoid splattering paint on the wall. Lastly, using a razor blade, remove excess paint from the window panes.

REMOVING WALLPAPER

It is feasible to paint over wallpaper, if there is only one firmly bonded, smooth-surfaced layer. The wallpaper must first be sealed with a pigmented shellac. If the wallpaper has an embossed finish, however, the embossing will show through. Textured wallpaper, vinyl, and fabric wallcoverings must be entirely removed. If there are several layers of paper or if the paper is bubbled or loose, it must be removed. Rent a wallpaper steamer, or buy glue-loosening chemicals made especially for wallpaper removal. Both methods will loosen the paper, which must then be removed with a wallpaper scraper. When all the paper is off, scrub the wall with a solution of water and trisodium phosphate (TSP), available at most paint and hardware stores or home centers.

Wallcovering

The term *wallcovering* applies to a number of materials, from traditional papers and vinyl to fabric, grass cloths, and other exotic formats. Wallcovering can bring elegance and distinction to a room and usually requires minimal upkeep. Though not difficult, covering a wall requires patience, skill at matching patterns, and the ability to maintain tight material seams.

If the area to be covered is subject to a lot of wear and tear, a washable and durable covering, such as solid vinyl, is preferred. For areas of moderate wear, such as bedrooms and hallways, vinyl-coated coverings will do well. Low-traffic areas may accommodate more-delicate wallcoverings, such as flock-faced papers, paper-backed foils, or grass cloths, which bring texture to walls.

Some wallcoverings are available prepasted, while others must be pasted as they are applied, sheet by sheet. No matter how it is pasted, the wallcovering must always be applied to a smooth, clean surface. Bumps and uneven areas on the surface of the wall will probably show through, spoiling the appearance of the wallcovering. It is advisable to strip the walls of old wallpaper before applying any new wallcoverings. If the wall isn't sufficiently smooth, first apply a layer of thick wallpaper liner to the wall, which will provide a smooth base for the finish.

Contemporary wallcoverings can provide old-fashioned grace to a room without the messy, old-fashioned pasting techniques.

Wallcovering Basics

Difficulty Level: 🔨🔨

Required Tools:

❏ **Basic Tools: chalk-line box with plumb bob, drywall taping knife, shears, spirit level, straightedge or metal ruler**

❏ **Special Tools: paste brush, pasting table, razor-blade trimming knife, seam roller, smoothing brushes, wallpaper tray**

1 **Plan the project.** Wallpaper is sold in rolls of varying widths, typically comprising 36 square feet of material. After you are done matching seam patterns and trimming off excess, you will most likely hang about 30 square feet per roll, throwing the rest away as scrap. Consequently, to figure out how many rolls of material you will need, first determine the area to be covered in square feet, subtracting openings such as windows, doors, and fireplaces. Divide this total area by 30 square feet. Round the result up to the nearest whole number, adding 15 percent for wastage. This is how many rolls you will need to complete the project.

If you are covering an entire room, chances are you won't be able to match the pattern where the wallcovering job starts and ends. Plan the project so that this meeting place is in the least conspicuous part of the room, such as over a door or in a corner.

2 **Mark a plumb line.** Beginning in a corner, start on the left side if you are right-handed or on the right side if you are left-handed. Measure a horizontal distance equal to the width of the wallcovering, minus ½ inch. Make a plumb line here, from the ceiling to the floor.

Beginning Point

1. The point where you begin and end wallcovering should be in an inconspicuous place, such as over a door, to hide a potential mismatch.

2. Beginning in a corner of the room, measure out a horizontal distance equal to the width of the wallcovering, minus 2 in. Make a plumb line at this point.

3. Rough-cut the wallcovering rolls into measured strips, leaving about 2 in. of allowance at both the top and bottom ends of each strip.

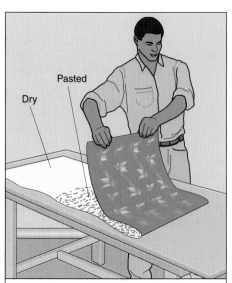

4. Lay a sheet of wallcovering on a pasting table. Brush on the paste, working from the center out toward the edges of the wallcovering.

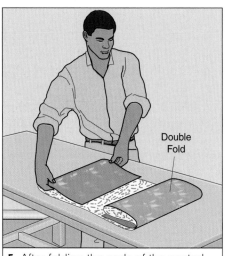

5. After folding the ends of the pasted wallcovering toward the center, fold each end toward the center again, making a double fold, as shown.

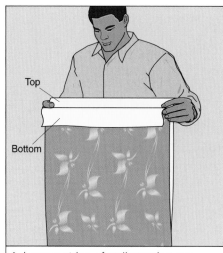

6. Longer strips of wallcovering are much easier to handle when they are folded for transporting, paste side to paste side, as shown above.

flush edge, about half the paper's length. (If the paper is prepasted, just brush on water.) Shift the paper across the table so that the opposite edges of the wallcovering and table become flush, and then paste the other edge. Align the paper with the table edge to prevent paste from getting on the table.

5 **Fold the pasted wallcovering.** Fold the pasted half of the wallcovering over on itself. Loosely roll up the section, pulling the remainder onto the table for pasting. When all of the sheet is pasted, fold it as you did the first section, and then set it aside for a while to allow the paste to soften the paper.

6 **Transport the pasted wallcovering.** Unroll the pasted wallcovering in the same manner that you might unroll a papyrus scroll if you were going to read it. Gently grasp the edges of the wallcovering, where the top and bottom meet, and hold it as shown, with the top corners between your thumb and forefinger and your other fingers supporting the fold and the bottom edge of the wallcovering. This will allow you to position the wallcovering along the ceiling edge as you permit the remainder of the sheet to unfurl.

3 **Cut the wallcovering.** Rough cut the wallcovering about 4 inches longer than the height of the wall. This permits adjusting the sheet up or down a bit to match seam patterns. Use a sharp pair of shears to cut the paper evenly across its width and long enough to leave about 2 inches of overlap at the top and bottom of the wall. Trim off this excess once the wallcovering is on the wall.

4 **Brush on the paste.** Wallcovering paste is available either as

a premixed liquid or as a dry mix to which water must be added at the time of use. Dry mix is more economical, and you need make only the amount you will actually use. If you mix your own paste, manufacturers usually recommend that you mix the paste about 30 minutes before you begin the job. Lay out a precut sheet of wallcovering on the pasting table, with one edge flush to a long edge of the table. Using a pasting brush, paste the wallcovering, brushing from the center outward to the

7 **Position the wallcovering.** Place the top of the wallcovering against the ceiling, leaving a couple of inches of overlap, and shift it into position along the marked plumb line.

8 **Smooth the wrinkles.** Once the sheet is in position, first smooth it out by hand, and then use a wallpaper brush to smooth out the remaining wrinkles. Brushing from the middle of the sheet toward the edges, use the brush to push the wallcovering firmly into the corners, along the ceiling-to-wall edge, above the baseboard, and along door and window casings. Lastly, wipe down the wallcovering with a dampened sponge, to remove excess paste.

9 **Trim the excess material.** After you've brushed out the wallcovering, use a drywall taping knife with a wide blade to push the wallcovering tightly into the joints at the ceiling, baseboard, wall corners, and door and window casings. Then, using the blade as a straightedge, cut along the crease with a trimming knife. Lastly, wipe away the excess wallpaper paste.

10 **Cut around windows and doors.** Hang a full sheet of wallcovering over a window or door, positioning the sheet so that the pattern is properly aligned. Using shears, cut a rough opening 2 inches in from the casing, and then make 45-degree relief cuts out to the casing edge, brushing the wallcovering into place. Score and cut as above.

11 **Hang tight seams.** Position the next sheet along the edge of the first so that the pattern is aligned. Butt the edges of the sheets tightly, neither overlapped nor sepa-

7. Position the first sheet of wallcovering flush with the guideline at your starting point. Leave a 2-in. allowance at the top for adjustment and edge trimming.

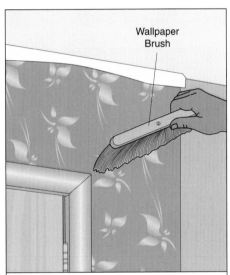

8. Using a wallpaper brush, brush out wrinkles and air bubbles, moving the brush from the center of the sheet toward the outside edges.

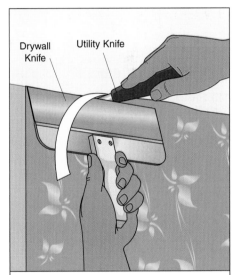

9. Using a drywall knife as your guide, press the wallpaper into place at the ceiling line (or crown molding), and trim off the excess with a utility knife.

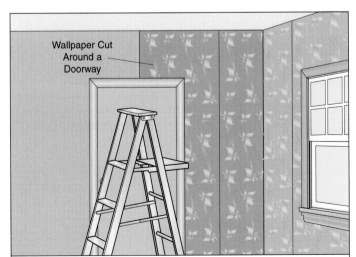

10. Install a full sheet of wallcovering over a door or window, and then rough-cut the opening with scissors, leaving a few inches' allowance to make relief cuts into the corners.

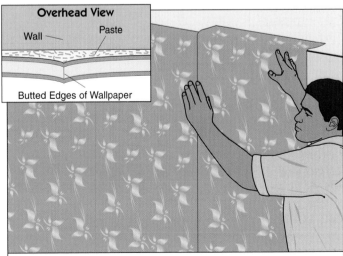

11. Butt adjoining sheets tightly against one another so that the edges of the two pieces create a slight ridge, but do not overlap the sheets or leave a gap between them.

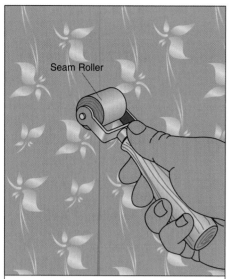

12. Once the seams have shrunk tightly to the wall, use a seam roller to flatten them. However, do not roll wallpaper if it has a raised pattern or texture.

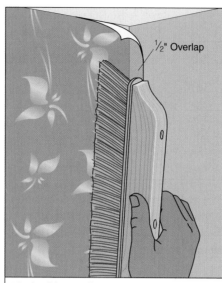

13. Avoid rounding an inside corner with a whole sheet. It will eventually pull away from the corner. Instead, cut the first corner piece with a ½ in. overlap.

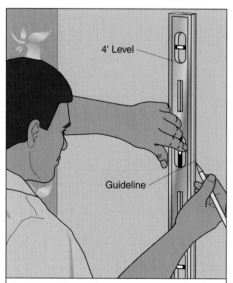

14. You will need to trim a second strip to fit into the corner. Measure the waste of the previous sheet (minus ½ in.) Mark a guideline for this second piece.

15. Install the second sheet in the corner, with one edge flush to the corner and the other at the guideline. Smooth the sheet out, and then trim away the excess.

14 Mark vertical guidelines. Measure the width of the narrow strip of wallcovering that was cut from the last sheet hung. Subtracting ½ inch, transfer this dimension to the uncovered part of the wall corner. Next, using a spirit level, make a vertical line at this dimension point. This guideline will represent the leading edge of the following strip of wallcovering.

15 Hang and trim the adjacent sheets. Hang the second, narrow strip of wallcovering, positioning it against the guideline. Brush out the sheet, smoothing it, and tucking it into the corner edge. Where the second sheet of wallcovering overlaps the one previously hung, cut through both sheets, using a razor-blade trimming knife, making the cut at least ¼ inch in from the trailing edge of the top sheet. After this cut is made, pull back the upper sheet slightly, and then peel out the cut strip of the lower sheet. Brush the top sheet back into place, and then roll the seam, using the roller to push the edges of both sheets toward each other, making a tight joint.

rated, for a professional look. Leave a slight ridge at the joints between sheets. This ridge will shrink as the wallcovering dries.

12 Roll the seams. After the wallcovering paste has begun to dry and the seams have shrunk back to the wall, use a roller to flatten the seams, pressing the edges of the sheets firmly into the paste. Roll one time only, up and down. Repeated rollings may cause a shine to develop along the seams.

13 Fit the corners. Patterned wallcovering must be cut so that the pattern will carry around a corner. Measure from the edge of the last sheet to the corner, at both the top and bottom of the wall. Add ½ inch to the larger measurement; then transfer this to a sheet of wallcovering. Cut it lengthwise, and then hang it along the edge of the previously hung sheet, overlapping the corner with the extra ½ inch, and then brush out the sheet.

Value Tip

- ✦ Add interest to a space by using wallcovering as an accent or for a border, instead of covering entire walls or rooms with the same material.

- ✦ Form a visual "chair-rail" in a room by papering the lower half of the wall and painting the upper half, separating them with a 4-inch border strip.

- ✦ Run a wallpaper border at the ceiling or above a kitchen or bath countertop.

- ✦ Protect walls in high-traffic areas by applying a heavy-weight wallcovering.

- ✦ Use the highest-quality pre-pasted wallcovering you can afford to buy.

Wall Tiling

Ceramic tile is a versatile material that is often used to form dramatic designs on wall surfaces. Ceramic tiles are long-lasting, and they come in a sizable assortment of colors, patterns, shapes, textures, and styles. In a kitchen, tiles can be used as an accent material when applied to a wall behind a countertop. Indeed, they are sometimes substituted for laminates when covering countertops. In a bathroom, few surface materials compare favorably with tile for covering walls. The rich look of tile not only adds value to a home but also provides attractive, easily maintained wall surfaces.

Ceramic tiles are produced in a variety of surface textures. Most tiles, however, can be classified as either *glazed* or *unglazed*. Glazed tile is available with either a matte or a gloss finish. Although usually impervious to staining, glazed tile is vulnerable to scratching. Nevertheless, it is the standard tile used around sinks, bathtubs, and shower stalls. Unglazed tile, produced only in matte finish, is subject to staining from grease and oil but is scratch-resistant. It is commonly selected as a finish for floors. Both types of tile are suitable for most wall applications.

Tiles are also made in a variety of pieces to serve specific purposes. The flat tiles, for example, are called *field* tiles; tiles for finished edges are called *bullnose* tiles; tiles shaped to fit around corners are called r*adius bullnose* tiles; and the tiles at floor-to-wall joints are called *cove base* tiles. Larger dimensioned tiles are usually sold loose while the smaller tiles are often purchased in sheets of tile pre-bonded to a thin webbed backer.

Before installing ceramic tile, be sure the receiving surface is clean, smooth, and structurally sound. Strip all wallcoverings, and repair damaged areas before tiling over older walls. Cement board and plywood are both good backing surfaces for tiling applications, especially in high-moisture areas like bathrooms. First, mark the guidelines for positioning the tile, and then apply adhesive to the surface being tiled. Press the tiles into place. After the adhesive dries, grout the joints.

Setting tile is not particularly difficult, but it does require a high degree of concentration, attention to detail, and a considerable amount of patience. It is also important to shop around. Find a tile store or home-improvement center with knowledgeable salespeople who can give advice and answer your questions. If you're doing a small tiling job or accent tiling, look for discontinued patterns or closeouts. You can sometimes find great bargains, getting beautiful tilework at a substantially reduced cost.

Tile Layout

Difficulty Level: 🔨

Required Tools:

❏ **Basic Tools:** chalk-line box, measuring tape, pencil, plumb bob, spirit level, sponge, water bucket

Lay Out the job. There are, basically, two ways to set wall tile: gradually build up the tiles in a triangular shape, starting from the center of a wall, or apply an entire bottom row, and then work from one corner, stepping tiles up the wall. Before beginning, you must decide whether you want to set tiles with unbroken vertical grout lines (jack-on-jack) or would prefer to stagger the vertical grout lines (running bond). Although the illustrations show a particular setting method, you may apply whichever one that you find to be the most suitable.

1 **Establish guidelines.** Establish a centerline by measuring the wall length and then dividing it in half. Mark this midpoint on the wall. Lay out a course of tiles at the desired grout spacing. Tiles with self-spacing lugs may be butted together. Mark the centerlines of the grout spaces on the wall. The last tile, at either end from the midpoint, should be at least one half-tile wide. If it is less, make a pencil mark at half the width of a tile to the right or left of the midpoint. Use this as a new guideline.

2 **Mark the vertical guideline.** Using a 4-foot long spirit level, mark the vertical guideline at the proper point.

3 **Mark the horizontal guideline.** Place one field tile over a cove base, as shown, allowing for one

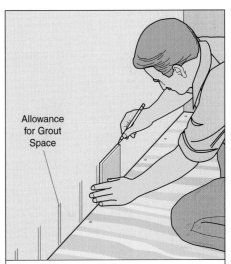

1. Establish a midpoint on the wall, and then lay out a tile pattern, including the grout space. Avoid layouts that require pieces to be cut in less than half width.

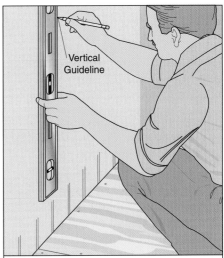

2. Using a 4-ft. spirit level or a chalk-line box with a plumb bob, make a vertical guideline at the centerpoint of your tile layout.

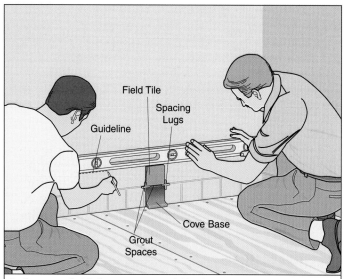

Field Tile

Spacing
Lugs

Guideline

Cove Base

Grout
Spaces

3. Space a field tile one grout width above a cove base. Set a level one grout width above the tile to fix a horizontal guideline.

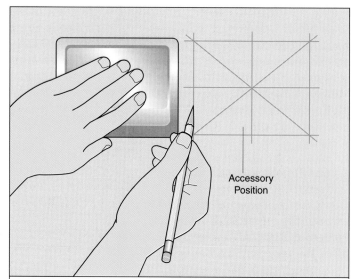

Accessory
Position

4. Determine the place where an accessory will be located, and then mark its position on the wall.

grout space above each tile. (A typical grout space is $\frac{3}{16}$ inch wide.) Exactly where to set your horizontal guideline depends on the dimensional difference between the highest and lowest groutline points determined for the base row of tiles. If this difference is less than $\frac{1}{4}$ inch, mark the highest point; you can make up the difference by varying the size of the grout joints. If the difference is greater than $\frac{1}{4}$ inch, mark the wall at the lowest point. Then use a line level or spirit level to transfer this mark onto all of the walls you are planning to tile. Connect the marks by snapping a chalk line. These lines establish your horizontal guidelines.

If you use the lowest point on the wall to establish the horizontal guideline, you may need to cut one course of tiles so that they align with the established horizontal guideline. This may also be necessary if you are tiling the entire wall and the ceiling joint is uneven. Check this by measuring the height of one tile, plus a grout joint. Mark this dimension incrementally down the wall to the horizontal guideline. The difference between the bottom of the last measured increment and the horizontal guideline is the amount by which the one course of field tiles must be trimmed. It is

best to trim the row just above the base or above a trim course.

As an alternative to having to cut so many tiles, you may prefer to end the tiling halfway up the wall, forming a tile wainscot. In this case, measure the height of one tile, plus a grout joint, and then mark off this height in increments, going from the horizontal guideline up the wall to the height you establish as the top edge of your wainscot. Snap a level chalk line. Remember, if you are tiling a shower surround, the tiles should extend at least one full tile course above the shower head.

4 **Mark accessory positions.** If you are installing a recessed soap dish that will sit flush with the wall, or if you are installing other similar ceramic-tile accessories, establish the position where the accessory will be located, and then mark its outline on the wall. Most tile accessories will have flanges to fit over the adjoining tiles.

Installing Tile

Difficulty Level: 🔨🔨

Required Tools:

❏ **Special Tools:** notched trowel, spacing lugs, tile cutter, tile nippers

1 **Apply tile adhesive.** You can adhere tile to a surface with either a mix-it-yourself cement-based adhesive or a premixed mastic adhesive. The usual way to apply a mastic adhesive is to spread it with the long edge of a notched trowel across the surface to be tiled. The depth of the tile adhesive should be consistent. If you have the right trowel, the proper amount of adhesive should squeeze through the notches as you run the trowel across the surface. Begin at your established guidelines, and then work in an outward direction, leaving the guidelines visible. The adhesive will dry slowly enough to give you time for adjustments, but don't cover so large an area that the adhesive

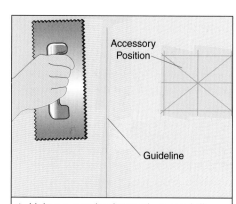

Accessory
Position

Guideline

1. Using a notched trowel, spread tile adhesive across the wall surface. Avoid spreading so much that it begins to dry out before you can apply the tiles.

loses its tackiness before you can get to it. When starting out, cover just a small area, about 4 feet by 4 feet, and be sure that the surface is covered entirely and evenly. As you become more skilled at setting tile you may begin to cover larger areas. Be careful not to spread tile adhesive on areas outlined for tile accessories.

2 **Set the tiles.** Install the course of cove base or other trim tiles along the floor-to-wall joint, lining up the first tile with the vertical guideline and then tipping it into position. Give the tile a slight twist to spread the adhesive beneath it more evenly. Settle the tile half of one grouting space away from the horizontal and vertical lines. If the tiles have lugs along the edges, they should be set even with the guidelines. Set another tile to the other side of the vertical guideline

in the same manner. Again, if the tiles have lugs, they should be butted to the lugs of the previously installed tile. Otherwise, you can position for the grouting space by eye, if you have confidence in doing this, or you may use temporary cross-shaped plastic spacers to keep the tiles one grout joint apart. If these methods don't work well, and the tiles begin to get out of line, you may need to space them with screws or nails driven partially into the substrate.

Use either the triangular or diagonal method described earlier to position tiles. If you lay the tiles carefully along a guideline, their edges will serve as guides for the next row or column of tiles, and so on. Be sure to measure for any tiles that will require cutting, and then set them in place only after all the whole tiles have been installed.

Cutting Tile

Making Straight Cuts. Use a tile cutter to make straight cuts. The tile cutter holds the tile in place while the surface is scored with a cutting wheel mounted on a fixed track. Pull the cutting wheel toward you along the cut line, applying some pressure to cut the surface, and then tip the handle sideways to break the tile along the scored line. Tiles with ridged backing should always be cut in the same direction that the ridges run. The rough-cut edge may be smoothed by rubbing it over a piece of metal lath.

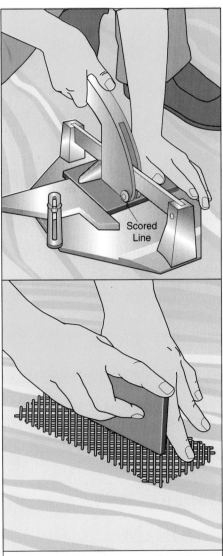

Making Straight Cuts. Use a tile cutter to hold the tile in place while the surface is scored with the cutting wheel. Smooth the rough edges against a scrap of wire lath.

2. Use either a triangular or diagonal pattern to position ceramic wall tiles, carefully keeping to your guidelines.

Making Curved Cuts. To fit tile around curved edges, like shower heads and pipes, you must nip the tile bit by bit with tile nippers. This requires a strong grip and not a little patience, because numerous nips through the very tough tile may have to be made to cut out the necessary shape. Most pipe holes and other areas that you must cut around will most likely be covered later by an escutcheon or flange, concealing the edges of the cut. For this reason, a slightly jagged edge on a nipped piece of tile is of little concern. To fit neatly around pipe holes and other openings, either match together the edges of whole tiles, or cut one tile into two sections that will meet at the centerline of the pipe opening. Nip out a semicircle on mating pieces of tile to fit them snugly around the pipe opening. If a very precise circular cut is needed, you can drill a hole in tile using a carbide-tipped hole saw, cutting from the back of the tile.

Grouting

Difficulty Level:

Required Tools:

❑ <u>Basic Tools:</u> rubber float, sponge and bucket

1 Spread the grout. Mix the grout, and then apply it with a rubber float, spreading it diagonally across the joints between the tiles. Make sure that the grout is packed firmly into every joint.

As soon as the grout becomes firm, use a wet sponge to wipe off excess grout from the tile surface. Shape the grout joints with a softer-than-tile striking tool.

2 Clean the tiles. Wipe the tiles down, and smooth over the tile joints with a damp sponge. Permit a dry haze to form on the tile surface; then polish the tiles with a clean, damp cloth. In most cases, the grout will take several days to set completely.

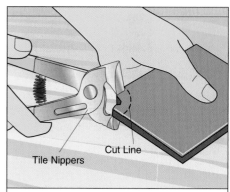

Tile Nippers

Cut Line

Making Curved Cuts. Cutting curves in tile requires nipping the tile bit by bit with tile nippers.

1. Using a rubber float, spread tile grout diagonally across the surface of the tiles. Make sure that the grout is fully packed into every joint, and then wipe off excess grout with a sponge.

2. After the grout has dried, use a clean, damp sponge to wipe down the tile. When a dry haze forms on the surface, polish the tile using a clean dry cloth.

Chapter 10
Floors

The appearance of the flooring in your home is more than a reflection of your taste in decoration; it is also an expression of the value you place on your home. If carpeting appears worn or damaged, if vinyl sheet flooring is yellowed or curling at the edges, or if wood floorboards are in need of refinishing or polishing, then it's time to change the "lived-in" look of your home to one of luxury and comfort.

Repairing or replacing flooring is a simple, sensible, and value-enhancing way to dramatically improve the appearance of your home. In fact, the most difficult aspect of installing new flooring is that of having to select from among the many types of flooring materials available. Each has it's own set of advantages and disadvantages with regard to cost effectiveness, durability, ease of installation, and stylistic variations.

IN THIS CHAPTER

Repairing Floors

Fixing Squeaky Floors 140

Fixing Squeaky Stairs 141

Replacing Damaged
Wood Flooring 142

Refinishing Wood Floors 144

Replacing Flooring

Installing Underlayment 145

Installing New Vinyl Flooring . . .146

Installing Laminate
Flooring 147

Ceramic Tile Flooring

Repairing Ceramic Tile 149

Installing Cement-Board
Underlayment 149

Laying Out Ceramic-
Tile Flooring 150

Installing Ceramic-
Tile Flooring 152

TODAY'S TRENDS

Parquet Wood Tiles

Area Rugs Over Carpeting

Quarry Tiled
Kitchens & Bathrooms

Imported Accent Tiles

Non-slip Surfaces

Repairing Floors

Whether you choose to refinish an existing floor or to install new floor tile, vinyl flooring, or carpeting, it is extremely important that you correct any structural problems first. Repair squeaky, spongy, and water-damaged sub-flooring before attempting to install new flooring.

Fixing Squeaky Floors

Difficulty Level:

Required Tools:

- ❑ **Basic tools:** hammer, mallet, power drill
- ❑ **Special tools:** wood or steel bridging ties, wood screws, wood shims

Normally, squeaky floors don't cause a great deal of concern. To some people, though, a minor squeak can be a major annoyance. Whether or not you are one of these people, fixing a floor squeak is a relatively simple task to perform, and there are a number of different ways to approach the job. The method you choose may be determined by the type of subflooring

you have in your home, as well as its accessibility.

To fix a squeaky floor, you must first find the source of the squeak. Frequently, floor squeaks are caused by two warped boards rocking when stepped on or by badly milled floorboards that have tongues and grooves that don't fit together tightly. Sometimes, the squeak may be caused by subflooring that has separated from joists because of settling or because the joists have dried out and shrunk. Depending on the situation, you may have to shim and/or reinforce the flooring.

To prevent squeaks in the new strip oak flooring being installed above, each piece is machine-nailed at a preset angle into the subfloor below.

Locate a squeak in an accessible floor by having someone walk over the noisy section of the flooring as you listen and observe from below. Look for springy boards, joist movement, or bridging that seems to bend under loading. Be sure to inspect the area around the squeak for structural damage that may require more extensive repair, such as new girders, posts, or bridging.

Shimming Floor Joists. Use wood shims to get rid of squeaks caused by movement between the floor joists and the subflooring. After locating the source of a squeak, gently tap a wood shim or two into the space between the subfloor and the joist below. This will restrict potential board movement. Do not drive the shims too forcefully, however, or they may widen the gap, causing more squeaking elsewhere. Instead, wedge the shims in just tightly enough to fill the space. Glue them in place to eliminate the movement causing the squeak.

Bracing Floor Joists. If the floor squeaking spans a large area, the problem may be caused by a shifting of the floor joist. You can reinforce structural joists laterally by installing wood or steel bridging between joists at 6 to 8 feet on center. You can even install some types of steel bridging without nails, by simply driving pronged ends into the joists. Begin by hammering the straight-pronged end of the bridging into one joist, near the top, and then driving the curled-pronged end into the neighboring joist, near the bottom. Install a second section of steel bridging immediately adjacent to the first but in the reverse direction, so that when they are completely installed, the bridging ties will criss-cross. Brace the remaining joists using the same method. Once firmly braced, the joists will be much less likely to move under the weight of the floor loading.

Board Fastening from Below. When individual floorboards are either loose or protruding, pull them down tight by screwing into them through the subflooring below, if it is accessible. Use round-head wood screws that will reach no farther than ¾ of the way into the finish floorboards. Choose a drill bit with a diameter equal to that of the screw, including the threads. Use the bit to drill a pilot hole through the subfloor and part of the way into the finish floorboard. Place a washer on the screw, and then screw it into the pilot hole. Tighten the screw, letting it bite into and draw down the finish floorboard.

Fixing Squeaky Stairs

Difficulty Level: 🔨

Required Tools:

- ❑ **Basic tools:** chisel, mallet, power drill
- ❑ **Special tools:** wood screws, wooden wedges and blocks

Some people may find squeaky stairs to be charming in an older house. Yet, like squeaky floors, they too can prove annoying, and they too can be just as easily repaired.

Most commonly, squeaky stairs are caused by loose treads rubbing against the risers or stringers. To eliminate this type of problem, first determine how the tread and riser are assembled, and then tighten the joint where the two come together. This may be accomplished by tightening or replacing loose wedging under the stairs, by gluing together

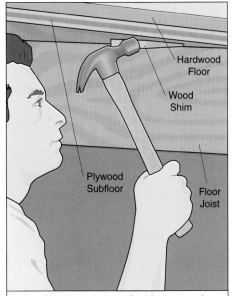
Shimming Floor Joists. A shim tapped and glued between a squeaky floor and the joist below will stop the floor from moving and silence the squeak.

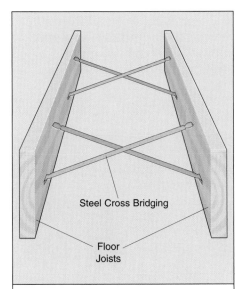
Bracing Floor Joists. Shifting floor joists may cause squeaking over a large area. You can prevent this by installing bridging between the joists at 6 to 8 ft. on center. The criss-cross bridging ties will keep the joists from racking and should eliminate any noise.

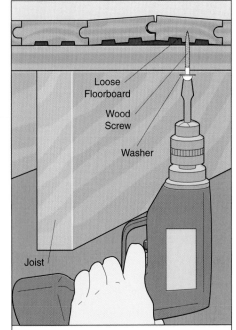
Board Fastening from Below. Fix raised floorboards by pulling them down from below using screws and a power drill.

loose treads and risers, or by reinforcing treads and risers with glued-in-place wooden blocking.

If you find that a tread is rubbing on a stringer or carriage supporting the risers and treads, locate the exact source of the squeak by having someone rock back and forth as they step on each tread. Closely watch the middle and both ends of the tread to determine where the greatest movement occurs. Stairs that are open or accessible from below are easier to fix because you will neither have to open existing walls and ceilings nor have to repair the subsequent damage.

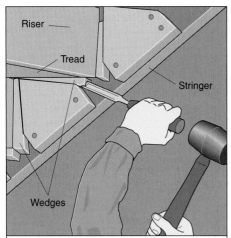

Replacing Loose Wedges. Split an old wooden wedge with a chisel, remove the pieces, clean out any dried glue, and then glue a new wedge tightly into place.

Tightening or Replacing Loose Wedges. In many staircases, the treads and risers are wedged into the stringer housings beneath the stairs. Occasionally, you may eliminate a squeak by simply using a hammer to tap the appropriate wedge(s) tightly back into place. Add glue for a more secure joint. At other times, though, you may find that the wedges cannot be moved because they are already glued in place. In this case, split the old wedge with a chisel, remove it, and clean out the dried glue. Cut a replacement wedge to size, apply wood glue to the housing, and then hammer the new wedge firmly into place—but not so hard that it lifts the stair tread.

Wedging a Loose Tread. If there is quarter-round molding at the back of the tread, remove it. Determine the existing type of tread joint by inserting a knife between the tread and the riser. If the knife goes through, the joint is butted; if it does not, the joint is probably rabbeted. Whittle 1- or 2-inch-long sharply pointed wedges, and then drive them into the gap between the tread and riser at the points shown. Insert them just far enough to eliminate the squeak. To conceal the wedges, cut off their exposed ends with a utility knife, and then add or replace quarter-round molding over the joint.

Gluing Wood Blocks. Working beneath the stairs, apply wood glue to two sides of a 2x2 wood block, and then press the block into the area between the tread and riser that is the source of the squeak. Drill pilot holes, and then drive two 2-inch drywall screws through the glued block into the riser, and one screw up through the glued block into the tread. Add as many blocks as necessary to remove the squeak.

Replacing Damaged Wood Flooring

Difficulty Level: 𝕋 𝕋

Required Tools:

❑ **Basic tools:** chisel (1-in.), finishing nails (8d), framing square, hammer, mallet

❑ **Special tools:** circular saw or handsaw, power drill, pry bar

Before recovering or refinishing a wood floor, it is extremely important to replace water-damaged and worn-out flooring.

The reasons for damage are usually obvious, including burns, food spills, pet stains, marring, cracking, and scratching of wood from the movement of furniture and heavy appliances. If the cause is not immediately obvious, examine

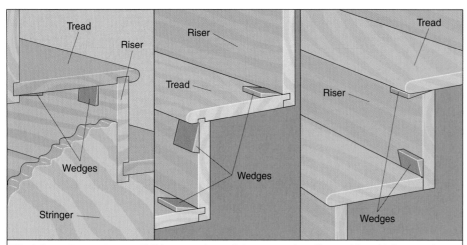

Wedging a Loose Tread. Shifting treads and risers can be silenced by driving wedges into the gaps between them. Gently insert a small wooden wedge, as shown at left, to silence dadoed treads. If the treads are rabbeted, insert the wedges as shown at center. If the treads are butted, use the method shown at right.

Gluing Wood Blocks. Squeaky stairs are usually caused by moving treads. Blocks glued and nailed or screwed behind them may solve the problem.

the entire floor, not just the damaged area. Also inspect the substructure for sagging girders, settling posts, moisture-laden and rotting wood caused by water leaks, or damage caused by wood-boring insects.

When purchasing replacement flooring, bring a sample of the old planks or strips to your lumber supplier so that a close match can be made. Be prepared for the possibility that nothing can be found to closely match your flooring. If this happens, refinish the floor when the new pieces are in place. Flooring constructed of prefinished wood may be somewhat less difficult to match, though over time even these pieces will alter in appearance because of normal wear and tear or the natural aging process.

There are two ways to replace flooring. (They are the same for strip or plank flooring. *Boards* here refers to strips or planks.) The simplest method is to cut out a rectangular area around the damaged boards, but the resulting straight line where old and new flooring meet will be obvious, as well as unsightly. The preferred method of replacing flooring, therefore, is to remove individual boards in a staggered pattern. Although it is somewhat more difficult, this technique will make the repaired section of the flooring much less noticeable.

Drill and pry out bad boards.
Mark the floorboards that you wish to remove. Instead of drawing a straight line across the boards, stagger the cut-lines so that each one will be cut to a different length. Cut the ends with a chisel. Drill a series of

holes, close together, down the center of the board but not into the subfloor. Using the chisel, carefully crack the board into two halves. Pry them up slightly, not enough to damage adjacent boards, and lift them out. Remove the remainder of the damaged boards by cutting their ends and then splitting them out. Set or extract any nails protruding from the remaining boards.

Tap new boards into place.
Cut the replacement flooring to the various lengths required. Using a scrap of flooring as a pounding block, tap a new board into place so that the grooved side will mate with the tongue on the edge of the last original board that remains in place. Next, drill angled pilot holes

for nails through the tongue of the new board. Lastly, anchor the floorboard into place with 8d finishing nails countersunk into the wood.

Install the final board.
To install the final floorboard, remove the lower lip of its grooved side, mate the tongued side with the flooring already in place, and then tap down the other end of the new floorboard. In this instance, drill the pilot holes through the top of the new floorboard, and then carefully nail the board into position using 8d finishing nails. After setting the nails, fill the nailholes with wood putty in a matching color, and then sand and finish the new flooring. (See the following section on refinishing wood floors.)

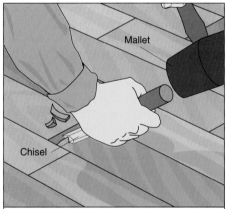

1. Using a hammer and a 1-in. chisel, score a line to mark the sections of the boards that you are removing. Chip the wood toward the damaged area.

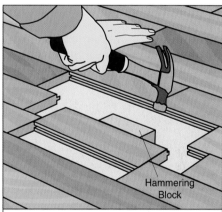

2. Measure and cut the replacement floorboards. Install the first piece by fitting a grooved edge onto the tongue of an original board; then nail it into place.

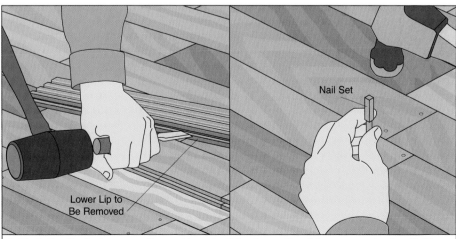

3. To fit the final piece, you'll need to cut off the lower lip of the grooved edge (left). Insert the tongue, and then tap the grooved side in place. Drill pilot holes through the top, and secure the board in place with finishing nails.

Refinishing Wood Floors

Difficulty Level: ⌐⌐

Required Tools:

- ❑ <u>Basic tools:</u> **clean cloth or mop, gloves, natural-bristle brush, pad applicator, scraper**
- ❑ <u>Special tools:</u> **drum and edge sanders, buffer, respirator**

If you decide to refinish your own scuffed, scratched, or worn out floors, follow these three basic steps: (1) sand off the old finish; (2) apply a sealer; and then (3) apply the new top coat. Water-based sealers and finishes are recommended because they emit less odor and tend to dry faster than oil-based products. You must still wear rubber gloves and an organic charcoal respirator to protect yourself against toxic fumes.

To begin, remove heat registers, seal doorways into other rooms, and remove the base shoe moldings. Open windows for ventilation; otherwise, dust will settle everywhere. Wood dust is extremely flammable, so be sure also to turn off pilot lights.

1 **Use a drum sander.** Tilt the sander back so that the drum rises off the floor, and then turn on the motor. When the machine reaches top speed, lower it, letting it pull you slowly forward, parallel to the grain. (On parquet or herringbone patterns, sand at an angle of 45 degrees to the wood grain.) Never let the drum linger too long in one spot, or it will gouge the wood.

When you reach a wall, tilt the sander up, walk it back to where you began, and then shift it 3 or 4 inches over to the side so that the second pass will overlap the first. When the sander becomes ineffective, replace the sandpaper.

2 **Use an edger.** After drum sanding, use an edge sander to reach areas along the wall that could not be reached by the larger machine. Again, work parallel to the grain with a semicircular motion.

3 **Scrape hard-to-reach areas.** Using a scraper, finish areas that you couldn't reach with a power sander. Scrape with the grain where possible, being careful not to gouge the wood. If the scraper becomes dull, sharpen it with a file. After removing most of the old finish, sand the area using a sanding block and 80-grit sandpaper.

4 **Seal the floor.** After vacuuming thoroughly, wipe the floor down with a damp cloth or mop. Allow a day for drying, and then use a natural-bristle brush to seal the floor along walls and in hard-to-reach areas. Brush parallel to the grain of the wood. Seal the remainder of the floor with a tubular-pad applicator. Begin at the wall opposite the door so that you won't inadvertently back yourself into a corner.

5 **Apply the top coat.** Apply a urethane finish by brushing it along the walls, corners, and other hard-to-reach areas. Roll the rest of the floor. Allow it to dry, buff it, and then apply another coat. Allow the final coat to dry for at least one day and buff it again before replacing furnishings or allowing foot traffic.

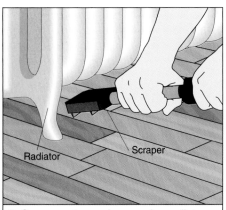

1. Run a drum sander parallel to the wood grain. Make at least three passes, using 60-, 80-, and 120-grit sandpaper.

2. Edge sanding should overlap slightly into the area sanded by the drum sander. Use semi-circular strokes.

3. Some spots, such as under radiators and toe kicks, will have to be done by hand, using a scraper and sandpaper.

4. When applying the finish, align the applicator with the joints between the boards to avoid leaving lap marks.

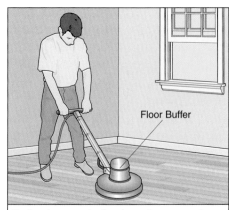

5. Apply a coat of polyurethane, and then buff the floor. Apply and buff additional coats, leaving no air bubbles.

Replacing Flooring

If your home-upgrade plans include new vinyl flooring, for example, you may wish to install new underlayment to prevent irregularities in the old floor surface from showing through the vinyl or to eliminate flexing that could cause the vinyl to loosen or crack.

Typically, ¼-inch lauan plywood is used as underlayment. Be sure, however, that the plywood is rated as an underlayment, that it has no voids in the center plies, and that it has a smooth surface. If the floor to be replaced is subject to moisture, then cement board is recommended as the underlayment. (See page 149.)

Installing Underlayment

Difficulty Level:

Required Tools:

- ❏ **Basic tools:** circular saw, hammer or screw gun, measuring tape, putty knife, 1-in. ring-shank nails or screws
- ❏ **Special materials:** plywood underlayment, wood filler

Value Tip

Overworked Wood

Wood flooring can enhance any home, but if the wood is badly damaged or sanded and refinished too many times, it may be more cost-effective to cover it with new carpeting, vinyl, or ceramic tiling, eliminating the work and expense of removing it.

1 Prepare the floor. The first step in preparing a room for floor replacement is to separate the baseboard molding from the walls. After this has been completed, if your intention is to reinstall the same baseboard, be sure to remove any nails projecting from the molding. Next, measure and cut the underlayment, and then arrange it on the floor to guarantee proper fit.

2 Install the panels. If you have existing subflooring or old vinyl flooring that is in reasonably good condition, then an APA-graded plywood underlayment at least ¼-inch thick can be applied directly over the existing material. However, in any areas that are typically subjected to heavy moisture, such as bathrooms, bear in mind that either an exterior-grade plywood or a cement board underlayment should be used.

Install the underlayment panels perpendicular to the lengthwise joints in the subfloor material. Screw or nail the panels into the subflooring at 8 inches on center across the field of each panel and 6 inches on center around the perimeter, at ⅜ inch in from the edges. Leave about ¹⁄₃₂-inch clearance between panels and ⅛-inch clearance between the panels and the walls.

3 Fill and sand the seams. The underlayment surface must be level, smooth, and free of any irregularities. Small bumps will invariably show through the finish floor, ruining an otherwise perfect installation. Dents, holes, or gaps greater than ¹⁄₁₆ inch should be filled with wood filler and sanded smooth.

Value Tip

Carpeting

If you are installing new carpeting, install the best underlayment padding available, as well as the highest grade of carpeting you can afford. This will not only guarantee a feeling of softness beneath your feet but also protect your investment for years to come by reducing wear and tear on the carpeting.

1. Remove the base and shoe moldings for later reinstallation, after pulling out any protruding nails. Next, measure and carefully cut the underlayment.

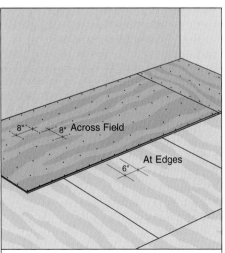

8" | 8" Across Field
At Edges
6"

2. Install the underlayment over the existing material or subfloor so that the underlayment joints do not coincide with any of the joints in the subflooring.

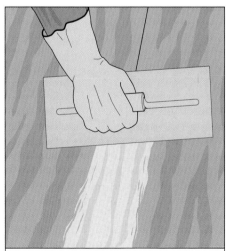

3. Imperfections in the underlayment and all gaps at seams should be filled with a wood filler. Sand these areas until they are level and smooth.

Installing New Vinyl Flooring

Difficulty Level: 🔨

Required Tools:

❑ **Basic tools:** framing square, hammer and nails, utility knife

❑ **Special tools:** linoleum roller, solvent, threshold reducers

Vinyl flooring is commonly used to cover kitchen and bathroom floors. The range of patterns and colors available is seemingly endless. It is also an economical and relatively easy way to rejuvenate dated-looking rooms without extensive remodeling. Although the cost per square yard of vinyl flooring increases with the thickness and quality of the finish, it is typically more economical to choose a vinyl flooring of midgrade quality in a well-known brand name. Cheaper, thinner grades of vinyl will have less durable finishes and will not hold up to heavy traffic. If you shop for discounts and end-of-roll remnants, you may find some remarkably good bargains. Look for vinyls that may be installed with a perimeter adhesive.

Vinyl flooring usually comes in rolls 6 or 12 feet wide. If you are covering a room less than 12 feet wide, you should have little trouble doing the work yourself. But if your layout will require several angle cuts and seams, it might be more sensible for you to do the under-layment yourself, and then hire a professional to do the final flooring application. Very often, seaming and cutting can be problematic, and hiring a professional in the first place is likely to be much less expensive than having to replace ruined vinyl sheet flooring.

1 **Trim outside corners.** Trim excess vinyl away from the out-side corners by cutting the vinyl straight down the joint where it meets and laps the corner on the wall. Beginning at the top edge, cut the vinyl down to the floor.

Installing New Vinyl Flooring. Old flooring in high-traffic areas may look worn and dirty. Brighten the room with new vinyl.

2 **Trim the inside corners.** Trim vinyl for an inside corner by cutting away the excess flooring with progressively descending

diagonal cuts on each side of the corner joint. Gradually, these cuts will produce a wide enough split for the flooring to lie flat at the corner.

3 **Trim the wall-to-floor joint.** Where excess vinyl flooring curls up at a wall-to-floor joint, press the vinyl down tightly into the joint, using a 2x4 about 2 feet long, until a sharp crease develops. Place a metal straightedge into this crease, and then cut along the straightedge using a utility knife. Leave a ⅛-inch gap between the wall and the vinyl edge so that the flooring can expand without buckling.

4 **Cut the flooring at jambs.** The best way to make vinyl flooring abut a door jamb is to cut the curled-up edge of the flooring to match the profile of the door jamb. Make vertical cuts down to the floor, and then cut the resulting strips along the creases created by forcing the strips tightly against the jamb and the floor.

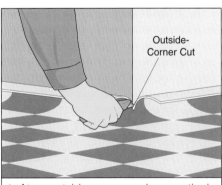

1. At an outside corner, make a vertical slit through the excess flooring using a utility knife.

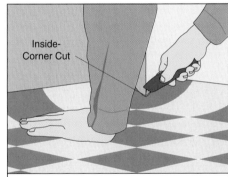

2. At an inside corner, make a V- or U-shaped cut, with the point of the cut ending at the floor.

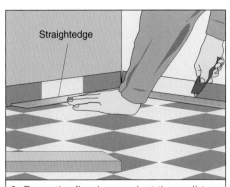

3. Press the flooring against the wall-to-floor joint using a 2x4. Trim the excess using a straightedge as your guide.

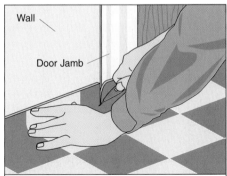

4. Make vertical cuts for a jamb protru-sion the same width as the door jamb, and then cut the strip at the floor crease.

5 Complete the work. Using a solvent approved by the vinyl manufacturer, clean away any adhesive residue remaining on the flooring material. Next, using a linoleum roller, press the flooring down firmly into the adhesive. Finally, replace the base molding, and then cover the exposed edges in doorways with wood or metal threshold reducers.

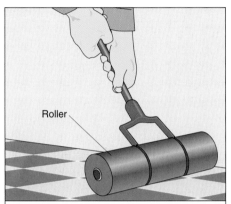

Roller

5. To complete the work, clean up excess adhesive, roll out the air bubbles, and then add threshold strips as needed.

Installing Laminate Flooring

Difficulty Level: 𝕋

Required Tools:

- ❏ **Basic tools:** carpenter's glue, duct tape, handsaw, rubber mallet, utility knife

- ❏ **Required materials:** foam underlayment, 6-mil polyethylene vapor barrier

Laminate flooring—both wood and non-wood—has rapidly become a popular alternative for homeowners. Wood laminates, for example, provide the warmth and beauty of wood flooring without the difficulty of sanding and finishing. Laminate flooring is usually installed as a floating floor system over a ⅛-inch thick layer of high-density foam underlayment. The tongue-and-groove joints are fastened with glue instead of nails. Because laminate flooring *floats*, it may be directly installed where standard wood flooring would require extensive preparation, such as over pre-existing vinyl or concrete floors.

Laminate wood flooring is easy to install, requiring no nailing and much less preparation than hardwood flooring. Its relative economy also makes it a good value.

SPECIAL SITUATIONS

Pro Tip

Thresholds. To finish a doorway where floors meet at different levels, install a saddle, or *threshold*, face-nailing it into the subflooring. Some thresholds, called *reducer strips*, are made so that one side will fit over the tongue of the adjoining board. Also, the strip can be butted to meet boards that run perpendicular to the doorway.

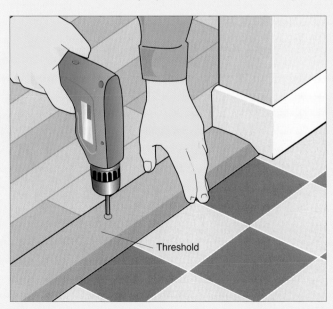

Threshold

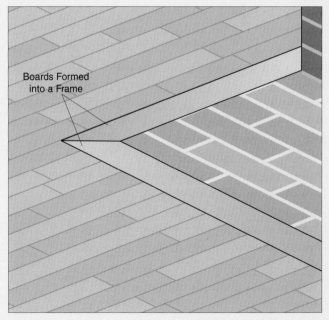

Boards Formed into a Frame

Framing Borders. To create a professional look at odd junctures, such as at fireplace hearths, use a miter box to cut boards at a 45-degree angle to make a framed border. Remove the tongues from boards that run perpendicular to the flooring or that must be butted against hearthstones.

Laminate flooring is manufactured in strips 2 to 4 inches wide or in planks up to 10 inches wide. It may be applied over almost any level sub-flooring that is smooth and dry.

The cost of laminate flooring is relatively competitive with other types of flooring. However, as is true of the other types, variations in price depend upon product quality and local economic conditions.

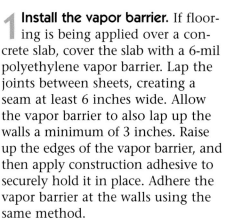

1. Install a 6-mil polyethylene vapor bar-rier over concrete subfloors to keep moisture away from finish flooring.

2. Roll out the foam underlayment, emplace it with butted joints, and then seal the joints with waterproof tape.

4. Join planks by running beads of glue along the lower lip of the grooved edges and tapping the planks gently together.

1 **Install the vapor barrier.** If floor-ing is being applied over a con-crete slab, cover the slab with a 6-mil polyethylene vapor barrier. Lap the joints between sheets, creating a seam at least 6 inches wide. Allow the vapor barrier to also lap up the walls a minimum of 3 inches. Raise up the edges of the vapor barrier, and then apply construction adhesive to securely hold it in place. Adhere the vapor barrier at the walls using the same method.

2 **Install the foam underlayment.** Roll out the foam underlay-ment, then cut it to fit the room. Butt the joints and seal them with duct tape.

3 **Install the laminate flooring.** Begin the flooring installation at one of the longer walls in the room, facing the tongue edge of the plank away from the wall. Leave a ½-inch wide expansion joint around the perimeter of the room.

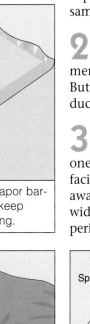
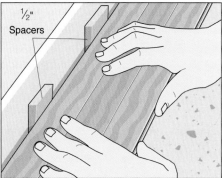

3. Install the laminate flooring with the groove facing toward the wall. Use ½-in. wood shims to set a uniform joint.

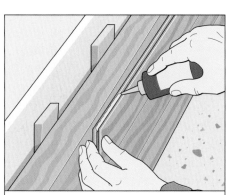

5. Use a rubber mallet against a scrap piece of flooring to tap the laminate planks together tightly before the glue sets.

4 **Join the planks.** Try to work in plank-runs that extend the full-length of a room. To join adjacent planks, run a bead of carpenter's glue along the lower lip of a grooved edge, on one of the planks, and then insert it into place against the tongue of the adjoining plank.

5 **Complete the work.** Knock the installed plank sections together tightly by tapping a rubber mallet against a scrap piece of flooring used as a hammering block. For odd-shaped areas, create a card-board template to mark the lami-nate planks, and then cut and install them.

Ceramic Tile Flooring

Ceramic tiles are often viewed as an expression of luxury, imparting the richness of color and texture to a residential space. From a pragmatic view, however, tile may also be used in spaces, such as bathrooms and kitchens, to provide a durable, water-resistant surface. For these reasons, ceramic tile is a desirable feature in a home. Clearly, if you have a slightly damaged tile floor, it is probably worthwhile to consider the value that would be added to your home by a simple, inexpensive tile repair.

Ceramic tiles add richness of texture as well as color to a room. Add painted or glazed tiles for special accenting.

Repairing Ceramic Tile

Difficulty Level: 🔨

Required Tools:

❏ **Basic tools:** cold chisel, hammer, putty knife, scraper

❏ **Special tools & materials:** glass cutter, grout, replacement tiles, sealer, tile adhesive

A number of cracked or broken tiles in one area may indicate some type of underlying structural problem. If this appears to be the case, remove all of the tiles. Install a rigid cement-board underlayment, and then set the new tiles in place.

If only a few tiles are cracked or broken, carefully dislodge and replace the ones that are damaged.

1 Remove the damaged tiles. Scrape away the grout around damaged tiles. If the tiles are glazed, score them across their surface with a glass cutter. They will then break apart quite easily. Wearing safety glasses, use a hammer and a cold chisel to break the tiles into small pieces. Working from the center of each one, chip them out. Be careful not to damage adjoining tiles.

2 Replace the tile. Using a putty knife, scrape dried adhesive off the substrate. Spread fresh adhesive on the back of the new tiles, and into the empty tile space. Press the new tiles into position, and then grout and seal them. (See page 154.)

Installing Cement-Board Underlayment

Difficulty Level: 🔨

Required Tools:

❏ **Basic tools:** construction adhesive, 4-ft. straightedge or framing square, 1½-in.

coated cement-board screws, power drill, utility knife

❏ **Special tools & materials:** fiberglass mesh drywall tape, notched trowel, power drill with carbide-tipped drill bit, saber saw with a tungsten-carbide blade or keyhole saw

The success or failure of any floor-tile application will depend almost entirely on the type and quality of the subsurface material to which the tiles will be adhered. An appropriate type of backer board or underlayment is an absolute necessity for some types of flooring, and it is especially recommended for ceramic tile flooring. A high-quality underlayment will provide protection against impact loads, as well as a smooth tiling surface. Cement-board underlayment, in particular, not only provides a tile base that is smooth and level but one that is also waterproof.

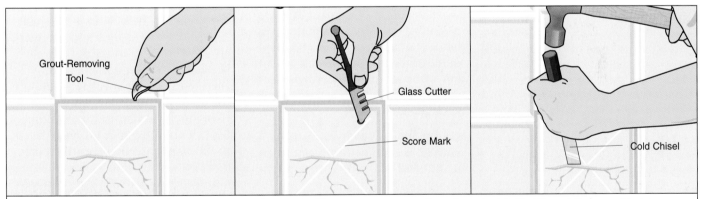

1. To remove a damaged tile, first scrape away the grout with a can opener or other sharp tool (left). Glazed tiles need to be scored with a glass cutter (center). You can then easily knock out the tile using a cold chisel and a hammer (right).

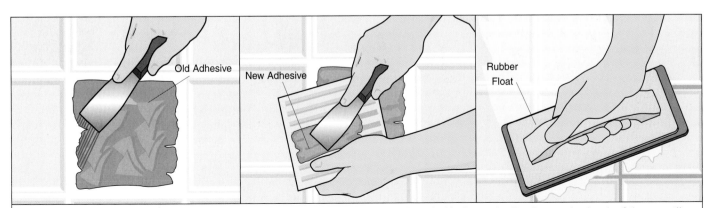

2. Use a putty knife to scrape away the remaining dried adhesive from the floor (left). Spread adhesive on the back of the new tile and on the floor (center), and then press the tile gently into place (right). Grout and seal the tile to finish the work.

1 Cut the cement board. Mark your cut lines directly onto the cement board. Using a straightedge as a guide, score a 1/16- to 1/8-inch deep groove along the line with a utility knife. Insert a length of lumber (2x4) under the cut line, and then press down on the panel to snap it apart. Use a utility knife to cut through the reinforcing mesh, and then separate the pieces. To cut openings for waste and supply pipes, use a saber saw with a tungsten-carbide blade or a hole saw.

2 Set the cement board. Using a notched trowel, apply thin-set adhesive to the substrate on which the first sheet of underlayment will

be located. Next, set the cement board into the adhesive with the smooth side down.

3 Fasten and tape the boards. Drill pilot holes 4 inches on center at the perimeter edges and 8 to 12 inches on center across the field of the cement board. Using a drill or screw gun, drive backer-board screws (non-corrosive, Phillips-head screws) into each pre-drilled hole, fastening the board in place. Cover all cement-board joints with fiberglass-mesh drywall tape. Simply cut, and then press the adhesive-backed tape into position.

Laying Out Ceramic-Tile Flooring

Installing a tile floor correctly takes a great deal of patience and planning, but it is a fairly easy way to upgrade the appearance of a kitchen or bathroom. Furthermore, if you search for discontinued lines, colors, or styles, you may realize significant savings, increasing the return on your investment. Tile suppliers are also a good source of technical information, and they often sell professional-grade tools that will make your tiling job much less difficult.

Making Scale Drawings. A scale drawing is a tremendous aid in laying out and estimating the amount

of material required for a tiling project. To begin with, measure the overall dimensions of the floor to be tiled, and then draw the space to scale on graph paper. Be sure to indicate the location of entryways and to add built-in cabinets and other permanent fixtures to your drawing. Note the dimensions of the tile itself, including the width of one full grout joint. This dimension is the base unit of measurement that you will use to plan the tile layout and to estimate the amount of tile needed.

If you are using square tiles, plan the drawing so that each square on the graph paper represents one tile plus its grout joint. If the tile is rectangular, have one square represent the smaller dimension, and have two squares represent the longer dimension. You may also lay down a pattern of two or more tiles to each vertical or horizontal dimension in order to create larger squares or other shapes.

Odd-Shaped Tiles. Non-rectangular tiles, such as hexagons and octagons, are more difficult to lay out. However, because they are generally sold by the square foot, it is easy to compute the quantity needed. For an accurate estimate, lay out a few tiles on the floor, including space for grout joints, to determine how many full and partial tiles fill a square of an arbitrary area. Divide the room by this area, and then calculate the number of squares it would take to cover the room. Multiply the number of squares by the number of tiles needed to fill each square and add 15 percent extra.

Base Drawing and Overlays. Using the base unit of area measurement determined earlier, construct a scale drawing of the room to be tiled, including openings and built-in fixtures. On a tracing-paper overlay, draw the proposed tile design. Use as many overlay sheets as are necessary to establish a satisfactory layout pattern. Use colored pencils to help you visualize the finished floor pattern.

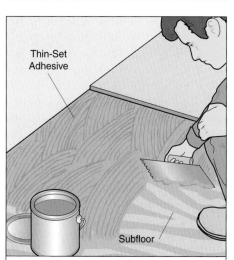

1. Use a straightedge or framing square to guide your utility knife along the cut-line. Then snap the panel along the line.

2. Using a notched trowel, apply a layer of adhesive to one board at a time, and then set the board in place.

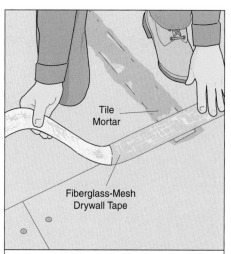

3. Cover all the joints with fiberglass dry-wall tape, and then *spackle* them with tile mortar spread with a drywall knife.

Adjusting the Layout. Almost certainly, some tiles will need to be cut. Using your base drawing, determine where the cut tiles will occur. Plan the tile layout so that a row of tiles that is less than half the width of a full tile will not end up in a conspicuous location, such as in a doorway.

Principles of good layout dictate that cut tiles be equal to at least half the width of a full tile. Cut tiles at opposite sides of a room should also be equal in width, providing a symmetrical layout. Try, also, to center tiles across wide openings, such as archways, or beneath focal points, such as pic-

ture windows and fireplaces, particularly for larger tile sizes. If the tiles extend into an adjacent room, make an effort to lay out the floor tiles in both of the rooms so that the grout joints will be aligned in the connecting passageway.

Snapping Guidelines. If the room to be tiled is relatively square, snap a chalk line lengthwise down the center of the room, and then snap another across the width. The chalk lines should intersect in the center of the room. Check the intersection with a framing square to be sure that it forms a 90-degree angle. These lines will be used for positioning the tile layout.

Beginning at the intersection, either dry-lay a row of tiles along each layout line or use a layout stick to determine where any cut tiles will occur. Make a note of what the cut tile dimensions will be, making sure to include the width of grout joints when positioning the tiles. If a row of partial tiles along one wall is less than half of one tile width, reposition the tiling so that the cut row will be at least one-half of one tile

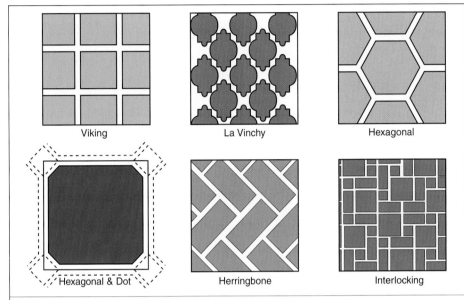

Viking   La Vinchy   Hexagonal

Hexagonal & Dot   Herringbone   Interlocking

Odd-Shaped Tiles. Non-rectangular shapes are more difficult to lay out and to estimate. Determine how many tiles fill a given area, and divide the room by this area.

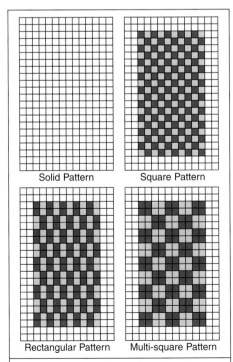

Solid Pattern   Square Pattern

Rectangular Pattern   Multi-square Pattern

Making Scale Drawings. A variety of patterns may be laid down with square tiles to create larger squares or other shapes.

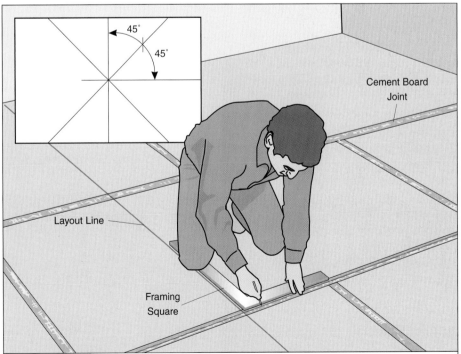

45°
45°

Cement Board Joint

Layout Line

Framing Square

Snapping Guidelines. Snap chalk lines parallel to each wall if you are installing tiles in a square or rectangular pattern layout. Verify that all of the perpendicular lines form 90-deg. angles by using a framing square to check them.

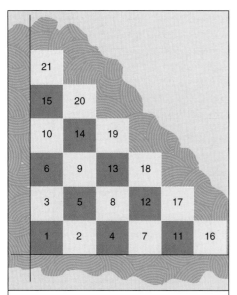

Jack-on-Jack. Install tiles in a jack-on-jack pattern as shown above.

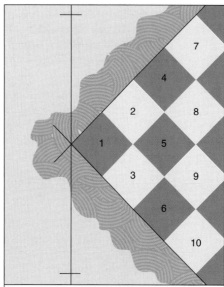

Diagonal Jack-on-Jack. Snap 45-deg. chalk lines and install tiles as shown.

Lay down subsequent tiles to each side of the first tile, alternating from side to side until you reach the side walls. Continue in this manner with a second horizontal row of tiles, either above or below the first row, staggering the tiles by one-half the tile width at the beginning of each additional course.

Installing Ceramic-Tile Flooring

Difficulty Level: 🔨🔨

Required Tools:

❑ **Basic tools:** glass or tile cutter, jointing tool, layout stick, notched trowel, plywood or particleboard sheet, rubber float, rubber mallet, sponge

❑ **Special materials:** grout, tile adhesive, tile beater (homemade), tile sealer

Before setting tiles you should lay them out in a dry run. For a large room, lay a single row of tiles along each guideline, all the way to the walls. Use spacers or a layout stick that includes the width of the grout joints to dry-lay the tiles. The dry run will check the accuracy of layout lines so that all tiles will be positioned properly, and so that all cut tiles at walls will be at least one-half of one tile width. For rooms of modest size, dry-lay all of the tiles to determine how well they fit together, and then do any necessary tile cutting before the final installa-

width or wider. If the layout results in a narrower row of tiles, you can sometimes make grout joints a bit wider to eliminate that row. The alternative would be to reposition the layout lines entirely. Likewise, if the last row of tiles against a wall is almost the full width of a tile, you can make grout joints a bit narrower, to fit a full row of tiles into that space. Working from the center of the room, dry-lay the tiles on the floor, one quadrant at a time.

There are a variety of sequential patterns from which to choose when laying out floor tiles, including jack-on-jack, diagonal jack-on-jack, and horizontal running-bond.

Jack-on-Jack. Lay out tiling in a jack-on-jack pattern by beginning where the vertical and horizontal guidelines intersect, choosing a quadrant, and then laying down diagonal rows of tile all the way into the corner of the selected room quadrant. Do the same with each of the remaining three quadrants, frequently checking the straightness of tile and grout lines with a framing square.

Diagonal Jack-on-Jack. In a diagonal jack-on-jack layout, cut tiles will always end up against the walls. Ideally, these cut tiles would be perfect diagonal half-tiles. More

often, however, if you extend diagonal tiles all the way to the walls, you will end up with only tile fragments at the perimeter of the room. For this reason, diagonal patterns usually look best when they are framed by a border of square tiles. Install tiles in a diagonal jack-on-jack pattern by drawing new guidelines at a 45-degree angle to the original vertical and horizontal guidelines. Using the new guidelines, lay down diagonal rows of tile in the same manner as before, this time working toward the side walls instead of the corners.

Horizontal Running Bond. Lay out tile in a running bond pattern by centering the first tile on the vertical guideline while using the horizontal guideline as the baseline.

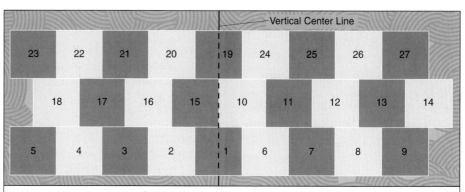

Horizontal Running Bond. Center the first tile on a vertical guideline while using a horizontal guideline as a base. Lay subsequent tiles as shown above.

1. Using a notched trowel, spread adhesive over a small area of the floor. Be certain not to cover your guidelines.

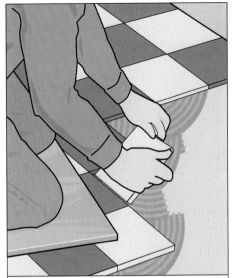

2. Set each tile in place by aligning one edge and then dropping it into position. Avoid sliding the tile across the adhesive.

Bedding Block

3. Place a bedding block over a section of the floor, and then, using a rubber mallet, pound uniformly across its surface.

tion. Be certain to key each dry-laid tile to its precise location on the floor, assigning it a number, and then recording the number both on the back of the tile and on the floor. Dry-laying tiles is an effective way to see variations in the color and texture of certain kinds of tiles before they are permanently set in place, making it possible to blend the varied tiles in an inconspicuous manner.

1 **Spread the adhesive.** After you snap the lines for your layout, you're ready to start spreading adhesive. Be careful not to spread too much on the floor at once. Tile only one small area at a time so that the adhesive will not set before tiles are in position. The amount of area that can be tiled at one time depends on both the *working time* of the adhesive and on the speed of the tile setter. Begin by covering 1 square yard of floor at a time and then progressing to larger areas as you gain more experience. Consult the tile manufacturer's literature for the suggested method of tile installation. Also, use the size and type of trowel recommended to apply tile adhesive. Some adhesives are applied at an angle to the tile, while others are spread in overlapping arcs. Be certain not to cover your guidelines

with adhesive. If you have used wood battens to align the tiles, keep adhesive a safe distance away from them. For thick tiles or for tiles with deep ridges on the back, apply adhesive both to the back side of the tile and to the floor.

2 **Set the full tiles.** After applying the tile adhesive, press each tile into position, twisting it slightly to bed it firmly. Don't allow the tiles to slide against each other, because this will cause excess adhesive to accumulate in the grout joints. Examine tile alignment frequently, using a straightedge or framing square. If tiles are a bit out of line, wiggle them on the setting bed until they are properly aligned. If it is necessary to walk on tiles that are already positioned, then set a sheet of plywood or particleboard over them, to distribute the load evenly.

CAUTION: When working with organic adhesives and other volatile or toxic materials, provide adequate ventilation, wear gloves, and use a respirator.

3 **Embed the tiles.** Wrap a 24-inch length of 2x4 lumber with scrap carpeting or other soft material to make a *bedding block*. Place the bedding block over a section of floor tile, and then pound uniformly

across its surface, using a rubber mallet, to level and firmly embed the tiles in the adhesive. Slide the bedding block across the floor until you've pounded the entire floor surface, continuing to level and embed the tile as you proceed. Check tiles frequently with a straightedge to be sure that they are all level. If the surface of one tile should fall below the surface of adjoining tiles, remove it, add more adhesive, and then reset it.

4 **Cut the tiles.** After you've set all the full tiles in place, cut the partial tiles that go around the perimeter of the room. Unless you plan to install either a cove base or a border band of trim, the cut tiles will abut the wall, leaving only a narrow expansion joint between the wall and the tiles. However, if you install trim tile, the space between the last row of full-size tiles and the trim band must be filled in with a row of partial tiles cut to fill the gap. To mark a tile for cutting, take two loose tiles, designated A and B, and then place tile A directly on top of the last full tile preceding the space to be filled. Place tile B on top of tile A, and then slide tile B up to the wall. Using the edge of tile B as a guide, scribe a pencil line on the surface of tile A. The exposed portion of tile A is the piece that you will cut and install. Before cutting this piece, however, be certain that you measure back from the cut line the full width of two grout joints. Mark a new line at this location. This will be the actual cut line. This method may also be used for cutting L-shaped tiles at the outside corners and for fitting partial tiles in between full tiles and either a cove base or a trim band.

5 Grout the tiles. Be sure to provide at least 24 to 48 hours of curing time for the tile adhesive prior to grouting the tile joints. Carefully read the adhesive manufacturer's literature to see whether there is a particular curing time that is recommended. When it is time to do the grouting, make sure that all of the tile joints are cleared of dust and debris, and that you have removed all of the tile spacers.

To prevent grout from staining the tile surfaces, protect them with a sealer. Be certain that the sealer is fully cured before applying the grout. Do not use grout to fill in the joint between the last row of floor tiles and the wall. Instead, use flexible silicone caulking, which will form an expansion joint. Mix the grout in accordance with the manufacturer's recommendations.

Using a rubber float or a squeegee, spread the grout diagonally across the tile joints, packing the grout firmly into each joint.

As it begins to set, use a wet sponge to wipe any excess grout from the face of the flooring tiles.

Shape grout joints with a jointing tool or a handy substitute, such as a toothbrush handle or spoon. Clean the tiles one more time, and

then smooth the joints using a damp sponge. Permit a dull *haze* to develop on the surface of the tiles. When the haze is completely dry, polish the tiles with a clean, damp cloth.

Sealing. If the tile or grout joints require a finish sealer, apply the sealer to the tile and grout joints in strict compliance with the manufacturer's recommendations. Two or more weeks of curing time are usually required prior to applying sealer to grout. When it is the proper time for sealing, be certain that the floor tile is clean and dry. Begin by applying sealer at the corner farthest from the door. Using a foam rubber paint roller or a sponge, spread a thin, even coat of sealer over the tile. Wipe off any excess sealer as you proceed, in order to prevent possible discoloration of the tile.

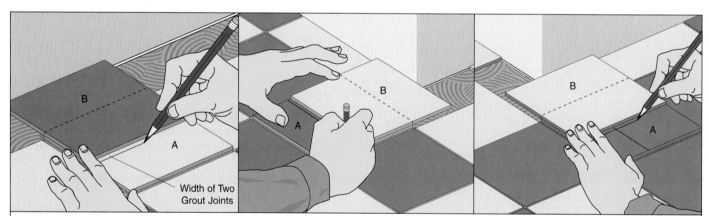

4. To cut tiles along a wall (left), slide the top one against the wall and score the one beneath—this will become the tile that abuts the wall. To cut around a corner, set one tile atop another at one side of the corner (center), and mark that dimension; then shift these two tiles into position on the other side of the corner (right) to mark the other cut line.

5. Use a rubber float to spread grout between the tiles. Move in a direction diagonally across the tile joints (left.) Next, wipe excess grout from the face of the tile with a wet sponge (center.) Lastly, shape the grout joints with a jointing tool (right), and then apply a sealer when the grout has thoroughly dried.

Chapter 11
Architectural Woodwork

Architectural woodwork is usually associated with the wealthiest of homes. Wood moldings, seemingly "molded" of plaster, were originally designed to mimic the stonework found on ancient Greek and Roman temples. Today they are often used to unify the interiors of fine homes. The purpose of woodwork, however, is more than purely decorative. Aside from paneling and edging, moldings also serve to protect and conceal. Chair rails protect plaster and gypsum wallboard from chipping and marring. Base moldings not only protect walls but hide irregularities and joint gaps. Whatever the purpose, the richness of architectural wood moldings will enhance the value of even the simplest of homes.

IN THIS CHAPTER

Architectural Woodwork

Decorative Style 156

Tooling Up 157

Door & Window Casings

Casing a Door 157

Casing a Window 158

Floor & Ceiling Trim

Installing Base Trim 159

Coping Inside Corners 160

Crown Moldings 160

Laying Out
Crown Moldings 160

Installing Crown Moldings 161

Wainscoting

Installing Simple
Wainscoting 163

Creating Elaborate
Wainscoting 164

TODAY'S TRENDS

Classical-style moldings

Corner and plinth blocks

Intricate jamb reveals

Panel moldings

Decorative molding on
door fronts

Architectural Woodwork

Decorative Style

Before settling on a style of decorative trim, first investigate the appropriateness of various trim styles and sub-elements readily available within your regional marketplace. Although special moldings can be obtained or made to order, custom millwork can be prohibitively expensive. Decorative trim is commonly sold by the linear foot, in lengths ranging from 6 to 14 feet. Ideally, you should plan to buy trim in sizes that will span the length of an entire wall, even though it is possible to bevel-splice, or scarf, shorter pieces together. When shopping for decorative trim, take note that many profiles are available in either clear or fingerjointed stock.

Today, home centers carry oak, pine, and even extruded polyurethane moldings in a broad range of profiles for a variety of specific applications. Polyurethane moldings are becoming a popular, inexpensive alternative to wood. They usually come preprimed and ready to paint.

If your intention is to use a wood stain or a clear finish, you will need clear stock. Finger-jointed stock is less expensive because it's made from shorter pieces spliced together. Because these splices are visible, this type of trim is intended only for painted finishes.

> **Pro Tip**
>
> ## PAINTING WOODWORK
>
> Save time and obtain better results by priming and painting woodwork before installation. If you stack trim on sawhorses, you can paint enough for an entire room in less time than it would take to paint already installed moldings. To prevent moisture absorption and warping, also prime the back of the trim. Fill in nailholes with wood filler, and then touch-up the filler with a small foam brush.

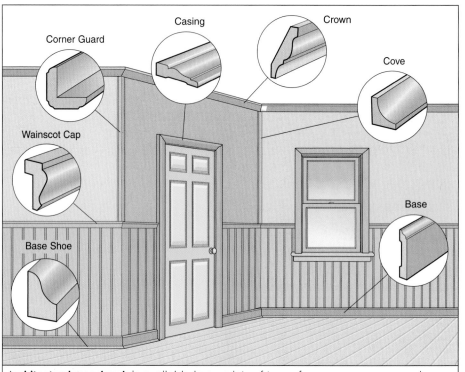

Architectural woodwork is available in a variety of types for use as corner guards, door and window trim, base and crown moldings, chair rails, and wainscoting.

Tooling Up

Aside from standard carpentry tools, one special tool worth acquiring is a power miter saw. If this tool is too expensive for you to purchase, you can rent one. A power miter saw is, simply, a portable circular saw attached to an L-shaped metal table with a pivot mount. Miter saws can be rotated to the right or left for cuts at angles of 45 to 90 degrees. A *compound* miter saw can even be tilted to make beveled miter cuts as well. Furnished with a carbide finish blade, there is no tool that can make a crisper, cleaner cut with a more consistent degree of precision in virtually any type of molding.

Few miter saws have high enough fences to adequately support extra-wide trim sizes. To raise the fence height of a miter saw, clamp a taller piece of wood to either fence. For cutting crown molding, consider adding a wooden stop to position the molding correctly as you make the cut.

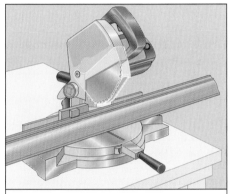

A power miter saw is used to make mitered and beveled cuts in decorative trim, quickly and accurately.

Door and Window Casings

Casing a Door

The architectural trim that surrounds an interior door or window is called a *casing*. Casings are used decoratively to set doors and windows off from an adjoining wall. They are also used to anchor door and window frames to a wall and to conceal the gaps between the frame and the finished wall. Casings add value to a home by improving its appearance and by bringing warmth and richness to the interior space.

Door casings add the quality of natural woods to a decorating motif, blending well with virtually any color scheme.

Difficulty Level: 🔨 🔨

Required Tools:

- ❑ **Basic tools: combination square, file, hammer, handsaw, measuring tape, nail set, nails, pencil, spirit level**

- ❑ **Special tools: block plane, miter saw or backsaw and miter box**

1 Set reveals. The inside edge of the casing should be offset from the inside edge of the jambs by approximately $\frac{3}{16}$ inch. The small edge caused by offsetting the two is called a *reveal*. Set a combination square for $\frac{3}{16}$ inch, and use it to

1. You may use a combination square to guide your pencil when laying out the inside edge of a reveal. Set the depth of the reveal to $\frac{3}{16}$ in.

Pro Tip — CUTTING ARCHITECTURAL TRIMWORK

Whether using a miter box (below, left) or power miter saw to cut trimwork, the best method for making a cut of any kind is to slowly *inch up* on the layout mark. First, cut slightly outside the reference mark, and then readjust the saw setting to shave the line. Test-fit the trim piece before installing it, and if the joint doesn't come together properly, shave the back end using a block plane. Coped joints can be fitted better by chiseling or filing (below, right.)

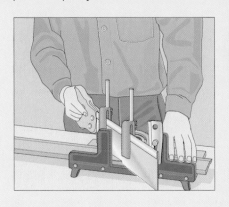

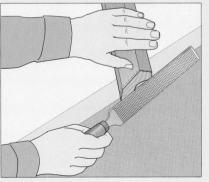

guide your pencil around the jamb, leaving a line ³⁄₁₆ inch out from the jamb edge.

2 Miter the casings. Cut a length of casing square at one end. Place the casing against the reveal line, mark it at the point where the vertical and horizontal reveal lines intersect, and cut a 45-degree angle at this point. Nail the side casing to the jamb with 4d casing nails spaced 12 inches on center. Cut a 45-degree angle on another piece of casing, and then fit it at the head of the doorway. Mark the head casing for the opposite 45-degree miter at the opposite jamb. Cut and install the head casing.

3 Complete the trim. Square-cut the bottom end of the other jamb casing, hold it along the reveal line on the jamb, and mark it even with the bottom of the head casing. Make the 45-degree miter cut, check the fit, and then make necessary adjustments. Nail the second jamb casing in place. Using a nail set and a lightweight hammer, set the nails just below the surface of the wood, and then fill the nailholes with wood putty. When the putty is dry, sand it smooth.

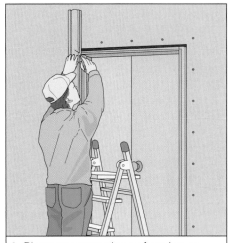

2. Place an uncut piece of casing at your reveal line, with the trim edge flush at the line. Mark the casing at the inside corner, and cut it at a 45-deg. angle.

3. Nail the casing in place. Set the finishing nails below the surface of the casing using a nail set. Fill the holes with wood putty, and sand them smooth.

Casing a Window

As with doors, window casings are used for both decorative purposes and the concealment of joints. Like those for exterior doors, however, window casings also serve to seal out the outside air. Although you may select varying styles, window casing is usually chosen to match the trim around interior doorways.

A *stool* is often placed along the bottom edge of a window opening, to deepen the sill and give it a more traditional appearance. You should install the stool first, followed by the jamb and the head casings. Windows without stools are said to be *picture-framed*, with four lengths of casing *mitered* at the corners. *Square-edged* trim may be butt-joined. In this case, base blocks (plinths) and corner blocks (rosettes) may be used as

decorative elements and to make neat transitions within corners. Windows with stools may be similarly trimmed at the jambs and the head. At the sill, an *apron* is usually installed, lastly, beneath the stool. Each end of the apron may be coped, returned, or cut square. Occasionally, jamb extensions may be required to bring a window jamb flush with adjoining wall surfaces before you place the casings.

$ Value Tip

Trim Accessories

Consider adding plinth and corner blocks to door and window casings. These relatively inexpensive elements add a decorative flourish to wall openings, bringing depth and richness to an interior space.

Casing a Window. The casing around windows generally matches the style of the casing around the interior doorways, except for the stool and apron at the sill.

Floor and Ceiling Trim

Installing Base Trim

Difficulty Level: 🔨

Required Tools:

- ❑ **Basic tools:** file, hammer, nail set, nails, measuring tape, pencil, spirit level

- ❑ **Special tools:** block plane, miter saw or backsaw and miter box

1 Cut the baseboards. Rough-cut baseboards to the right length; then place them in position around the perimeter of the room. Using a measuring tape, mark the rough-cut sections for more precise cutting.

2 Miter the baseboards. Beginning at an outside corner, place a section of baseboard in a miter box, right-side up, and make the appropriate cut. To cut outside corners, angle the saw 45 degrees so that the front face of the baseboard will be longer than the rear face. When cutting inside corners, angle the saw 45 degrees so that the back will be longer than the front face. Fit the piece against the base of the wall, tack it in place temporarily, and then cut the adjoining piece.

3 Install the baseboards. Working your way around the room, cut and then tack each piece of baseboard in place. Using pairs of 8d finishing nails 16 inches on center, fasten the baseboard to the studs and the sole plate. Hammer in the nails just far enough to hold the baseboard in place so that it will not be damaged if you need to remove the nails to adjust its position. After all the base molding is properly fitted in place, hammer the nails completely in, and then set them using a nail set.

Joining Sections of Baseboard. Base trim can usually be purchased in sizes long enough to span the length of wall. However, in rooms

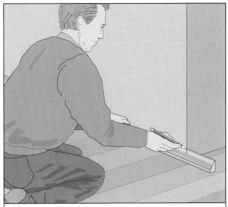

1. Cut baseboard to rough sections, and set them into position. Fitting outside corners first, mark the true cuts carefully.

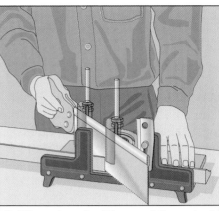

2. Miter-cut each of the carefully marked sections using a power miter saw or a backsaw with a miter box.

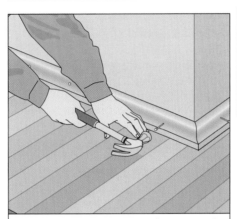

3. Nail baseboards with 8d finishing nails at 16 in. on center, one nail into the wall stud and one nail into the sole plate.

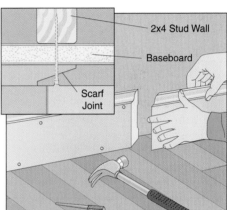

2x4 Stud Wall

Baseboard

Scarf Joint

Joining Sections of Baseboard. Longer baseboards may be formed by joining shorter sections with a scarf joint.

Pro Tip

INSTALLING BASE SHOE MOLDINGS

Where base trim and door casings form a butt joint, set a base shoe molding in place against the baseboard. Mark it with a guideline extending 45 degrees out and away from the joint. Using this guideline, bevel the end of the base shoe molding with a block plane. Using 4d finishing nails, attach the base shoe molding to the baseboard, but do not nail it into the floorboards. (Hardwoods should be predrilled.)

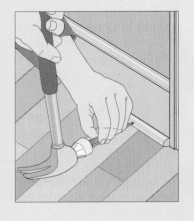

with particularly long walls, you may have to splice sections end to end. To do this, place the sections being spliced right-side up and face forward in a miter box. Allow the joining ends to overlap enough so that you can make a 45-degree cut through both sections of base trim at the same time. This will create a smooth splice that can be fastened together using only one nail. Ideally these joints should be planned to line up over wall studs to make a stronger nailing connection.

Coping Inside Corners

Difficulty Level: 🔩

Required Tools:

❑ **Basic tools: coping saw, rasp**

1 Bevel the ends. Rather than mitering an inside corner, an experienced carpenter will often shape one section of baseboard trim to fit the contours of another, creating a tight joint that won't shrink or open. This type of joint is called a coped joint. To cope a joint, first cut one baseboard section with a squared end that butts into the adjacent wall, and then cut the adjoining baseboard section with a 45 degree beveled end so that the rear face will be longer than the front face.

2 Cope the ends. Place the square-ended board perpendicular to the front face of the beveled board. Trace the profile of the square-ended board onto the beveled board. Using a coping saw, back-cut the beveled end slightly along the curve of the trace line. The resulting shape will fit neatly over the face of the abutting baseboard. Adjust the fit by trimming or rasping the rear edge of the coped board, forming a seamless joint.

Crown Moldings

Crown moldings are commonly used both for concealment and for decoration. Milled from a variety of wood species, they are available in standard as well as custom shapes and lengths. Their top edges may sometimes be rabbeted, forming a reveal to hide irregularities in the ceiling-to-wall joint. Because crown moldings are also cut with narrow cross sections, ceiling irregularities are further hidden by the angle of the installed trim to the wall and ceiling surfaces. Installing crown molding is considerably more complicated than installing other types of decorative molding. Nevertheless, it is a good way to add worth to a home, and one that is well within the ability of the average homeowner.

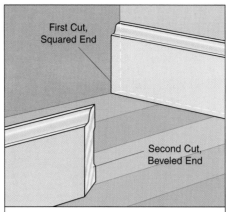

1. To create a coped joint at an inside corner, square the first piece against the wall. Then bevel-cut the second piece.

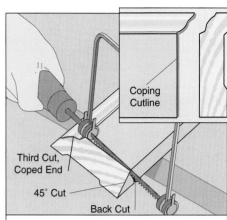

2. Outline the contour of the molding's profile with a pencil. Then cut along the line with a coping saw. Rasp as needed.

The most critical step in applying crown molding is marking the molding's depth on the wall. Once you have successfully accomplished this, simply cut the molding to fit the layout. You will need an assistant to hold one end of the molding while you fit the other end into place.

Value Tip

Built-up Cornices

Combine various base, crown, and cove moldings to create an elaborate cornice that is both imaginative and tasteful. Use the pattern throughout your home to establish a unique architectural element having the appearance of being professionally designed.

A built-up cornice can add a decorative flourish to an interior space. It also serves to hide imperfections at the ceiling.

Laying Out Crown Moldings

Difficulty Level: 🔩🔩

Required Tools:

❑ **Basic tools: chalk-line box, hammer, measuring tape, nail set, nails, pencil**

❑ **Special tools: framing square, line level**

1 Establish the molding depth. Use a framing square to represent the vertical and horizontal planes of the wall and the ceiling. Holding a piece of crown molding, as shown, determine how far below the ceiling its bottom edge will rest on the wall. This dimension is termed the *molding depth*.

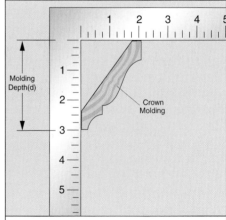

1. A framing square may be used as a corner to establish the vertical depth of the crown molding.

2 **Mark the guidelines.** Measure the height from floor to ceiling at various points in the room to determine the location of the low point. Mark a reference line below this point, at a distance equal to the molding depth.

Measure the distance from the floor to the molding-depth reference line using a line level. Extend this reference line around the perimeter of the room, and then snap a new chalk line at this height.

3 **Install the molding.** Line up the bottom edge of the molding on the chalked reference line. Nail the top edge directly into the ceiling joists or blocking and the bottom edge to the top plate or the wall

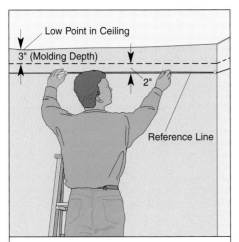

2. Find the low point along the ceiling, and measure down from here to establish the molding depth reference line.

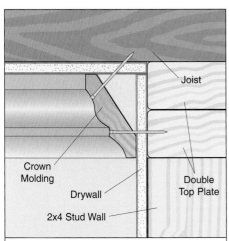

3. Nail in the molding, with the top nail going into the ceiling joists and the bottom nail going into the top plate.

stud. Fill any gaps between the wall and the crown molding with drywall compound or caulk. If the ceiling is very uneven, install the molding parallel to the ceiling rather than parallel to the guidelines.

Cutting Crown Molding. Unlike window casings or base moldings, crown moldings cannot be cut flat against an edge of a miter box. Crowns must be held at the exact angle at which they will be applied. To do this, draw a mark on the miter box (or fence, if you're using a power miter saw), indicating the molding depth. Clamp a wooden stop to the back fence at the molding depth. Set the edge of the molding against the stop, and then cut. If you're cutting an inside or outside miter joint, set the bottom edge of the molding against the stop with the face toward you. For a coped inside joint, the back will be longer than the front. Use a coping saw to cut along the profile line created by the cut. If you are making an outside joint, then the front face will be longer than the back. Be aware that corner joints seldom meet at exactly 90 degrees. Cut some short test sections of molding at a 45-degree angle. Before you cut a section of molding, apply the test sections for fit, and then adjust the angle of their cuts until you get the proper fit. Make the cuts slightly long so you can fit the joints as described in "Cutting Architectural Trimwork," on page 157.

Installing Crown Moldings

Difficulty Level: 🔧🔧

Required Tools:

☐ **Basic tools: coping saw, hammer, handsaw, measuring tape, nail set, nails, pencil, power drill, rasp, stud finder**

☐ **Special tools: miter saw or backsaw with miter box**

1 **Install the first section.** If the molding-depth line is 2¼ inches

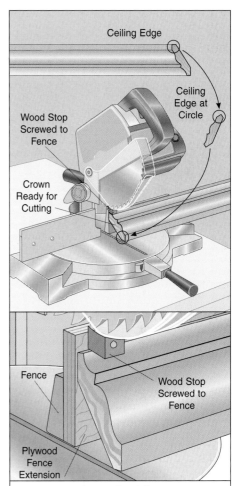

Cutting Crown Molding. Miter cut crown molding using a miter saw with a wood stop attached. If the molding is too deep to be nailed to the top plate alone, locate and mark the studs ahead of time, and add nails at the stud line.

or less below the ceiling height, nail the crown molding into the top plate, if it is deep enough. If the molding is so deep that it misses the top plate, install blocking behind the molding, or fasten the trim to the wall studs. Where you must find studs, use an electronic stud finder or probe with a hammer and a 6d finishing nail. Set the probe holes above the molding depth on the wall so that the crown molding will cover them when it is installed. Mark the stud locations on the wall surface with small pencil lines just below the molding-depth line.

After measuring the wall, square-cut both ends of a section of molding so that it fits snugly from one wall to the opposite wall. Rest the bottom edge of the molding on temporary nails along the layout line. Drill pilot holes, and then nail the crown into the studs or top plate.

2 Cope the corner section of molding. Place a section of molding upside down in a miter box with its face toward you and the ceiling edge placed against the bottom of the miter box. Miter-cut the end at a 45-degree angle so that the back edge of the molding will be longer than the front edge. Using a coping saw, back-cut along the profile line created by the miter cut. The profile line of the coped section of molding forms an edge that will butt and contour to the profile of the square cut edge of molding already in place.

Butt the coped section of molding against the section already installed to test-fit it. Using a rasp or file, trim the back side of the molding, as required, to make a cleaner, tighter-fitting joint.

3 Cut the other end of the coped molding. If the other end of the coped molding will be on an inside corner, simply cut it with a square edge to butt against the opposite wall, and then cope the next piece of crown molding to contour-fit against it. If the other end will be on an outside corner, hold the molding in position against the outside corner, and then make a guideline on the back face of the molding. Next, place the marked molding in a miter box with its front face toward you and with the top edge of the molding resting on the saw table. Miter-cut the end at a 45-degree angle so that the face of the molding will be longer than the back. Tack the section of molding in place using 8d finishing nails. Do not set the nails. You may yet need to adjust the molding so that the next section will fit properly in place.

4 Complete the work. After all the crown molding is tacked in place, go back and do the finish nailing. Hammer an 8d nail into each stud or at 16 inches on center

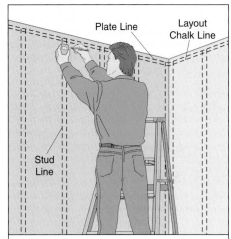
1. Use a stud finder to locate studs. Mark their location just below the depth-of-molding line for later nailing.

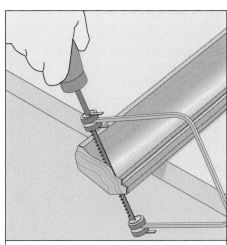
2. Bevel-cut an end at a 45° angle. Use a coping saw to back cut along the profile line created by the bevel cut.

3. Hold the crown molding at an outside corner, and then mark a guideline on the back edge for mitering.

4. When all the crown molding is tacked into place, do the finish nailing. Set the nails, and then putty the holes.

into the top plate. Set the nails, and then fill the holes with putty. At outside corners, drill pilot holes through the molding, and then join the top edges of the miter together with 4d finishing nails.

Blocking Note: If the studs or the top plate are difficult to locate, leaving you with nothing solid to nail into, then use construction adhesive. Tack the molding into place and allow the adhesive to set. If there is only one top plate, install wood blocking at the wall-to-ceiling joint in one of the two ways shown, and then nail and glue the crown molding to the blocking. The blocking may consist of either solid wood or plywood strips.

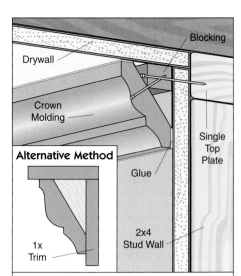
Blocking. If there is only one top plate, then install blocking at the wall-to-ceiling joint or nail the crown into the wall studs.

Wainscoting

Wainscoting consists of decorative and protective wood paneling applied to the lower portion of a wall. Although there is no set rule governing wainscoting height, a wainscot with panels 32 to 36 inches high (representing the height of a typical chair rail, which is often used to cap wainscoting) is customary for a room with a standard 8-foot ceiling height. A wainscot of this height creates a division of the wall surface that is visually balanced and well proportioned.

In planning your project, there are three important rules to remember: (1) Plan your project so that the wainscoting will complement the decor of your home and tie spaces together thematically. Balance is sometimes achieved by carrying wainscoting through adjoining rooms or hallways. (2) Select colors carefully. Lighter colors tend to make rooms appear larger, while darker colors sometimes deaden a room and make it look smaller. (3) Plan your layout so that vertical elements line up with window and door trim and meet symmetrically in corners. Make a scaled drawing to guarantee the desired end result.

An inexpensive way to create a wainscot is to use standard 4x8 wood panels cut into three equal sections about 32 inches high and 48 inches wide. Panel sections may easily be glued and nailed to an existing wall, and the addition of baseboard, base shoe, and corner and cap moldings will add a look of elegance.

Installing Simple Wainscoting

Difficulty Level: 🕇

Required Tools:

❏ **Basic tools:** caulking gun and adhesive, chalk-line box, circular saw, 4-ft. straight-edge, measuring tape, hammer, nail set, nails, level, power drill and drill bit for predrilling nailholes, pry bar, stud finder

❏ **Special tools:** drywall saw or saber saw, keyhole saw, miter saw, wire shields, electrical box extenders

1 Establish a reference line. The first step is to lay out a reference line the length of the wall, 32 inches from the floor. Mark the wall 32 inches above the floor every 3 feet, and use a 4-foot level to draw a continuous reference line from wall to wall.

2 Cutting panels. Remove existing baseboard and shoe molding using a pry bar—you don't want to damage the wallboard too much; a block of wood between the wallboard and pry bar will usually prevent this. If you expose the studs, mark their location on the wall above the wainscot height so that you will know where to nail the panels later.

Cut each 8-foot length of wood paneling into 32x48-inch sections. Use a straightedge or jig to keep the panel cuts straight. Before you install the panels, you'll also need to cut out sections for electrical boxes and phone jacks. A quick way to mark where to cut is to coat the rim of receptacle boxes with chalk or lipstick, put the panel in place, and press it so that it contacts the box. An outline will transfer to the back of the panel. Drill a hole in one corner, and then cut along the outline using a keyhole saw or an electric saber saw.

When moving a box farther than you've got wiring for, turn the existing outlet into a junction box: Splice in the same-size wire, and run it through holes drilled in the studs 1¼ inches from the face, or notch the studs and protect the wire with metal plates designed for that purpose. If you need to relocate an electrical box, cut a section out of

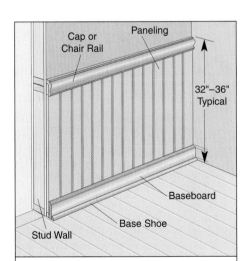

Wainscoting. Various wood moldings and panels may be combined to create a balanced division of wall space with the resulting wainscot design.

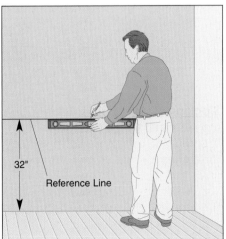

1. Lay out a reference line on the wall, customarily at about 32 in. above the floor. Use a spirit level to extend this line around the room.

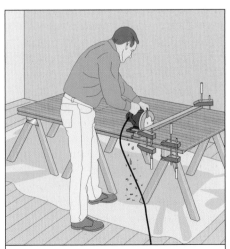

2. Simple yet effective wainscoting may be created with lengths of wood paneling cut into three 32x48-in. sections. Cover the joints with vertical boards.

the wallboard at the new location. Don't worry about cutting access channels in the wallboard—it will be covered up by the wainscoting.

Leave about 12 inches of wire extending from the new boxes. You can trim the excess wire when you wire the receptacles. If you don't feel confident moving the wiring, consult an electrician or electrical inspector. If you're lucky and you don't need to move any receptacles, you will probably still need to use UL-listed box extenders equal to the thickness of the paneling.

3 **Attach the paneling.** Using a caulking gun and panel adhesive, run three or four beads of caulk from the floor to the reference line on each panel section. Press each panel into place, and then nail the corners and midsection with 4d finishing nails nailed into the studs at 16 inches on center vertically.

If your panel cuts are jagged and don't butt together neatly, you can add a 2- or 3-inch cover strip (stile) to hide the joints, creating an attractive sectioned look.

Other extras you may add are a chair rail, base, and bed molding to create a transition from the top rail to the chair rail.

Fancy wainscoting creates a look of elegance and refinement.

Creating Elaborate Wainscoting

You can easily increase the elegance, as well as the value, of wainscoting by selecting richly contrasting exotic woods, more ambitious designs, or additional layers of moldings. Where you draw the line depends upon your budget, aesthetic sensitivity, and skill level. Panels can be made from solid wood, plywood, or sheetrock. Stiles and railings can be solid wood, veneered wood, or plywood.

Consider mitering and installing overlay molding inside the stiles to create a shadowbox effect. Fancy molding or quarter round may be used to create a look of elegance and refinement.

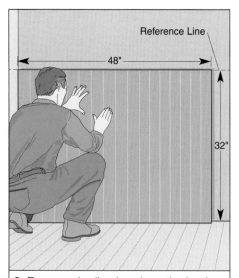

3. Run panel adhesive along the back surface of each panel section, and then press them into place. Nail the panels into the studs with 4d finishing nails.

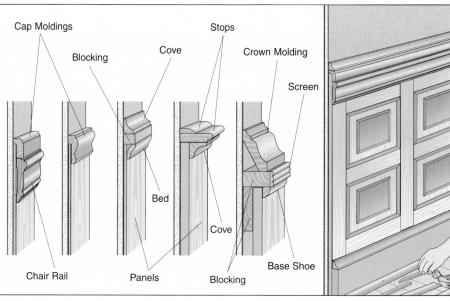

Elaborate wainscoting may be developed by combining different types of architectural trimwork with exotic wood veneers in imaginative and contrasting patterns.

Chapter 12
Investment Benefits

Generally, we place a high premium on our possessions; we worship our automobiles, covet designer clothes, pay homage to stock portfolios, and lavish our income on the latest technology. But how much attention do we pay to the one investment that yields us the greatest potential for personal satisfaction and financial gain—our home?

Can we really afford to be so blasé? It may not matter if we plan on living in one place forever, but "forever" now averages less than six years. Jobs change, people change. You never know when you may need to move. It's a smart idea to be prepared—not only to know but to influence what your choices may be. In the long run, it pays to treat your home as the valuable investment it is.

IN THIS CHAPTER

Your Home as an Investment 166

Renting or Selling

Making the Down Payment 167

To Be or Not to Be
a Landlord 167

Short-Term or
Long-Term Investing 167

Selling Your Home

Determining Fair Market Value ..167

Selling without a Broker 168

Advertising Your Home 168

Types of Real
Estate Agencies 170

Renting Your Home

Your Home as a
Rental Property 171

Protective Interiors 171

Protective Exteriors 171

Finding Tenants 172

TODAY'S TRENDS

Owning to Rent

Selling to Trade Up

Selling to Trade Down
at Retirement

Your Home as an Investment

Of all the investments made in life, perhaps the most far-reaching in importance, and the most emotionally stressful, is the investment made in one's home.

Most of life's purchases, like last year's car model, seem to depreciate in value faster than you can finish paying for them. But a house is different. You not only expect your home to appreciate in value, you depend upon it.

Unfortunately, nothing is guaranteed in life. Markets fluctuate, neighborhoods change. Possibly the most important decisions you can make with regard to your home are the ones concerning how best to protect your investment. Certainly, the first decision, and commitment, you must make is to ensure that your home is well maintained so that it will hold its value. But sometimes, this alone is not enough. Somewhere down the line you may intend to sell your home and retire to a less-expensive or more-temperate region. Or perhaps you may choose to use your home as an income property by renting or leasing it to someone else. In either case, you may ask yourself, "How can I protect and increase the value of my house?"

Though there are no guarantees in economics, just as there are no guarantees in life, there are certain things you, as a homeowner, can do to hedge your bets. As mentioned earlier, home maintenance is absolutely fundamental. Much of the book has addressed this issue. But another, equally significant means of adding value to a home is that of home improvement.

Remodeling a home offers no assurance of added value. But as any Realtor or home remodeler will tell you, if planned with utmost care

Home-Improvement Cost vs. Value Recovered

Project	Cost Return*
Minor Kitchen Remodel	94%
Bathroom Addition	89%
Major Kitchen Remodel	87%
Family-Room Addition	84%
Two-Story Addition	84%
Attic Bedroom	83%
Master Suite	82%
Bathroom Remodel	73%
Siding Replacement	71%
Deck Addition	70%
Window Replacement	68%
Home Office	64%

*National average return on investment one (1) year after project completion.

Source: The 1998–1999 Cost vs. Value Report from the Nov. 1998 issue of *Remodeling* magazine ©Hanley-Wood, Inc.

and critical attention to regional building trends and market characteristics, nothing can add value to a home more effectively than the *right* remodeling project.

But which remodeling project is the right one? And will it pay off in the long run? These are the hard questions to answer, and some might respond that only you know what is right for you. This may be true, but only if you plan on living in the same house forever. If you plan on selling or renting, you had better develop a strategy for putting the odds in your favor. What does your home need most to make it appealing to a likely buyer or tenant? Don't underestimate the value of painstaking research. Use every resource at your disposal: the local library, newspapers, magazines, architects, builders, realtors, interior designers, mortgage bankers, school administrators, even your neighbors. Consult anyone who can offer you a fresh perspective on which type of project will be likely to generate the greatest return on your investment.

The chart at left serves only as a starting point, but it will give you a snapshot view of how some average remodeling projects, according to a national survey, are currently adding value to homes.

The remainder of this chapter focuses on developing strategies for either selling or renting a home for financial gain. Beyond that, the hard work is yours to do.

Renting or Selling?

Decisions, decisions! Should you rent your home? Or should you sell it? Sometimes the answers to one set of questions will come by first finding the answers to another. Specifically, there are three sets of questions that you should answer before you decide whether to rent or to sell your house.

Making the Down Payment

If you need to come up with a down payment on a second home before you can sell the first, can you take out a second mortgage or refinance your mortgage for an amount large enough to get you safely into your next residence? Or will rental income be enough to cover the new mortgage payment? If either one of these two questions can be answered in the affirmative, you have the option of selling or renting. Before making the final decision, however, you should probably sit down with a reputable mortgage lender and carefully review the numbers to ensure that they are correct.

To Be or Not to Be a Landlord

Do you think you have the necessary skills and temperament to be a landlord? Renting or leasing can be an effective means of generating income, but it requires considerable skill, time, and commitment. Are you willing to deal with tenant complaints on weekends or in the middle of the night? Do you have the skill and time to do necessary repairs and maintenance? Or will you have to hire construction contractors? Will you have the nerve to collect late rents or to evict troublesome tenants through court appearances? Or will you have to rely on expensive property managers and attorneys? You must answer these questions carefully and honestly, thinking twice before taking on the demanding responsibilities of being a landlord.

Short-Term or Long-Term Investing

Are you seeking a long-term investment? Or are you hoping for a quick return on your money? Many people have made quick profits, even in volatile real estate markets. Probably a greater number, however, have lost money because of bad timing at the difficult-to-recognize end of an economic boom, when property values often plummet drastically. Real estate investing is not a scheme for getting rich quickly. It is a risky business, even for professional investors. It is easy for an amateur to wait too long to sell a property or to buy high and then get stuck in an economic downturn. Whether renting or selling, real estate is best thought of as a long-term investment. Most properties will, eventually, appreciate in value.

Selling Your Home

Ultimately, if you decide to sell your home, it is important to be aware of the way homes are sold in today's real estate market. Today, most home sales are contingent upon an inspection by a professional architect or certified home inspector. Buyers are better educated than ever before, and they know value when they see it. You can be sure they will comparison-shop, and if your home comes up short, you may be the loser. To get an acceptable offer for your home, it must be in top condition and priced competitively for the market in which it is selling.

Determining Fair Market Value

The first step in determining a fair asking price for your house is to do some market research. Find out how much similar homes have recently sold for in your area. Contact a realtor for this information. Your local Multiple Listing Service (MLS) lists all home sales, as well as homes currently for sale. This list is computer generated, and it can be easily printed out. If the selling price of similar homes is close to the amount you hope to get for your house, then you know that your established price is fair. If not, then you must adjust accordingly. Another strategy is to look through similarly priced houses for sale in your region. As you examine them, note their advantages and disadvantages in relation to your own home. Assess the comparative pluses and minuses, and gauge your asking price accordingly.

Value Tip

Setting the Stage for Selling Your Home

Buying a home is an emotionally charged experience, and first impressions count for almost everything. Every detail becomes important, so *set the stage* in order to evoke positive emotions when showing your house to prospective buyers. Note the features that a buyer will see when first entering a room. Remove or rearrange furnishings to create a sense of spaciousness. And remember, also, to appeal to the senses—with flowers, cookies baking in the oven, or even a roaring fireplace in the wintertime. Place plants and decorative vases on countertops. Use light, both natural and artificial, to highlight a special painting or an heirloom antique. In short, make your home seem not only livable but also warm and inviting to all who enter.

F.Y.I.

BUILDING EQUITY

Even with an unpaid mortgage, renting or leasing a property can make financial sense. Rental income may be used to make mortgage payments at the same time that the property continues to appreciate in value. Once the mortgage is paid in full, monthly income converts to a positive cash flow, increasing your net worth considerably.

Few homeowners realize that they can build real estate equity even when their first mortgage is not yet paid off. One way to do this is by living in a home for a while, making improvements on the property, and then turning it into a rental property. Buying a home for yourself, as a property to be *owner-occupied* for a minimum period of time, allows you to acquire a mortgage for a much lower down payment than would be required for a property purchased directly as an investment. After living in the house for at least two years, you may then use the property as equity to negotiate a mortgage for your next owner-occupied investment property. As you build equity on each subsequent investment, financing becomes easier because many lenders will permit you to apply as much as 80 percent of rental income as *qualifying* income in your loan application.

How many times you can repeat this depends on many variables. The Federal Homeowner Agency (FHA) allows borrowers to retain their current loan and finance another loan, provided that the borrower moves up to a larger home and has 25-percent equity. Fannie Mae will underwrite up to four homes. Investigate lenders also, such as banks and mortgage companies, which may be eager to work with an investor having a sound track record. Whatever you do, always be sure to consult professionals, such as real estate lawyers, accountants, and bankers, before making any risky decisions.

If you have made improvements to your home that are not in character with neighboring houses, you may have priced yourself out of the market. Your chances of getting back a return on your investment will be diminished.

Selling without a Broker

If you wish to maximize the profit from your home sale, you may want to sell it directly, without a broker. Realtors typically require a seven-percent commission on the selling price of a home, which can be a considerable chunk of money. However, this must be weighed against the resources of a regional or national real estate franchise and its ability not only to handle all the details for you but to effect the timely sale of your home.

The success of a personally directed sale depends entirely on the time and energy you have to put into its organization. It is best to list a home with the local MLS if time is short or if you are too busy to tackle advertising and showing your home. If you have months to work with, then it may be worthwhile to run a few ads yourself before resorting to a real estate agency.

Advertising Your Home

Posting a Sign. The first order of business, when selling your own home, is to put a *For Sale* sign on your front lawn. This is important, because it not only tells the ad responders that they are in the right place, but it catches the attention of casual passersby who may be looking for a home in your neighborhood.

A For Sale sign on the front lawn tells a prospective buyer that they are in the right place and gets the attention of casual house seekers.

Consider placing corner directional signs, as well, along the routes to your home.

Writing a Classified Ad.
A well-written ad is one that tells your story concisely and effectively. Serious homeowners want the facts, stated as truthfully as possible. No homebuyer wants to be drawn into a wild-goose chase by flowery descriptions that end with extreme disappointment when the actual house is seen first-hand. Don't exaggerate, merely state the facts. Embellishments may get the prospective buyer to your home, but they will not get them to buy. How trustworthy will they think you are to execute a fair transaction if you lie about the condition or environment of your home? Make a list of what is important to the buyer: the square-foot area of the house, the architectural style, the number of floors and rooms, special features like fireplaces or extra baths, the truth about the view (assuming there is one), and the asking price. Leave out the fluffy stuff.

Handling the Calls.
Once your sign and your ads are in place, the phone will ring—you hope. This can happen on any day and at any time. Be prepared. Callers will have questions about the neighborhood, the distance to the nearest train station, area shopping malls, schools, and every manner of thing you can imagine. So imagine them and be ready to give your caller a truthful answer. Keep a sheet handy by your phone with answers to the most frequently asked questions.

Be prepared, also, to receive phone calls from brokers who see your ad and try to solicit your business. Most contracts with brokers extend for a specified period of time. Even if you find the buyer, you will still have to pay the realtor a commission, unless you negotiate an agreement to the contrary.

Potential buyers may occasionally ask if you will carry the mortgage or if they can assume your loan. Ask them to bring proof that they have been approved by a bank for a loan. If their credit and income aren't good enough for their bank, they shouldn't be acceptable to you. Deal only with potential buyers who have been prequalified by a lender and who need a home within a time frame acceptable to you.

If you don't have time to take endless phone calls or put up with buyers who make appointments and don't show up, and you don't want to deal with the stress of making a sale,

THE HOME INSPECTION

F.Y.I. A home inspector may be employed by either a homebuyer or a home seller. As a home seller, you may benefit by having an inspector highlight problems that may later become an obstacle to the sale of your home. A thorough inspection will uncover areas in need of repair. Either make these repairs or at least reveal their need to prospective buyers, and then adjust the asking price accordingly. It does little or no good to hide problems that will most likely return later to haunt you in the form of legal liabilities.

The buyer, on the other hand, may employ a home inspector to check the condition of a home for sale, in order to avoid any nasty surprises after the closing. If problem areas are found, these may become bargaining chips in negotiating a fair market price for the house. In fact, most lenders will insist on a certified home inspection before approving a mortgage.

Areas of concern, for buyers and sellers alike, include the condition of water heaters, gas connections and pipes, furnaces, chimney flues, drains, sewer lines and septic systems, roof shingles, electrical wiring, driveways and walkways, plumbing fixtures, siding, wall finishes, etc., and whether there is a leak or standing water of any kind in or around the house.

then listing with a real estate agent is the best way to go. A good agent will handle the details of finding and negotiating with a buyer, as well as follow through on the paperwork to a successful closing.

How do you find a good agent? First, if neighbors have sold their homes in your area recently, ask for their recommendation. Second, look for agents who have listings in your area. They are showing and advertising these homes already, so this can benefit you.

Because almost all real estate companies are now computerized, and their listings must be posted on the MLS computer, the size of the company is not as important as the competence of the agent. Also important, specify in the listing agreement that you can cancel unconditionally if you're not happy with the company's service. The last thing you want is to get locked into a listing agreement for several months with an unsupportive agent. A good agent will not object to this request.

Choosing a competent agent requires more than finding a good real estate agency; it also requires that you know which type of real estate agency is best suited to your needs. There are basically three classes of agencies chartered by state legislatures: seller agencies, buyer agencies, and dual (or limited) agencies. A fourth type, called a transaction broker, or facilitator, where the real estate agent represents neither the buyer nor the seller, is gaining in popularity in some states.

From a consumer's point of view, knowing whom an agent represents guards against misrepresentation and allows the homebuyer or seller to take the fullest advantage of the real estate agent's expertise.

Types of Real Estate Agencies

Seller Agency. When you list your home for sale through an agent, you establish a "seller agency." You may limit that agency to your broker of choice or offer "sub-agency" status to any or all agents listed on the MLS. Because you may be held liable for the misrepresentations of agents from other brokerages, sub-agency status is typically limited to the listing agent or broker.

Buyer Agency. As a home buyer, you may engage a real estate agent to represent you. These kinds of agents have no duty or loyalty to the seller and give you the advantage of their expertise and experience when evaluating a home for purchase. You may agree to work with one of these agents *exclusively* or choose non-exclusive representation, leaving yourself with the

F.Y.I.

SHOWING YOUR HOME

To get the most out of an opportunity to sell your home, be prepared when a prospective buyer comes looking. If you cannot answer simple, fair, easily anticipated questions, you will sell yourself short and perhaps not sell your home at all. There are certain things a buyer will want to see. You may even take the initiative and gain an advantage by presenting these items for review without waiting to be asked. For example, have documentation showing the average annual cost of your gas and electric utilities. If you haven't kept a record, obtain one from your utility company. Other items include water bills, tax receipts, subdivision maps or lot surveys, covenants, etc. … As for the home itself, present it in the best possible light by making sure it is clean and neat. Be sure your agent can show your house even when you are not around so that delays and missed opportunities can be avoided. Be explicitly clear about what items are and are not included in the sale of your home. Add homey touches, like fresh flowers, when your home will be shown, and be certain to eliminate smoke and pet odors, etc. On gray, wintry days, open the shades or blinds, or light the fireplace if you have one. Make your home seem cheery, but not noisy or distracting. Turn off stereos, television sets, and kitchen appliances. And by all means, keep your pet(s) under control or out of the way. Finally, if an agent is showing your home, find somewhere else to be so that you won't be a distraction. Many buyers prefer to look at a home when the seller isn't around.

option of working with as many different agents as you wish.

Dual, or Limited, Agency. With the written consent of both parties, a realtor may represent both the buyer and the seller. This type of agent must remain neutral and may not say or do anything that will harm the bargaining position of either party. Because of the great potential for liability, many brokers choose to avoid this option.

Transaction Broker, or Facilitator. This type of agent establishes no allegiance to either the buyer or the seller but rather works solely as a *facilitator* in putting together a deal. Not all states currently permit facilitator agencies, but the concept is growing in popularity because it limits liability for both the agent and the seller.

Renting Your Home

Selling a home, although it can be a somewhat emotional, even traumatic, experience, is a process. It has a beginning, in the decision to sell, and an end, at the closing when the checks are all exchanged and the papers signed, sealed, and delivered. Deciding to rent or lease a home, by comparison, evokes an entirely different set of emotions and thought processes. Putting emotions aside, you must acquire an ability to see your house not as your home but rather as an income-producing business, a business that has as its goal the earning of profit and the building of equity.

Your Home as a Rental Property

The key to successfully renting a home lies in recognizing that the investment is long-term. It is also tangible. It has physical properties, and like all things physical, it is subject to degradation and deterio-

ration. Keeping it in good condition is very much like maintaining your own health. Without it, you have nothing. So keep your house, and yourself, in great shape, and the rewards will come when you are ready to sell your home as an income-producing property.

Because renters will not have the same emotional attachment to your home as you do, begin thinking about making exterior and interior changes that will turn your house into a quality rental property that will be both trouble-free and resistant to damage.

Protective Interiors

Ceramic Tile. Tile is a good choice for a conversion upgrade. It's an attractive, inexpensive, damage-resistant, and easy-to-install material. On countertops, ceramic tile will resist heat from hot pans that would easily destroy plastic laminates. And quality tile flooring will stand up to punishment better than linoleum, vinyl, carpeting, or wood. Keeping extra tiles on hand will make replacing a cracked tile easier later on. Keep enough to cover 10 to 15 percent of the floor, wall, or counter area that is tiled.

Bathrooms. The bathroom is probably the room in a house that is most susceptible to water damage. Be sure bathtubs and showers are carefully caulked at all wall and floor joints. Install plastic water guards where the wall meets the bathtub. Inspect the bathroom thoroughly for leaks on a semiannual schedule. Even a small leak, if undetected early on, can cause major damage to subflooring and ceilings below.

Corner Guards. Install corner guards on every corner to protect against banging and chipping. They may be strictly utilitarian, clear plastic protectors or elaborate wood moldings. At the very least, use metal drywall corner guards, finish them with joint compound, and then paint them to match the walls.

Walls. Because the lower half of a wall is more vulnerable to damage than the upper half, consider installing wainscoting in key rooms, such as the living room, family room, or kitchen. Even a simple chair rail will afford some protection to your walls.

Equipment. Because it is dangerous for certain types of appliances or mechanical equipment to be moved, secure such devices to the floor or wall structure as a precaution against potential gas or fire hazards. Have a professional inspect gas appliances, water heaters, furnaces, electric panels, and the like.

Life Safety. Install smoke detectors on every floor and in every bedroom. Check them semiannually, and replace the batteries. Some states require that hard-wired detectors also be installed. Carbon monoxide detectors should be installed in homes with gas heating or appliances.

Fireplaces/Wood Stoves. It is best not to permit the use of a fireplace or wood stove, but if this is part of the charm that makes your home rentable, be sure it meets code requirements for clearances and fireproofing. Install a firebrick hearth to protect flooring and carpeting.

Protective Exteriors

Roofs. It is not likely that a tenant will notice a roof problem until the water comes pouring through the ceiling. Inspect the roofing, the roof edge, gutters, leaders, and flashing at least once a year.

Landscaping. Plant hardy, low-maintenance plants, shrubs, and trees that are appropriate to your region. Use ground covers to reduce lawn area and the need for mowing and pesticides. If the climate is dry, consider an automatic sprinkler system to protect the lawn and plantings. Drive by occasionally during the summer to see that the sprinkler is being used and to replace or recalibrate sprinkler heads. Use pop-up type heads to minimize damage and the need for replacements.

Glazing. Protect sliding glass doors from accidental walk-throughs with a horizontal glass protector at latch level, or adapt a screen-door protector for this purpose. Avoid using interior glass doors.

Garage Doors. If there is a garage, install an automatic garage-door opener. Mechanically operated garage doors tend to sustain less damage than do doors that are opened and shut manually. It is also a good idea to bolt a 4x4 timber to the garage floor as a car stop. The same can be done for a carport or at the end of a driveway to prevent potential damage to car and house alike from overshooting.

Accessories. Add a touch of class to your home while protecting it from damage. Install brass kickplates on heavily used exterior doors. If the budget permits, consider brass switch plates and receptacles, doorknobs, and so on.

Finding Tenants

Finding a tenant may be as simple as putting up a *For Rent* sign or placing an ad in the classifieds. One of the best ways to get tenants, however, is by word of mouth or referrals through people you know. Whatever

A **low-maintenance landscape** not only adds to the appeal of a rental property but also makes its upkeep both easier and less costly.

you do, always be aware of federal and local fair-housing laws against categorical discrimination.

If you decide to place an ad, keep it brief, listing the address, a short description of the house, and your phone number. Develop a clearly written application form, and insist that all prospective tenants fill it out. This will ensure that everyone is treated equally. The form should include the applicant's name, address, phone number, place of employment, length of employment, previous landlords (if any), and Social Security number.

Applicants. What should you look for in an applicant? Probably the single most important consideration is length and stability of employment. It is also a good idea to know how long the applicant has lived at their previous address and why he or she is moving.

Rent. How much should you charge for rent? Check the classifieds for similar homes renting in your area. Or contact property managers who have a firsthand knowledge of the local market.

Should you lease? Do so only after carefully considering the potential consequences. A long-term lease is not always a wise choice. In a rising economy you may be locked in for the length of the lease. In a declining economy, your tenant may forfeit the deposit and move. It is probably best to keep leases short. Six months to a year is typical.

Rental Agreements. It is important to have a signed rental agreement that spells out everything agreed to by all parties. This will help you if it becomes necessary to go to small-claims court to collect back rent or to evict a tenant.

Deposits. The market in your area will determine what you can charge the tenant for move-in costs. At the very least, get one-half month's rent as a deposit and the first and last month's rent in advance. If your prospective tenant does not have enough money to cover this cost, keep looking. And good luck!

Get a signed rental agreement that specifies everything agreed to by all parties to ensure good tenant-landlord relations.

Glossary

Adhesive Mastic A pastelike cement used for applying floor and wall tiles; a waterproof caulking compound used in roofing.

Air Gap The distance between the outlet of a faucet and the overflow level of the fixture.

Apron Architectural trim beneath a window stool.

Asphaltic Concrete A mixture of liquid asphalt and aggregate used as a paving material.

Ball Cock A self-regulating valve that controls the supply of water in a toilet.

Batter Boards Boards that support the string marking an excavation or construction outline or the elevation level of a construction form.

Baseplate A plate that distributes vertical loads.

Bay Window A window or group of windows that project from a house, forming an interior niche.

Bedding Block A wood block covered with carpeting used to press tiles into adhesive.

Bevel Gauge Tool with two arms that adjust to any angle for marking where materials are to be cut.

Black Iron Pipe Galvanized pipe that has not been zinc-coated, used for gas lines.

Bow Window A rounded bay or bowed window projecting out from a building in an arced shape.

Braided Stainless Steel Flexible supply pipe made of stainless-steel strands woven together.

Broom Finish Texture created when concrete is swept with a stiff broom while it is still curing.

Brown Coat The second coat of plaster applied over a scratch coat as a base for the final coat.

Bullnose Tile A trim tile with one rounded edge used to finish outside corners.

Buyer Agency A real estate agency that represents the interests of the homebuyer.

Casing Trim around windows and doors.

Caulking An impermeable yet flexible substance used to make joints between materials watertight.

Cement Board Fiberglass-reinforced, cement-based backer board used as underlayment for tile.

Chair Small support used to maintain the position of reinforcing steel during concrete placement.

Chair Rail Horizontal molding that protects a wall from chair backs or that caps a wainscot.

China Bristle Natural bristles used in the manufacture of paintbrushes for solvent-based paints.

Closed Valley Roof valley covered with roofing woven in a way so that flashing does not show.

Compound Miter Saw A power saw that can cut angles in two directions simultaneously.

Compression Faucet A faucet in which compressed rubber washers prevent water flow.

Coped Joint Joint between two pieces of molding, one of which is cut to fit the contour of the other.

Cornice The horizontal molding that crowns or caps a building or the top of an interior wall.

Cove Base Tile Trim tile that makes a smooth joint between a wall and a floor or other surface.

Crown Architectural molding around a room at the joint between the wall and the ceiling.

Cutting-in Painting by brush those areas of a surface that cannot be reached with a paint roller.

Darby Flat, wide board with a handle, used to smooth concrete after an initial pour.

Dash Coat A slurry of plaster applied with a brush as the finish coat in a three coat process.

Disk Faucet A faucet containing plastic or ceramic disks that move up and down to regulate water flow and rotate to control water temperature.

Dual Agency Limited agency in which a real estate agent represents the buyer and the seller.

Eaves Roof edge that projects over the outside wall.

Edging Board Formwork for containing the spread of concrete on flat surfaces such as walkways.

Elastomeric Having the elastic property of rubber.

Epoxy Thermosetting resin that provides strong adhesion and tough, low-shrink fillers and coatings.

Equity Residual value of a property, calculated by deducting liens or mortgages from its gross value.

Escutcheon Plate A decorative and protective plate, as around a keyhole or pipe stubout.

Exclusive Agency Agreement wherein a property owner uses one broker during the listing period.

Felt Paper Compressed organic fibers impregnated with asphalt, used as a moisture barrier.

Ferrule Spacer used in hanging metal gutters; metal sleeve binding bristles to a brush handle.

Flashing Material used to avert water passage at door, window, roof and other joint intersections.

Float To smooth poured concrete with a trowel made of steel, aluminum, magnesium, or wood.

Furring Leveling a wall or other surface by means of wood strips before adding a finish.

Gable Vent A louvered opening on the gable end of an attic serving as an inlet and outlet for air.

Galvanized Protected by a coating of zinc, either by immersion or electroplating.

Glazed Tile Ceramic or masonry tile with an impervious, glossy surface.

Green Board Moisture-resistant drywall for use in areas of high moisture, such as bathrooms.

Grout Material used to fill voids between tiles.

Head The top of a door or window opening.

Holiday A spot missed while painting a surface.

Jamb The vertical side of a door or window frame.

Keyway A recess or groove cast in a concrete pour or cut into concrete, which when filled by the next pour, will form a lock in the concrete joint.

Laminate Material formed by bonding together several layers with adhesive under pressure.

Ledger A horizontal framing member that serves to seat joists and support them.

Lift Rod A rod that is pulled up or pushed down to control a lavatory pop-up stopper, or drain plug.

Market Value The cash price that a buyer and seller would be willing to agree upon.

Mason's Sand A fine, dry prescreened sand.

Miter Cut A beveled cut, usually at 45 degrees, that is used to form a mitered joint.

Mitered Joint A joint formed between two surfaces, usually beveled at 45 degrees each.

Molding Depth Distance between the bottom edge of a crown molding and the ceiling plane.

Open Valley A valley on a roof in which roofing is trimmed back, exposing the valley flashing.

Paver Block or tile unit used as a wearing surface.

Pivot Rod The rod connecting a lavatory lift rod to a pop-up stopper, or drain plug.

Plate A flat, horizontal framing member at the top and bottom of studs or posts.

Plinth A square block base that serves as a stop for the vertical casing around a door or window.

P-Trap P-shaped trap providing a water seal in a waste or soil pipe, primarily at sinks or lavatories.

PVC Polyvinyl chloride thermoplastic resin, often used to make plumbing supply and drain pipes.

Rake Slope of a roof; the molding placed along the sloping edge of a gable to cover the edges of siding.

Reducer Strip Trim used to make a smooth transition between varying floor heights or materials.

Reveal Portion of jamb (usually 3/16 inch) that is "revealed" at the edge of a window or door casing.

Ridge Vent A linear vent running the length of a roof ridge, serving as an inlet and outlet for air.

Riser Vertical surface between stair treads; pipe connecting a shutoff valve to a plumbing fixture.

Rosette Circular or oval ornamental plaque that serves as a terminus for vertical casings.

Rough Opening A framed opening into which a door, window, or other type frame will be fitted.

Sash The frame into which window glass is set.

Scratch Coat First coat of plaster or stucco, "scratched" to bond with a brown coat.

Screed A straight 2x4 moved across a concrete pour to strike off excess concrete.

Seller Agency A real estate agency that represents the interests of the homeseller.

Sill The bottom of a window or door frame; lowest member in the wood frame of a structure.

Slurry Mix of water and finely ground substances such as Portland cement, plaster, or clay particles.

Spall To chip or fragment; a flake detached by weathering, pressure, or expansion.

Step Flashing L-shaped flashing stepped along a sloped joint between a roof and wall or chimney.

Starter Course The first course of shingles applied along the eaves of a roof or at the base of a wall.

Stop Door jamb trim used to stop a door from overswinging; trim that secures a window sash.

Stool Window trim that provides a stop for the lower sash, and that extends the sill into a room.

Stubout Part of a pipe projecting from a wall.

Thin-Set Adhesive A cement-based or organic adhesive applied thinly, to set tiles.

Tongue-and-Groove Lumber milled with a groove on one side and a tongue on the other, so that joined pieces will fit snugly together.

Transaction Broker Real estate agent who has allegiance to neither the buyer nor the seller, but who serves as a facilitator for putting together a deal.

Trisodium Phosphate A crystalline compound mixed with water to make a cleaning agent.

Underlayment Plywood or backer board used as a base for surfacing materials.

Unglazed Tile Ceramic tile composed of the same material throughout, deriving it's color and texture from the material and the method of firing.

Vermiculite Loose-fill insulation, made from clay minerals, hydrous silicates, or aluminum, magnesium, and iron that have been expanded by heat.

Wainscoting The lower part of a wall that differs in finish or material from the upper part.

Wax-Ring Seal A ring of wax pressed between the drain and the horn of a toilet as a waterseal.

Welded-Wire Mesh Steel wires welded into a grid of squares, used to reinforce concrete slabs.

Working Time Length of time a substance such as cement can be manipulated before it dries enough to be unworkable.

Index

A

Advertising your home, 168–170
Aged wood flooring, 143
Aluminum siding: repairing, 58; replacing, 58–59
Architectural trimwork, cutting, 157
Architectural woodwork, 155–164; decorative style, 156; painting, 156; tooling up for, 157
Asphalt paving, 18; repairing, 18–19

B

Balusters, painting, 87–88
Base plan for landscape, 8
Base shoe moldings, installing, 159
Base trim, installing, 159
Bathroom accessories, 116; recessed medicine cabinet as, 116–117; wall mirror as, 117–118
Bathrooms, 109–122; faucets in, 14–16; lavatories in, 110-113; pedestal sinks in, 111–113; prefab vanity in, 110–111; shower enclosures in, 120–122; toilets in, 118–120;
Bay window, installing, 46–48
Brackets: corner, 87; sandwich, 87
Broker, selling without, 168
Brush bristles, 80
Brushes, selecting, 128–129; testing, 80

C

Carpeting, 145
Caulking, 86
Ceilings, 88; overlaying, 127; painting, 88, 128–130; repairing, 127–128; texturing, 127–128
Ceramic tile, 148; cement-board underlayment for, 149–150; installing, 152–154; laying out, 150–152; repairing, 149
Clapboard, replacing, 50–51
Color cards, 87
Color schemes, 87–88
Composite shingles, 64; installing, 70–71
Concrete driveways, 19; cleaning, 19–20; laying out new, 21–22; ordering concrete for, 22–24; repairing, 20–21
Concrete steps, 24–26; repairing corners, 25–26; repairing edges, 24–25
Concrete walkways, 26–30; building formwork for, 27–29; laying out new, 26–27; pouring and finishing, 29–30; resurfacing, 30

Corner brackets, painting, 87
Cornices, built-up, 160
Countertops, 98; installing custom, 99; installing prefabricated, 98–99
Crop seeds, 12–13
Crown moldings, 127, 160; installing, 161–162; laying out, 60–61
Cutting-in, 129

D

Damaged wood, repairing, 85–86
Dishwasher, installing, 105–107
Doors, 33-38; casing, 157–158; painting, 35; styles of, 37
Dormers, shingling around, 74
Down payment, 167
Drip edging, 70
Driveways, 17–24; asphalt paving, 18–19; concrete, 19–24; stain removal in, 20
Dry-laid walkways: edging systems, 30–31; installing brick, 31–32; paving units, 30
Drywall, repairing, 124–125

E

Electric ranges, 103–104
Epoxy, patching wood with, 53–54
Equity, building, 168
Extension ladders, 82–83
Exterior paint: damaged wood, repairing, 85–86; removing, 84–85
Exterior painting, 77–90; colors for, 86-88; preparation for, 83–86
Exterior repairs, 49–60; aluminum siding in, 58–59; fiber-reinforced cement shingles, 54; stucco, 59–60; vinyl siding, 55–57; wood siding, 50–54
Exteriors, protective, 171–172

F

Fair market value, 167–168
Faucet: installing new, 115–116; removing old, 114–115; selecting new, 114
Fertilizer, 15
Fiber-reinforced cement shingles, 54; repairing, 54
Fixtures and appliances, 100; installing dishwasher, 105–107; installing garbage disposal, 107–108; installing range, 103–105; installing sink, 100–101; replacing faucet, 101–103
Floor joists: bracing, 141; shimming, 141

Floors, 139–154; ceramic tile, 148–154; fixing squeaky, 140-141; painting porch, 88; refinishing wood, 144; repairing, 140–144; replacing, 145–148
Frieze, painting, 87
Front doorway: painting, 87; refinishing, 34–35; replacing door, 35–38

G

Gas ranges, 104–105
Germination, 12
Grass seed, 12–13
Grouting, 138
Gutters: maintaining, 76; repairing, 74–75; replacing, 75–76

H

Hardboard panels, replacing, 53
Home: inspection of, 169; as investment, 5–6, 166–167; selling your, 6, 167–171
Home improvements: percentage of return on, 5-6; surveys on, 6
Hydroseeding, 14

I

Inside corners, coping, 160
Investment, home as, 5–6, 166–167
Investment benefits, 165–172

K

Kitchen cabinet improvements, 92; refacing, 94–95; refinishing, 92–93
Kitchen cabinet replacements: installing base, 95–96; installing wall, 97
Kitchens, 91–108; countertops in, 98–99; fixtures and appliances in, 100–108

L

Ladder jack scaffolding, 83
Ladders, 82; extension, 82–83; scaffolding, 83; step, 82
Landscaping, 7–16; creative, 11; eye appeal in, 110; planning, 8–9
Landscape architect, 8
Landscape plan: balance in, 10; color in, 11; composition in, 10; harmony in, 11; proportion in, 11; scale in, 11; texture in, 11
Latex paints, 78
Lavatories, 110; installing new faucet, 115–116; installing pedestal sink, 111–113; installing prefab vanity, 110–111; removing old faucet, 114–115; selecting new faucet, 114

Lawns, 12; adding, 12; replacing, 12; seeding, 13–14; sodding, 14–15
Lead in paint, 78
Light, reflected, 117

M
Mason's sand, 32
Masonry, painting, 88, 90
Medicine cabinet, installing, 116–117
Metal flashing, installing, 69–70
Metes and bounds, 8
Miter saw, power 157

N
Nailing shingles, 71
Natural clustering, 10
Nesting shingles, 72
Nitrogen, 15

O
Overworked wood, 145

P
Paint brushes, 79–80; selecting, 128-129; testing, 80
Paint colors, 86; cards, 87; choices, 86; schemes, 87–88
Painting: balusters, 87-88; brick, 90; corner brackets, 87; foundations, 88; frieze, 87; floors and ceilings, 88; front entrances, 87; masonry, 88, 90; panel siding, 90; plywood, 90; posts, 87; rails, 87; room, 129–130; safety, 84; steps and risers, 88; stucco, 90; surface preparation, 129; and weather, 89; wood siding, 89–90
Painting tips, 88
Painting tools, 79, 128–129; brushes, 79–80, 128-129; rollers, 80–81, 129; sanders, 81–82; scrapers, 81
Paint rollers, 80–81
Paints: latex, 78; lead in, 78; solvent-based, 79; types of, 128
Paint scrapers, 81
Paint sheen, 79
Panel siding, painting, 90
Pavers, 30-32
Pedestal sink, installing, 111–113
Phosphorus, 15
Plaster cracks, repairing, 125–126
Plywood: painting, 90; replacing panels, 53
Popped nails, concealing, 124
Posts, painting, 87
Potash, 15
Primers/sealers, 79
Protective exteriors, 171–172
Pruning, 15

R
Rails, painting, 87
Range, installing a, 103–105
Real estate agencies, types of, 170–171
Reflected light, 117

Remodeling, 5-6
Rental agreements, 172
Renting: home for profit, 6; your home, 171–172
Replacement windows, 38; installing flange-supported, 42–43; installing jamb-supported, 41–42; replacing entire unit, 41; replacing sash and jambs, 38–40
Replacing: clapboard, 50–51; hard board panels, 53; plywood panels, 53
Replacing flooring, 145; installing laminate, 147–148; installing new vinyl, 146–147; installing underlayment, 145
Ridge shingle, repairing, 63
Risers, painting, 88
Roofing, 62; applying underlayment in, 68–69; built-up, repairs in, 63–64; composite shingles, 64, 70-74; inspecting, for damage, 62; inspecting shingle, 66; installing metal flashing in, 69–70; preparation for, 66-68; rake and eaves fascia and soffits, 65; removing shingle, 67–68; reshingling in, 67, 70-74
Roof repairs: installing metal flashing 69-70; preparation for, 66–68; repairing gutters, 74–76; shingle replacement, 70–74; underlayment in, 68-69
Roof venting, 67
Room, painting, 129–130
Rough opening, 36

S
Safety, painting 84
Sanders, 81–82
Sandwich brackets, 87
Scaffolding, ladder jack, 83
Screeding, 29, 32
Seeding: lawn, 13–14; vs. sodding, 12, 14
Selling, home for profit, 6
Shingle replacement: installing composite shingles, 70–74; roofing open valley, 72–73; roofing ridge, 73–74; sealing and trimming, 74
Shingle roof: inspecting, 66; preparing for reshingling, 67; removing, 67–68; repairing, 64; replacing, 70-74
Shingles, nailing, 71
Shingling around dormers, 74
Shower enclosures, 120–121; installing, 121–122
Shrubs, 15–16; planting, 16; thinning, 15
Siding: aluminum, 58–59
Skylight, installing, 44–46
Sodding: lawn, 14–15; vs. seeding, 12, 14
Soil, 12; testing of, 12

Solvent-based paints, 79
Specialty windows, 43; bay windows as, 46–48; skylights as, 44–46
Stains, exterior, 79; removal of, 20
Stairs, fixing squeaky, 141–142
Stepladders, 82
Steps, painting, 88
Stucco, 59; painting, 90; repairing, 59–60
Surface preparation, 129

T
Tenants, finding, 172
Toilets, 118–119; installing new, 119–120; removing old, 119
Trees, 15–16; planting, 16; pruning, 15–16
Trim accessories, 158

U
Underlayment, applying, 68–69

V
Value, fair market, 167–168
Venting, roof, 67
Vinyl, cleaning, 57; cutting, 56
Vinyl siding, 55; installing soffits and fascia, 57; repairing, 55–56; tools, 56

W
Wainscoting, 163–164; creating elaborate, 164; installing simple, 163–164
Walkways: concrete, 26–30; dry–laid, 30–32
Wallcovering, 131–134
Wall mirror, hanging, 117–118
Wallpaper, removing, 131
Walls: overlaying, 126; painting, 128–130; repairing, 124–126
Wall tiling, 135–138; cutting, 137–138; grouting, 138; installing tile, 136–137; layout, 135–136
Waste-disposal unit, installing, 107–108
Weather, exterior painting and, 89
Weed barrier, installing, 32
Weeds, 13
Windows: casing, 158; painting double–hung, 130; replacement, 38–43; smooth operating, 39; specialty, 43–48
Wood: overworked, 145; patching with epoxy, 53–54
Wood flooring: aged, 143; refinishing, 144; replacing, 142–143
Wood shingles, repairing, 51–53
Wood siding, 50; avoid splitting, 51; painting, 89–90; patching, with epoxy, 53–54; repairing shingles, 51–53; replacing clapboard, 50–51; replacing hardboard or plywood panels, 53

Have a home improvement, decorating, or gardening project? Look for these and other fine
Creative Homeowner Press books at your local home center or bookstore. . .

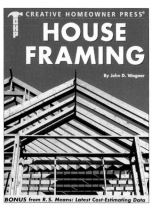

HOUSE FRAMING

Designed to walk you through the framing basics. Over 400 illustrations. 240 pp.; 8¹/₂"×10⁷/₈"
BOOK#: 277655

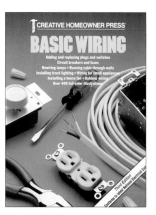

BASIC WIRING

Best–selling house–wiring manual. More than 350 color illustrations. 160 pp.; 8 1/2"×11"
BOOK #: 277048

FENCES, GATES & TRELLISES

Step–by–step instructions & projects. Over 395 color illustrations. 160 pp.; 8¹/₂"×10⁷/₈"
BOOK #: 277981

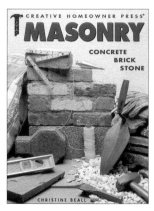

MASONRY

How to work with concrete brick and stone. Over 500 Illustrations. 176 pp.; 8¹/₂"×10⁷/₈"
BOOK#: 277106

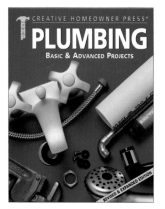

PLUMBING

Take the guesswork out of plumbing repair. More than 550 illustrations. 176 pp.; 8¹/₂"×10⁷/₈"
BOOK#: 277620

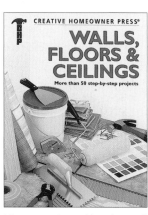

WALLS, FLOORS & CEILINGS

How to replace old surfaces with new ones. Over 500 illustrations. 176 pp.; 8¹/₂"×10⁷/₈"
BOOK#: 277697

Working with TILE

Install tile on walls, floors, patios, countertops, and more. Over 500 illustrations. 176 pp.; 8¹/₂"×10⁷/₈"
BOOK#: 277540

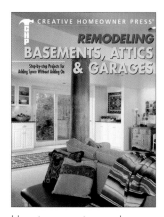

REMODELING BASEMENTS, ATTICS & GARAGES

How to convert unused space into useful living area. 570 illustrations. 192 pp.; 8¹/₂"×10⁷/₈"
BOOK#: 277680

KITCHEN DESIGN

How to create kitchen style like a pro. Over 150 color photographs. 176 pp.; 9"×10"
BOOK #: 279935

HOME DECORATING

How to work with space, color, pattern, texture. Over 300 photos. 256 pp.; 9"×10"
BOOK #: 279667

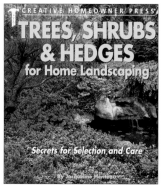

TREES, SHRUBS & HEDGES for Home Landscaping

How to select and care for landscaping plants. Over 500 illustrations. 208 pp.; 9"×10"
BOOK #: 274238

BETTER LAWNS Step by Step

Create more beautiful, healthier, lower–maintenance lawns. Over 300 illustrations. 160 pp.; 9"×10"
BOOK #: 274359

For more information, and to order direct, call 800-631-7795; in New Jersey 201-934-7100.
Please visit our Web site at www.creativehomeowner.com